Second Home

Life in a Boarding School

Second Edition

edited by
Craig Thorn IV

2003

AVOCUS PUBLISHING, INC.

GILSUM, NH

Second Home: Life in a Boarding School, 2d Edition

Avocus Publishing, Inc.
9 White Brook Rd.
Gilsum, NH 03448
Telephone: 800-345-6665
Fax: 603-357-2073
e-mail: info@avocus.com

Disclaimer:
Nothing in this book is intended in any way to be libelous in nature. Neither is it the intent of Avocus Publishing, Inc. to publish any accusatory statement, direct or implied, of improper motives or illegal actions by any individual or educational institution. Any other interpretation of our printing is erroneous and therefore misunderstood. We believe that the public interest in general, and education in particular, will be better served by the publication of the authors' experiences and opinions.

Copyright © 2003 by Avocus Publishing, Inc.

Printed in the United States of America

ISBN 1-890765-09-0 : $16.95 Softcover

Cover design by Michel Newkirk

To Judith and Laszlo Papp

Acknowledgments

I would like to thank Avocus Publishing for a great run. I would also like to thank Jean St. Pierre for all her support over the years. And, of course, I must thank my friend and colleague Tim Hillman.

Eight years ago, when Tim Hillman approached me about a book designed to introduce boarding school life to prospective students, I was initially skeptical. He was persistant and soon persuaded me that it was not only a workable idea, but a very good one. With this second edition, I am privileged to present an expanded version of *Second Home: Life in a Boarding School*. I hope that this second edition honors Tim's vision by bringing it to another generation of young students looking for a challenging and complete education.

Contents

INTRODUCTION

If you are reading this, you have already distinguished yourself as a young person willing to consider a grand adventure: living on a school campus. At first, "living at school" sounds awful. Who would want to live where you go to school? Movies, music, and even books frequently portray school, particularly high school, as a place most kids are in a big hurry to flee at the end of a school day. Who hasn't seen *Ferris Bueller's Day Off*, heard Pink Floyd's *The Wall*, or read J. D. Salinger's *Catcher in the Rye*? So why do so many kids go to boarding schools?

Perhaps you are looking at boarding schools because going off to boarding school is a family tradition. Perhaps your local school does not interest or challenge you. Perhaps you want to meet more people. Perhaps you think that you can get into a better college if you go to boarding school. Perhaps your family situation makes boarding school a logical choice. Perhaps you are having trouble in your current school. These are all good reasons to consider boarding school as an option, but *Second Home* is full of stories that will give you many more reasons for wanting to go to boarding school.

You will hear about all kinds of opportunities: amazing sports programs; great facilities like photo labs, recording studios, radio stations, indoor tracks, observatories, and libraries; incredible teachers who not only teach you biology, but also work alongside you on all kinds of projects; off-campus programs from France to the Grand Canyon; and motivated, interested kids from all over the country and sometimes the world. In essays by students and teachers from nearly fifty schools around the country, *Second Home* shows you that boarding schools take full advantage of the campus environment to create a supportive community that will challenge you to explore and excel, inside and outside of the classroom.

Second Home also shows you that there are many kinds of boarding schools, reflecting philosophies and programs that appeal to all kinds of kids. If you are dedicated to the arts, you will find a host of fine schools that will immerse you in music, theater, and everything from pottery to photography. If you want to develop your skills as an athlete, you will find schools with brilliant programs in every sport from lacrosse to fencing. There are boarding schools that focus on your religious faith, others that refine your skills in mathematics, and still others that nurture a profound awareness of and respect for the great outdoors. And if you just want a challenging general education that invites you to try new things, you will find boarding schools that answer the description.

However, when you find the right match, you still have to adjust to a whole new experience. Where do you do your laundry? What is it like to eat in a dining hall alongside faculty families? How do you get along with someone from Croatia? Why is there so much homework? Who can help you with problems you normally turned over to your parents to solve? When do people sleep in this dormitory? Right now, these questions might seem daunting. Be assured that very quickly after arriving on your campus, you will find answers to these questions and many more. For the time being, however, you have *Second Home*.

Second Home is not just a collection of amusing stories about boarding school life. It is filled with information that will help you adjust quickly and comfortably to this new experience. The teachers and students you meet in these pages tell you what you need to know. The book is divided into four sections: *Starting with You, Outside the Classroom, In and Around the Classroom,* and *Ending with You and Your Family*. Within each section, there are subsections. The writers in *Second Home* are not shy about any topic. There's help here on difficult questions about relationships, schoolwork, rules, and the crises, great and small, that every teenager faces. There's also good advice about managing your money, your room, and your roommate. And if you want to know about the rules of hanging out on a school campus, this is your source.

Designed to give you easy access to topics that interest you,

Second Home also provides you with insights into what other students might be interested in because the book reflects possible answers to questions asked in admissions offices and on campus tours all over the country. So as you read those essays that reflect your interests and concerns, consider reading a few that do not. You will learn something about kids and adults whom you will meet on campus. Filled with invitations to write in the book, *Second Home* offers exercises that help you to figure out what you might want out of boarding school. So you are going to learn something about yourself, too.

Have a great time with this book! You are going to meet fantastic faculty, parents, alumni, administrators, and especially fantastic kids that are happy they made this choice.

Craig Thorn
Thompson House
Phillips Academy
Andover, Massachusetts
December 17, 2002

Starting with You

Ultimately, any boarding school is about making connections, finding relationships between what defines you and what defines others. In fact, the boarding school life is just a microcosm of all social life. After all, we spend most of our lives figuring out how to balance our sense of self with our sense of belonging. In other words, we define ourselves as both a part of groups of people and apart from groups of people.

Starting with You is the longest section in the book because it is the most important. In four subsections—"First Friends," "Settling In," "Settling Into Relationships," and "Beyond the First Friends"—you will learn a lot about dorm life, starting with your room and your roommate and moving into expanding circles of social experiences that will at once invite you to examine what makes you who you are and what defines others. So you will hear about everything from socks to cliques. Whereas the next section will devote itself to more formal relationships—sports, extracurricular activities, community service, and the like—this section focuses on the personal relationships you develop. Remember that no matter how small the group you find yourself in at any given time—a dorm room, a dining hall, a playing field, club meeting, or classroom—everything starts and ends with you, a kind of community of one rich with experiences, ideas, feelings, anxieties, and dreams.

You will hear about "family" often, a word kids and adults use often to describe relationships that develop by accident and by design. And you will hear about situations that arise regarding romance, race, religion, and even nationality, some that you will experience yourself and others that you will witness when you become a student at boarding school. Along the way, all these stories tell a collective tale about learning how to get along with all kinds of people from all kinds of backgrounds. In some instances, one essay will raise questions that another essay will attempt to answer. And in some instances, one essay will pose some hypothetical challenges that the very next essay will dramatize in a personal story.

Regardless, *Starting with You* practically insists on your participation. What you get out of this section of the book depends mightily on what you are willing to put into it. In that respect, this first section of *Second Home* is much like boarding school itself. Who you are at school depends on the relationship between what you offer the school and what the school has to offer. Of course, you can put *this book* down at any time and watch a good movie or hang out with friends. Just come back to it later.

FIRST FRIENDS

First Home

Charlie Mitchell
Dean of Residential Life, Cheshire Academy

I moved into my first dorm room when I was three days old— Stebbins House at The Bement School. No, my parents were not eager to send me away to start my education early; they were dorm parents. We moved twice after that, ending up at Spaulding Hall at Lawrence Academy for fifteen years. Mom and Dad finally moved out of the dorm after twenty years as dorm parents, having spent most of their married life and raising two kids in an apartment surrounded by teenaged boys virtually 24/7. Now, at the age of thirty-one, I have found myself in a new home: Van-DerPorten Hall at Cheshire Academy. My sister is married and is raising her child in the New Dorm at Forman School. Of the fifteen or so kids that grew up "in my neighborhood," at least eight are back now working in boarding schools in one way or another. We are "fac brats" and most of us wear the title with pride (well, most of the time).

While most people involved in residential schools refer to the concept of "second home," for me it has always been my first and only home. The children who grow up on a campus are, in many if not most schools, integral to the tone and life of the school. The infants in the strollers out for a walk; the toddlers screaming in the dining hall; the preteens being extremely cute and playful (or totally obnoxious depending on the moment); the teens trying to be students and not children of faculty members; or the older ones coming home to visit the family—all have their places in our boarding school world and can make a campus much more like home for everyone. The fact that I grew up in a world where education was always the center of life, where I was surrounded by an incredible assortment of people, where I was exposed to art and theater and sports and lectures and music and games all the time has always been a major part of who I am.

There are many ways to judge the health of a school when you visit—college placement, faculty with advanced degrees, the size of the endowment, the attrition rate, admissions yields, the state and growth of the physical plant, scores on SATs, APs, ACTs, ISEEs, and SSATs.

Or you could just talk to the spouse or child of a dorm parent. They see things from a different point of view and often have a unique perspective on life on campus. Talk to them about respect and support, ask them about the food and entertainment, find out what roles they play in the community.

And then when you enroll in a school, get to know them—the kids, the dogs, the families, these are what make boarding schools truly special. A complete education in our schools can be most effective if we find ways to integrate the lives of those at their "second home" with those at their "first." You just may find that the people who don't have grade books may have as much to teach you as those that do. A dorm parent's spouse may be involved in a field you are interested in and be able to help you get started. Or he may have a skill or hobby that you want to learn more about. Or maybe has a way to explain that math problem her way that you understand better. Or perhaps he is just a great listener for those times you need a friendly ear.

The fac brats will look up to you, the dorm students, and see you as a large extended circle of almost-cousins—they will in fact want to be like you whether you know it or not. You are their models of scholars and athletes and citizens and they will remember you and what you did with them for a long time after. Most of the people I remember being influential in my life were the kids in the dorm—the ones who I not only watched play ball and sing in the play but also the ones who helped me with my math, the ones who made me feel important like only an older favorite "cousin" can.

Boarding schools are much more than the buildings and numbers and names and titles. They are families. Not everyone sees things the same way and not everything goes as planned—I don't know any families where they do. But our schools are great places to raise kids and help them grow and learn and have fun—whether it's the students or us fac brats. When a school makes the "home" part of their campus central and integral to their work then everyone benefits. For families of faculty, the opportunities are virtually boundless—where else can you raise your children with access to the resources that boarding schools provide? For students, the dimension this gives to your school can be more rewarding than any other—where else can you get to know your teacher as a coach, an adviser, a dorm parent, a father or mother, a spouse or bachelor/bachelorette? So make sure you do. It will mean a lot to both you and the families that live on your campus if you can make an effort to get to know them for who they are and what they bring to your new world.

Charlie Mitchell is currently the dean of residential life, a history teacher, and a varsity soccer coach at Cheshire Academy.

Random Acts of Rooming

Charlie Maule and Tyler Mixter '02
Phillips Academy

You probably know more about having a roommate than you think, if you've ever lived with siblings, traveled with someone, gone to summer camp, or cared for a pet. The only difference is that the court of law is not the family kitchen but your roommate's beady eyes staring at you across a tiny space. Nonetheless, some things about residential life will surprise you. For us, those least expected and inconsequential things were the most rewarding part of living together.

We first met as dormmates, not roommates, and spent a good part of that first year hating each other. Depending on whom you asked, Tyler had either ruined a comforter with his sneakered foot or innocently violated the six-inch "ring of safety" surrounding the bed. Since we were both studiously inconsiderate and vindictively OCD, the conflict dragged on for months, until the embarrassing perspective of winter vacation prompted us to call a truce. We spent the rest of the year cautiously befriending each other and by April had decided to be roommates.

We had our other great fight over socks. An errant argyle was discovered under the couch, and as Charlie searched for the other and tried to decide if the socks belonged to him, Tyler hid the original. Somehow yelling began, and at one point we actually tried to storm out of the room. But by then we were seniors, well-practiced roommates, and we couldn't even slam doors without doing it together. We ran into each other on the way out, and ended on the floor laughing rather than swinging.

By contrast, an episode involving Tyler's desk chair never threatened a serious rift. In one particularly intense session of roommate wrestling, he began to toggle his opponent's pinky back and forth, vigorously. Charlie pushed him away, and Tyler, who had been seated until this point, felt the back of his chair give way. He cried out in uncomprehending disbelief: "You have irreparably damaged my chair!" Surprised by the high drama of this proclamation, we both cracked up. Breaking the chair turned out to be a high point of our first year together; "irreparable damage" became a catchword between us, eliciting grins in the tensest moments, and persisting as a playful reminder.

We spent most of our time as roommates between extremes of brotherly love and rancorous hate. Our relationship played out in a rich array of events and emotions, most of which were experienced simultaneously: like Charlie making fun of Tyler the week before Thanksgiving vacation for having to stay an extra day to finish a last minute paper, then spending the ride home calling him to make sure he didn't fall asleep during his all-nighter; or

Tyler noting Charlie's ludicrously fanatic regard for his books even as he moved them off the couch so they wouldn't get "hurt." In two years of living together, we learned each other's endearing, deplorable idiosyncrasies. We perfected the art of brotherly hate.

And we did so while undergoing that succession of the trivial and mundane which characterizes real life. At the foundation of rooming are the dumbest little things. Probably, nothing very momentous will ever happen to you and your roommates. For us, anyway, the most potent invitation to come together came from the small and ambiguous. Incidents between roommates have a strange way of opening themselves to interpretation. The choice to joke or fight, to begrudge or forgive, is yours to make. That choice is in itself momentous.

For graduation, our parents sent us on a tour of Asia. The trip has evoked our favorite memories, and given us the chance to live new ones. Once Charlie took his roommate to the infirmary with a prostrating migraine. Now Tyler has had the chance to nurse Charlie, in a Beijing hotel bathroom. That our career as formal roommates is over makes us more aware of the grand opportunity that is sharing a room. We are now tormenting and celebrating and looking out for each other, which is especially important in a place where lane lines are primarily a loose suggestion and a flinch invites all kinds of unwanted attention in the market.

Yue Xiu Hotel
Beijing, China
Summer 2002

Charlie Maule graduated from Phillips Academy with reluctance in June 2002. He has since gone on to college in order to pursue his interest in rooming, and studies history on the side. **Tyler Mixter** is also going to college. He has no idea what he is going to do with his life.

GETTING READY FOR ROOMMATES

Take some time to answer these questions about what you like and the way you like to live. Be honest with yourself, then let your school's dean of students or residence know what kind of person you are, and what kind of person you would like to room with. Write your answers on this page, then after a month or at the end of the year, do it again and see if you would answer the same way. Have you changed?

1. Do you like to go to bed:
   ❑ Early   ❑ Late

2. Do you consider yourself:
   ❑ Messy   ❑ Neat   ❑ Slovenly

3. Do you like:
   ❑ Metal   ❑ Rap   ❑ Folk   ❑ Techno

4. Do you like your music:
   ❑ Quiet   ❑ Loud   ❑ Earth-shattering

5. Do you like to have music while you study?
   ❑ Yes   ❑ No

6. Do you consider yourself a social animal?
   ❑ Yes   ❑ No

7. Do you consider yourself a "jock"?
   ❑ Yes   ❑ No

8. Would you like a roommate from another country?
   ❑ Yes   ❑ No

9. Do you prefer to sleep in a:
   ❑ Cold room with a lot of blankets
   ❑ Warm room with next to no blankets

10. Are you self-conscious about your body?
    ❑ Yes   ❑ No

11. Do you like to wake up to:
    ❑ A loud buzzing alarm   ❑ Soft music
    ❑ Someone yelling at you to get out of bed

12. Do you find black light to be:
    ❑ Weird   ❑ Cool   ❑ Just plain silly

13. Do you like stuffed animals?
    ❑ Yes   ❑ No

14. Are you easily distracted when you study?
    ❑ Yes   ❑ Excuse me, what?

Go back over these questions, and you'll probably have a pretty good picture of yourself. Now, imagine having to room with yourself. Would you get along well?

❏ Yes   ❏ No

A Conversation with Roy

David P. DeSalvo
St. Andrew's School, Middletown, Delaware

It was in my second year of teaching in a boarding school that I had my conversation with Roy. The conversation was something of a wakeup call for me and as I look back upon it now, it rattles certain chords in my thinking about what being a teenager means. Roy was a good kid but someone other students saw as a bit of an outcast because he was too straight, too concerned with obeying school rules, too much a brownnoser. I liked Roy a lot, particularly because I knew he was having a hard time fitting in with the other students. Consequently, he spent much of his free time with teachers, probably more time with me than any other. I felt sorry for him and wanted very much to help him with his problems, but we rarely spoke of what I knew was his awkwardness with the other students.

I was very surprised when one night in my living room Roy wanted to talk about his inability to find a group of close friends. When he started to talk about some of the illicit activities that the boys engaged in, my antennae went up. I began to think about how I would have to respond, as a young, "responsible" teacher, to the information that I was hearing. But I soon realized that Roy was not giving me data so I could start an investigation; he was trying to tell me that he had finally succumbed after two years of refusal to their invitation to go out and smoke some marijuana, to be initiated in one of the rituals inherent in the school's subculture, to become "one of the fellas." Roy was feeling miserable, devastated by how he had compromised his own convictions, feeling guilty and needing to get it off his chest. He needed to tell someone about it, he needed to be forgiven. In his own mind, as he explained his feelings through tears and confusion, he felt he had let the school down, let me down; while on the other hand, as he put it: "It felt so good to be part of a group, to belong." It has been twelve years since Roy sat in my living room and told me his story, but I will never forget those powerful words of his, "It felt good . . . to belong."

Boarding schools are among the few remaining places where, for a small segment of society, there is protection from the forces and pressures of the greater world. At boarding school you will rarely find poverty, hunger, violence; boarding schools are one of the few havens where people are free to focus on community, to learn what it means to belong. If you look at the philosophies of different boarding schools, you will find they make clear what they are about. In each statement of philosophy or mission, you will find that the intention of the school includes something about each student developing his or her mind, body, and spirit as an individual, while at the same time striving to function as part of a community, learning to be responsible so that they can someday take their place as contributing members of society.

Within a few days of their arrival at school, new students will notice that groups are a big part of school life. Seeking connection with others is natural, and as Roy put it so painfully, to belong feels very good. At boarding school, groups form for a variety of reasons: from dress to race, from socioeconomic background to geographic background, from age to gender, from one dorm to another. At my school, the most prevalent grouping is the form group. You do not choose which form you belong to; it is decided by your age and grade level. Your roommate is a member of your form, you live in a dormitory with members of your form, you have English class with your form, in most cases you sit at cafeteria meals with other members of your form. The forms are set in such a way that the bond is solid and lasting. Ultimately you are referred to as "the Class of _____" and you are graduated on the same day, making way for a new form. The cycle is endless.

Within the larger structure of the school there is good deal of crossover between students of differing ages: sports, most obviously, and then there's band, and choir, and with the exception of English, classes contain some mixture of the forms. Major committees are comprised of students of various forms, the most predominant being the social activities, honor, discipline, and student life committees. All clubs contain a mixture of forms.

Although boarding schools offer a great many extracurricular activities, students will continue to seek opportunities to fill the "belonging" void. Students talk about the need for "bonding" experiences. This is especially true within the forms at my school. Form meetings are chaotic and too task-oriented; form trips tend to fragment the form, as small groups go off and "do their thing" together. What they like best is to be invited to someone's house for a form party, where everyone is confined to one location to share a variety of activities but still feel a part of the larger group. Camping out is another experience that allows for bonding within a form. We've also had the occasional form cookout and bonfire, which many students enjoy because they feel that everyone is together having fun with no specific purpose or agenda.

I have come to see that belonging has more to do with how one feels than what one does and for that reason belonging can have negative effects. Often, students trying to get "in" to a certain group will look for the "inside track" where they will try to remake themselves into whatever are the perceived needs or wants of the group. There is less commitment to being genuine and more adherence to acting like one of the group. In this sense, belonging removes your ability to choose. You no longer know what to do, nor do you need to know. You just do whatever the group does. As a result, you forget how to be yourself and lose the dynamic ability to take risks, the result of which is a slip into complacency, mediocrity, and emptiness. And herein lies a paradox: The energy you spend trying to be one of the crowd can be exhausting, leaving you feeling as though you are alone, feeling like you don't belong.

In the end, there is a delicate balance at work here. A boarding school must be above all a place where a student can flourish physically, intellectually, and spiritually. Such an environment must provide a variety of experiences to choose from. Aside from the academics and athletics, school government and other facets of the system, there are friendships and clubs and social groups. Choosing where to belong is difficult, but part of growing up means learning how to make choices. Identifying with this group or that means taking a stand, showing one's colors, testing one's convictions. Fortunately, it is very much in the nature of young people to be accepting and forgiving. If you make a mistake along the way, the key is to keep your options open, be honest with yourself, and try again.

Roy graduated back in 1982. He did so with a clean disciplinary record and a few close friends. In looking back, I now see that perhaps Roy was caught between two clearly defined school bodies: students and faculty. While he had friends in both groups, he needed to establish solidarity with the students before he could be fully accepted by them. We teachers were not the enemy, but we did have the responsibility for keeping the school rules enforced. Students saw Roy's relationship with the faculty as a threat, particularly because he refused to participate in their rule-breaking activities. Roy struggled with his need for a clear conscience and his need to belong. In the end, belonging won out. I admire him for the courage he maintained, for the struggle he endured, and for the seriousness with which he faced an important choice. Did he make the right choice? Who can say? Perhaps the fact that he struggled is what really matters.

David DeSalvo's hobbies are reading, playing guitar, and coaching baseball. He serves as bishop's chaplain and is currently a postulant for holy orders in the Diocese of Delaware. He teaches in the math department at St. Andrews.

What Makes Cliques Click?

Jesse Payne-Johnson '03 and James Gardner '03
Loomis Chaffee School

After the tragic spate of high school shootings which began with Columbine High School and ended with a nation's attention focused on its educational system and the sociological health of its younger generation, the word "clique" began to roll off the tongues of high school counselors, deans, students, and concerned parents alike. And, as such things do, the clique discussion became inexorably intertwined in the endless rubric of criteria for the public vs. private education debate. Like many aspects of private school, the essential forces that govern the creation and perpetuation of cliques remain the same, although perhaps less pronounced, in an independent school setting as in public high school. The universal determinants of money, intellectual ability, athleticism, race, ethnicity, creed, and background still govern much of the social dynamic at private school but a more mature and more homogenous student body usually prevents social distinctions from becoming as blatant, exclusive, and corrosive at independent schools as they might be at public institutions.

Many people believe that the student bodies of prep schools represent an exclusive clique in their own right, a privileged and elitist class of "blond-haired, blue-eyed, spoiled rich kids" convinced of their own socioeconomic superiority. While this may have been the case fifty years ago, today it couldn't be further from the truth. Thanks to generous financial aid programs (many of which have substantial budgets), concerted efforts to increase on-campus diversity, and the decreased importance of family lineage in the admissions process, the "old-boy" private school stereotype has all but evaporated. However, this new influx of diversity has led to student bodies with generally less in common and diversified interests and talents, and resultantly more distinct social and academic subgroups, or "cliques," have appeared on prep school campuses.

If this process of diversification sounds familiar, it should. It represents a general trend among youth and in education all across the country, and prep schools are in no way immune to the national social climate. Like any institution that dares to collect teenagers in large numbers, prep schools foster allegiances and alliances between students, which can be both beneficial and/or detrimental to the community at large. It's only natural for students to want to forge relationships with people who share their interests, experiences, or goals. Athletic ability, academic drive, race, ethnicity, and a myriad of other characteristics both unite and divide student bodies, and create groups of students with shared commonalities. As athletes share space on the field, academics share tables at the library, and thespians share center stage, students with similar interests are herded together and develop their relationships accordingly. This process is virtually identical to the way publicly educated students would go about developing their own social circle. If anything, the greater number of clubs, activities, teams, and programs at private schools may exacerbate the formation of cliques as students are put into contact with similar peers more quickly and permanently than they would be at public school.

However, the simple formation of social groups is neither unhealthy nor necessarily detrimental to the community. It's the way those groups interact with one another and with other members of the school that should be the focus of any discussion of cliques. The general concern about cliques is that they become so exclusive, elitist, and concentrated as to inspire envy, hatred, and even violence between themselves and other members of the school. While this has been the case at many public schools across the nation, it seems to be less of a problem at private institutions. Several factors contribute to this phenomenon. First, despite the aforementioned increased diversification of private school student bodies, they still fall far short of representing a true cross-section of the American population. Rigorous admissions processes do their best to cull a group of students who exemplify high standards of intelligence and maturity, but also attempt to ensure that any candidate who exhibits signs of aggressive antisocial behavior be rejected. Therefore, social interactions on boarding school campuses are generally conducted with a more mature respect for the interests and emotions of other students than would be found at public schools.

Second, boarding schools seem to make more of an effort to stress the importance of "tolerance" and "community" to their students, nearly to the point of overkill. From the initial prospectus to the final graduation speech, independent schools are eager to lecture students about open-mindedness and acceptance in social contexts. Perhaps the small size and the 24-hour-a-day closeness of boarding communities, along with the traditionally unpalatable cuisine, instill a universal sense of camaraderie in students. Perhaps a fear of negative publicity drives schools to stress the idea of community. Whatever the reason, this message seems to stick in the minds of students. The resultant climate of tolerance and mutual respect prevents the kind of rigid social divides and accompanying problems that might be found in public schools.

The analysis of private school cliques reveals both the vulnerability and the saving grace of the independent school system. Private schools are not immune to the problems that plague the national educational system, nor do they draw from such an elite group of students as to avoid widespread social trends. Sure, the students will naturally form cliques based on their mutual interests and personalities, in the same manner they would at public schools. However, the maturity, respect, and intelligence of students and faculty at private schools, and the school's intense desire to perpetuate those ideals, ensure that cutthroat social hierarchies and the psychological complexes they induce rarely invade the independent school environment.

Jesse Payne-Johnson is a senior at Loomis Chaffee School where he heads the debate team. **James Gardner** is the class president and also a senior at Loomis Chaffee.

Getting to Know Yourself and Everyone Else

Clara Kim '05
Milton Academy

Moving away from home and coming to a boarding school for some of the most important years of your life is really hard, harder than any glossy brochure or admissions officer can actually describe. Nobody I know who's been through it all would have it any other way, though—coming to Milton Academy was probably the best and the smartest thing I ever did, despite all the things I miss. It's not just that I got to meet some of the coolest people ever, or that I learned more in my first year at Milton than I had in the preceding thirteen years. It's a lot more than all the reasons that you probably have in your mind right now for considering boarding school; I know that when I was applying to schools, I was thinking more about the college matriculation stats and getting excited about living without my family, rather than how rewarding or fun it would be to try something completely new and different.

There are so many reasons that I'm glad I chose to go to boarding school, but I have to say that living in a dorm is at the top of my list. For one, living with a group of kids your age is a surefire way to learn to overcome people-phobia, of which I had a major case. It's hard to feel homesick or shy for very long when you spend virtually all of your time with the kids in your dorm and the rest of the boarding community. Another great part of living in a dorm is the diversity of the people that are around you all the time; a boarding school is bound to be full of kids from all over the world and from every stratum of the society. I had learned a lot of English in Korea before I came to Milton and I wasn't a complete stranger to the American culture, so I didn't expect too much trouble with adjusting to the system when I moved here in September—I couldn't have been more wrong. It seemed to me, after the first couple days, that I knew nothing at all about how these Americans lived—why did they have two sheets on the bed, and who in the world was Ferris Bueller? Watching the movie *Ferris Bueller's Day Off* in the dorm on a closed weekend with some senior girls actually turned out to be one of the more memorable events of the year. I'm not saying that watching a movie you've never heard of is a good way to make friends, or that being unfamiliar with the environment is an advantage—I'm just saying that living in a dormitory gives everyone plenty of chances to learn or discover something new.

When I first told my parents that I'd like to go to boarding school, their immediate reaction was one of anxiety or worry. There are many myths out there about boarding school that unsettle parents. My parents were especially worried because I am their youngest, and also because I was moving so far away from home—Korea is approximately halfway around the planet. I think it would have been a bit better for them if I had been a boy. My parents, however, need not have worried; being a girl in a boarding school is safe and a lot of fun. Personally, I think that the girls share a kind of rapport that doesn't really exist among the boys. The upperclassmen, especially the girls that I met in the dorm, were absolutely amazing when I first moved in. I came from a school where you must greet most upperclassmen with a bow and speak to them in the "formal" Korean that is used when addressing adults; it was a completely foreign experience for me to be addressed as an equal and as a friend by girls who were three years older than I. I relied on the support of the upperclassmen in the dorm to figure out exactly how things were done at Milton; it was to their rooms that I went before the first dance, and to complain about that horrible ancient civilization term paper due the next morning. The only real social tension exists between the boarders and the day students; for reasons unknown to the majority of the student body, the two groups just don't get along very well. Also, the inevitable formation of social "cliques" causes tension on a smaller scale; boarding schools, like public schools, are plagued with gossiping and other problems, especially among the girls. These are challenges, but I have found that you can overcome them in one-on-one situations.

I've noticed an interesting effect that boarding school seems to have on a lot of people, myself included. It seems as if through every part of the experience, one learns not only the ways of the "real world," but also how to focus inward on who he is as an individual. Intellectual growth doesn't hinder the process of self-discovery; in fact, the two complement each other perfectly. Moving to Milton taught me these things, both in and out of the classroom. Living in a dorm means that you constantly learn about other people and their ways, but it doesn't mean that you are forced to change what you believe in and who you are. My friends in Korea were surprised when I came back to Korea for the summer, speaking Korean much better than I used to; strangely enough, this improvement was caused by moving to America. There is nothing that makes one group of people more cohesive than severing them from their motherland—this goes for everyone, regardless of race or where you come from.

It's this sort of personal growth that makes me really happy to be where I am. I don't agree with the people who tell you things like "some people just aren't boarding school material." It's true that some enjoy it more than others, and that some benefit more from the experience than others, but don't let that stop you. No matter where you go or what you do afterward, the schools you attend will change your life—so do yourself a favor and choose wisely. Good luck!

Clara Kim was born in Chicago, but spent most of her life in Korea with her family before she decided to try boarding school. She attended Seoul International School for seven years. She enjoys listening to music (mostly classical and Korean pop), trying new foods, and spending time with her friends.

HOW YOU MIGHT DEFINE YOURSELF

First, try defining yourself as a composite of parts, but use an unusual metaphor. At the end of this book, Nadia Sarkis talks about herself in the context of photography. Try describing yourself in one of the following ways:

- a recipe
- a musical
- composition
- a country

- an animal
- a house
- a movie

- a painting
- an appliance
- a book

Why did you choose to make the comparisons you did?

Second, imagine yourself as someone else for a day. Of course, you cannot be someone else literally, but trying to put yourself in someone else's shoes can by an eye-opening experience. You might learn something about that person and yourself as well. Here are some people:

- a very poor person
- a computer whiz
- a devout Catholic
- a theater jock
- a Korean girl
- a skinhead
- a black woman
- a Latino man

- a short boy
- a Pakistani girl
- an overweight man
- a homosexual
- a very attractive girl
- an inner-city student
- a post-graduate athlete
- a very rich person

How does the school look to you as this person?

_____

_____

_____

_____

What do you do that most clearly defines who you are?

_____

_____

_____

_____

Where do you feel most comfortable?

_____

_____

_____

_____

When are you most like yourself?

_____

_____

_____

_____

Whom do you find most unapproachable?

_____

_____

_____

As you are considering these questions, what assumptions do you make about the person? Knowing that every person is somehow more than the sum of his parts and that no type totally defines a person, consider getting to know someone whose immediate appearance and/or most visible characteristics would normally keep you at a distance for whatever reason.

Third, seek out groups that seem to support and/or reflect who you are on your terms. Make an effort to get to know people in the group when they are outside the formal setting of that group. Make sure that the group does not become a limiting experience, confining you to only one point of view.

Fourth, pick the five inanimate objects that you most clearly identify with: for example, a soccer poster, your music collection, C. S. Lewis's *The Chronicles of Narnia*, your lamp, and the floor rug in the downstairs bathroom. Bring them to school.

Fifth, set aside at least half an hour during the day or early evening, if possible, when you can spend some time by yourself doing something you've always done: for example, building models, reading a magazine, listening to a favorite band on your headphones, doodling on a drawing pad, or watching a weekly television show. Work hard to protect this time.

Finding and Keeping Friends

Richard E. "Nick" Noble
The Fay School

"It was amazing! We just clicked! We're best friends now, completely simpatico. We tell each other everything."
—a ninth-grade boarding student
talking about her best friend

We use the word "friend" and the phrase "best friend" very seriously and quite casually throughout our lives. We are serious in the short run, when our friends, especially our best friends, seem so important to us. With our closest friends we can talk about those issues and incidents that we find difficult to broach with our parents or our teachers. We share our secret longings with our friends, and they share theirs with us. Our friends help us to feel safe, secure, and supported within our own peer group rather than having always to rely on the sometimes intimidating and often confusing security and support we get from even the best of adults.

For many of you, this will be the first time away from home. For others, overnight camps or similar programs are just not the same, as they are usually viewed as temporary experiences and their offerings are usually meant to be fun. Within this new boarding environment, friendships will be formed, there is no doubt at all about that. But concerns about how, and who, and when are quite normal under the circumstances.

"When I first got here, I didn't know anybody. At home, all the kids I went to school with I'd known since the first or second grade. I didn't have that advantage here. I worried a lot about how I was going to make any friends. No, I didn't tell anyone; that wouldn't have been cool. But I worried. I shouldn't have."
—a veteran boarding school student, discussing his first year away from home

There is nothing wrong with doing the best you can to keep up your old friendships back home. Write your friends letters, call them, get in touch on the Internet, see them during vacations. But for their sake as well as your own, don't refuse to make friends at boarding school because of your friends at home. It happens more frequently than you think: boarding students who refuse to get involved in activities at their school and resist making friends, who go home every single weekend or, if in a five-day boarding environment, spend virtually all of their free time in constant communication with old friends at a distance, never giving the new friends and the new place a chance. It is a mistake. If you have decided that a boarding experience is best for you, you should go out of your way to make the best of it.

The best way to make friends is to get involved. Friends can be found on teams, in clubs and organizations, at weekend activities and events. If you like computers, music, athletics, dramatics, or almost anything else you can think of, you have common ground with others around you. Sometimes, however, you will find friends and friendships will happen completely out of the blue. A student of mine once became, almost overnight, close friends with a classmate with whom I thought he had absolutely nothing in common. They were fast friends for the better part of two years, to the amazement of many faculty and more than a few students. At one point, a few weeks before graduation, I said to the student I had been teaching: "I have to ask: How can you and he be friends at all? What do you have in common?" He said: "Come on, Mr. N.! Friendship isn't computer dating. One night last year I came back to the dorm all depressed because of my grandmother dying. You remember the time? And he was the only one around. I had to talk with someone. And he listened. It turns out that he had a relative die too, not that long before. Someone he was really close to. So we talked. Sure, we hardly agree at all about a lot of things. But we listen to each other, we respect each other's feelings, and we trust each other."

You will encounter all kinds of friendships. The most obvious— boyfriend and girlfriend—are also the least likely to last. This is also, however, a period in your life when you discover that you can be close friends with a member of the opposite sex without there being any romantic or sexual involvement. You will discover that an adult can be your friend, and that the relationship of pupil to mentor can evolve throughout your boarding years and well into your life into a kind of friendship richer and deeper than many. Finally, it is the time in your life when you will learn that you can function well with your peers, even sympathetically, without their ever becoming your friends.

None of these aspects of friendship are unique to the boarding experience. What makes the boarding experience special is precisely that—you are boarding. You are living with these people, eating three meals a day with them, sharing a bathroom with them, sleeping in the next bed, seeing and hearing and encountering each other morning, noon, and night for three or four years. Everyone knows everything about you, and you know everything about everyone else: there is very little privacy. You might think this would put a terrific strain on friendships, and at times it does. But more often than not it makes for a real sense of community and a healthy sense of perspective. You learn to respect the privacy of others. You learn not to put people into stereotyped compartments, but to see them in three dimensions. Just as you never like to be pigeonholed into a category (jock, nerd, bimbo, goody-goody), it becomes harder to see others that way, and this includes teachers.

The friendships you make during your time at boarding school may be among the most important friendships in your life, whether or not they last beyond graduation. Some *will* last, of course, enriching our lives for days and years to come. Others will not, but even then you will have spent some serious time learning the valuable lesson of how to be a friend.

I learned a valuable lesson about friendship as a boarder in the mid-1970s. My first year away at school had been successful enough. I had made several friends and only one implacable enemy. He and I had at least three knock-down-and-drag-out fights, and by the end of the year we survived simply by steering clear of each other. The second year was, for us, one of uneasy truce. No more fights, but very little mutual respect, and an undercurrent of antagonism that kept a nasty edge on our relationship, no matter how pleasant and successful the remainder of our sophomore experiences. By the end of that year, however, when it came time to put in for rooms and roommates for next fall, each of us, unbeknownst to the other, took a kind of lackadaisical, wait-and-see approach to the process. The upshot of this was that when it came time to put up or shut up, we were all the other had left. We roomed together, then, our junior year, and to the surprise of both of us we became close friends. This friendship lasted throughout our school years and even a considerable way into college. For both of us, boarding school altered our perspective on what it takes to make a friendship.

Boarding schools like to call themselves "families." Families, of course, exist because of relationships, and relationships cannot exist in a vacuum. Forging the links that form the bonds of true relationships is what making friends is all about. By the end of their boarding experience, most students have crossed the legal threshold into adulthood. Most students, in my experience, tend to think that one can be friends only with one's peers. However, becoming an adult means in part that we are accepted as a peer by others. A boarding environment, with its close-knit sense of community and with the myriad responsibilities entrusted to its charges, creates good adults, good peers, good friends.

> *"Just because we're related doesn't mean we're a family. Here, with my friends, I feel like I've come home."*
>
> —a ninth-grade boarder

Nick Noble is the chair of history and chapel coordinator at The Fay School, where he had spent the previous fourteen years. He is the author of five books, and past director of Brantwood Camp.

SOME WAYS TO LOOK AT FRIENDSHIPS AND PEERS

1. The headings below represent the three most common ways we meet people. "Who You Are" refers to the basic features that define you (age, race, gender, religion, regional background). "What You Do" refers to your interests and activities (hockey, chess, drama, French, biking). "How You Appear" refers simply to the way you present yourself (preppy, punk, casual, formal, artsy).

Who You Are	What You Do	How You Appear
_____	_____	_____
_____	_____	_____
_____	_____	_____
Friends' names	Friends' names	Friends' names
_____	_____	_____
_____	_____	_____
_____	_____	_____

Now list your closest friends according to how you met them, under the appropriate column. If they all fall under only one column, then you might be limiting yourself and you might want to be more adventurous when making friends at your new school.

2. List the six most important qualities in a friend.

    A. _____   D. _____

    B. _____   E. _____

    C. _____   F. _____

Of these qualities, how many do you have? How many of your friends have all six qualities? Are any of the qualities based on gender, race, religion, ethnicity, class, or type? If not, can you say that you have friends who are not your gender, race, religion, ethnicity, class, or type?

3. Consider these questions as you think about the situations presented below:
    *   What would you do in each situation?
    *   What more would you need to know about each situation in order to feel comfortable with a course of action?
    *   Are there limits to a friendship?

The Situations:

A. Your friend changes for the worse when the two of you are with a group.
    *   What would you do?
    *   What more would you need to know about this situation in order to feel comfortable with a course of action?
    *   How does this situation impact your friendship?

B. Your friend is in serious trouble, but asks that you not tell anyone.
    *   What would you do?

- What more would you need to know about this situation in order to feel comfortable with a course of action?
- How does this situation impact your friendship?

C. Your friend tells racist jokes about someone.
  - What would you do?
  - What more would you need to know about this situation in order to feel comfortable with a course of action?
  - How does this situation impact your friendship?

D. Your friend pressures you to do something that you feel is morally wrong.
  - What would you do?
  - What more would you need to know about this situation in order to feel comfortable with a course of action?
  - How does this situation impact your friendship?

E. Your friend is ridiculed by people you like a lot.
  - What would you do?
  - What more would you need to know about this situation in order to feel comfortable with a course of action?
  - How does this situation impact your friendship?

F. Your friend puts incredible demands on your time.
  - What would you do?
  - What more would you need to know about this situation in order to feel comfortable with a course of action?
  - How does this situation impact your friendship?

Thinking about these questions prevents awkward situations in the future, especially in the dormitory when you cannot rely on the authority of your parents to help you out of a dilemma. The questions also help ensure that you will be a good, honest friend when your friend most needs a cool head to guide him or her, whether or not he or she knows it.

  4. How do you act around different kinds of people? Thinking about the way we change in order to accommodate different audiences can tell us a lot about ourselves.

How would you behave with people in:
  A. the dormitory
  B. the classroom
  C. cruising campus on Saturday night
  D. the dining hall
  E. the weight room
  F. the library

How would you behave with groups of people:
  A. at a gay/straight alliance meeting
  B. in a senior citizens' home
  C. from a popular girls' dorm
  D. who participate in the computer club
  E. in a meeting about racism
  F. at a party for hockey players
  G. who are extremely conservative
  H. at a senior music recital
  I. on the sidelines of a soccer game
  J. in a movie theater

If you change the way your present yourself, how many "faces" do you have? Is having many "faces" honest or dishonest, cynical or sensitive? Remember there are no right answers, just how you feel about it. Are there certain aspects of your personality that never change? Among your friends and/or peers, when are you most relaxed and least likely to feel the need to put on a "face"?

  5. How would you judge a group of people of which you are a member? Write in the name of the group you are thinking of. Then circle your answers.

  GROUP: _____

How I Feel in this Group

	STRONGLY AGREE 1	AGREE 2	NOT SURE 3	DISAGREE 4	STRONGLY DISAGREE 5
Most people in this group know me for who I really am.	____	____	____	____	____
I enjoy participating in group activities	____	____	____	____	____
I can be myself.	____	____	____	____	____
I feel that I am a valued and respected member.	____	____	____	____	____
I can approach someone if I have a problem.	____	____	____	____	____
I feel included in most things that go on.	____	____	____	____	____
I usually feel comfortable speaking my mind.	____	____	____	____	____
I know that criticism is fair and objective.	____	____	____	____	____

My Perception of the Group

	STRONGLY AGREE 1	AGREE 2	NOT SURE 3	DISAGREE 4	STRONGLY DISAGREE 5
Most people are proud to be in the group.	____	____	____	____	____
Individual talents and diversity are encouraged.	____	____	____	____	____

The group is respectful
of people not in it.   ____   ____   ____   ____   ____

All the members are
treated with respect.   ____   ____   ____   ____   ____

Conflicts and
disagreements are
handled openly in
this group.   ____   ____   ____   ____   ____

Leadership is shared
by all in the group.   ____   ____   ____   ____   ____

SETTLING IN

My Finances

Elizabeth Campbell '04
Milton Academy

Okay, I have a confession to make. I am a teenage miser. Well, I *was* a teenage miser, before I started going to boarding school. When I started living a thousand miles away from my home, parents, and piggy bank, I had to rid myself of that lifestyle option. It became necessary for me to, well, buy things on my own. Now, at first, this idea was abhorrent to me, but eventually, I came to the realization that, as a boarding school student, spending money was essential for my survival. So, my parents and I fashioned a budget that worked for me.

I know that most teenagers around my age do not seem to have my money-phobic problems. From observing my friends' budget woes (and my own), I quickly learned that making a successful budget has a whole lot to do with two things: flexibility and trust. Now, I'm not suggesting that you let Janie run amok with your Visa. (But if you are the sort of parent who would, let me know. My parents keep threatening to put me up for adoption, and I like you already.)

Seriously, though, every budget is different, because every student is different. I truly wish there were a special formula to tell every student just how much money to set aside for mechanical pencils every year, but there isn't. Planning a budget is entirely dependent on a whole lot of factors. So carefully consider these factors to see how (or if) they matter to you. Because it seems simplest to me, I'll just separate these items into a few categories: communication, academics, extracurricular, travel, personal maintenance, and social.

My mom always says that communication is an art. Let's just say that she is an unparalleled artist. It's really advantageous to have several venues of communication with home, in case one isn't accessible all of the time. First of all, think about telephones. Does the school have a long-distance plan? Also, after my first semester away from home, my parents purchased me a cell phone. While it took me a while to get used to the idea, I could call my parents from anywhere, if the need arose. An extra bonus is that my cell phone plan has a large number of weekend minutes, so I can still keep in touch with my friends, at no additional cost to my parents. In addition, consider bringing a laptop to school, or see if the school has an e-mail system. Communication through the Internet is fast and easy.

When I got to school, I was surprised to find how much money I still had to spend for academic purposes. At different points throughout the year, I needed various books for my classes, paper, and pens . . . and when my calculator broke (in the middle of my mid-year math exam), I needed to replace it. Lab materials and hardback textbooks (that dwarf encyclopedia volumes) can get pricey. My school does have student accounts to which one can charge academic items, and I've heard that similar accounts are common at comparable schools. If you are receiving financial aid to help with tuition costs, you may also merit aid to cover other expenses, such as bookstore bills or music lessons. Don't be afraid to deplete your school's endowment; that's why it's there. Call the financial aid office and ask a question or two. (If you're waiting for the aid office to call and offer you money—well, you'll be waiting a while. [Think Sophia from "The Golden Girls."])

The great thing about extracurricular activities is that one gets to meet new groups of people with diverse interests. I'm involved in music and sports, two extracurriculars that demand time, and in many cases, money. I play percussion, piano, and (try to) sing, so I take music lessons through my school. Also, musicians will need money to replace reeds, drumsticks, etc., while athletes may need a certain kind of shoe or equipment. For example, I play on the tennis team, so during the tennis season, I had to pay for part of my uniform and racquet restringing. However, there are *lots* of activities that require little or no financial commitment, such as culture groups or school publications. Last year, I was part of a school theatrical production and a member of the speech team; both yielded rewarding experiences that cost me little (except time and effort). Remember that some extracurricular obligations may require trips off-campus, and the school may not provide transportation.

The category of maintenance includes money for miscellaneous things. (I just called it "maintenance" because I like that word.) In my mind, it covers: hygiene items from the drugstore, laundry, grocery store visits to buy favorite foods (I like sushi and Oreos . . . but not at the same time), or offerings at a religious institution (especially around exam time). The money spent (or left unspent) in this category depends solely on the individual.

A student's social budget can vary greatly, depending on the school they choose to attend. My school, Milton Academy, is pretty good about scheduling weekend events, and I leave campus fairly frequently for extracurricular activities or to visit friends, so I don't need to have a lot of money for social outings. However, it's fun to go out to eat, or to order food delivery from local restaurants. Sometimes my friends and I go to see a concert or movie. All of these things depend on school location (are these activities available?) and personal interests.

The next thing one needs to consider is money access. At some school registrations, parents can set up a bank account, which they can tailor to their student's specific needs. Credit cards, debit cards, and checking accounts are very common at my school. However, these may not be practical in a school set in an extremely rural area. Many schools also have an allowance system, where students can receive, on a weekly basis, an amount of cash predetermined by their parents. This is a good system; however, it works best when combined with one of the other methods, so that a student always has a way to obtain money, even on weekends or in an emergency situation.

Now, before you start pulling your hair out, realize that many frustrated and clueless families have gone before you in this budgeting enigma. Maybe it would be a good idea to call a teacher who is knowledgeable about boarding life (or a student currently enrolled in your selected school). You aren't going to get the entire budgeting shebang right on the first try, so don't spend an obscene amount of time worrying about it. But, if in a weak moment, you do let Janie borrow your credit card, have her send some sushi and Oreos (the peanut butter kind) to Milton Academy . . . because you know I won't buy them on my own.

Elizabeth Campbell is currently a junior at Milton Academy. Her sister recently graduated from Idyllwild Arts Academy, also represented in this book. A native of rural Indiana, she was delighted to contribute to a book that would "help students with their very first home-to-school transition."

Make Your Room Your Own

Kiri Miller '96
The Putney School

My room at school did not strike me favorably. It was full of things that made me feel out of place—thumbtack holes all over the walls from generations of other students and their posters and art, various names and dates written in the ceiling of the closet and the inside of the dresser drawers, the bare light bulb, and, of course, the unfamiliar luggage piled on the bed opposite mine. I hadn't shared a room for years, and was apprehensive about living with a stranger who owned matching teal-and-purple baggage. My parents had already left to make the long drive from Vermont back to Philadelphia. I went out onto the fire escape and looked at the hills, feeling pretty bleak.

My experience was not unique to me or to my school. Dorm rooms do not give a good first impression. This is almost a guarantee. Even if, somehow, your dorm room is bigger than your room at home (highly unlikely, even for a double), it will be full of things that don't seem right to you—among other things, a roommate. It is absolutely necessary that you like being in your dorm; unless your parents live nearby, or you make friends with a lot of day students, you'll be spending long periods of time there. You will be required to be there after a certain time in the evening, and if you're not comfortable in the space you'll go crazy by mid-winter.

The best thing you can do for yourself when you're going to boarding school for the first time is to pack well. Clothes are not the important thing. There will be between ten and two hundred people in your dorm, depending on your school, and every one of them will probably bring more clothes than are really necessary. Trading clothes is an intrinsic part of dorm life, so don't worry too much about what you bring. Except socks. Something about dorm laundry rooms is fundamentally opposed to the existence of socks. Losing six or seven pair a month is pretty standard, and it gets worse from there. Be prepared.

You want to create a place where you can go when you're tired from sports and irritated from classes, the kind of place where you can stare at the ceiling and relax. The necessary components of such a haven are simple: stuff on the walls and good music. Once I got a poster and a couple of pictures up and plugged in my stereo, I didn't even feel like I needed to unpack the rest of my things. One of the questions on your roommate selection form will probably be about what music you like. Be honest. If your roommate has similar taste, your relationship will be infinitely improved. Bring a variety of music, and in the first week or so try to figure out what both of you can live with happily.

Put good things on the walls, being careful not to invade your roommate's space. Bring thumbtacks. They will make your life easier and also make you very popular in the dorm. You might also consider a hammer for tough old walls, and duct tape for when your boots start to leak and there's three feet of snow on the ground. On the cleanliness front, bring a laundry bag, detergent (unless your school provides it), and toiletries. Get a full bottle of shampoo and a new tube of toothpaste. Opportunities to buy more may be limited, and if you don't run out that's one less hassle.

If you have a computer or word processor, bring it. If not, don't bother buying one unless you can easily afford it. By the time you finish high school, there will be better machines available for less money. All most people need a computer for is typing papers, and your school will almost certainly be equipped with computer labs. If you learn to work in a shared lab, you will forever be able to block out unwanted distractions. If this is a skill you are unable to develop, at least you'll get some good social time while appearing to be working.

You make or break the ambiance of your room with the lighting. Many dorm rooms are lit by a single bulb, often the ecologically correct (also known as "dim") variety. Bring a lamp or two. A light with a clamp attachment and adjustable direction is particularly useful. You can clip it onto windowsills or beds, and direct it strategically when your roommate is trying to sleep. If your school experiences harsh winters, keeping your room bright and warm will do wonders for your mental state in mid-February.

Avoid the temptation to bring a whole wall's worth of pictures of your friends and family from home. It'll make you homesick, and it can be off-putting to your roommate and any potential friends who wander in. It's also important not to transplant your whole room at home to your dorm. For one thing, there probably isn't enough room. More significantly, you want your space in the dorm to be different. You are beginning a new kind of life at school, and your room should reflect that. Besides, if you leave your room at home intact, when you go back on breaks you'll feel relaxed and welcome. It's hard to let go of what you're used to, but unless you open yourself up to new people and possibilities you will be very unhappy at boarding school.

Pack fairly light, unless you've been guaranteed a huge single. You will definitely end the year with more stuff than you started with, and eventually you're going to have to take everything back home. Don't bring all your books because you won't have time to read them. Don't bring your skis because you can pick them up at Thanksgiving or Christmas break. Do bring a bike, if you have one, because sometimes classes are in unreasonably distant buildings from your dorm or each other.

When you're packing, don't worry too much. If you forget something or need something, someone can mail it. You won't be as cut off from your old life as you may feel. Your parents are probably not quite comfortable with leaving you. Call them, and let them know how things are going. At first, this won't be a struggle, but as you get more involved at school it'll be easy to forget that there's a world off-campus. Stay in touch. Prepare your parents to send you care packages, with brownies and good music. And socks.

Editor's Note: Kiri graciously agreed to write a follow-up to the piece she wrote in 1995.
One morning this summer I bought a rocking chair. There was a yard sale across the street and I kept looking out the window to see the wares—on the lookout for the practical and cheap, like all graduate students. A good portion of my furniture comes from alleys in Chicago on four successive June 15ths, the day the college student population moves and neighborhood goods are redistributed. Futons, wobbly fiberboard shelves, desks with missing drawer handles, infinite numbers of tall black halogen lamps, and massive couches with tattered 1970s upholstery move from fifth-floor walk-up to alley, then down the street and up the stairs again, year after year. Here in the Boston area the magic day is September 1st, when over 50,000 students change residence. The sidewalk treasures are the same.

I've moved twelve times in the last ten years, since I first left home for boarding school at thirteen. Granted, for the first four years the moves were only from dorm to dorm on a single campus, but nevertheless each year I had to take stock, dividing my possessions into the outgrown (the music I wouldn't be caught dead listening to by the end of the freshman year), the essential (all that hated long underwear for the next Vermont winter), and the so-essential-I-couldn't-be-without-it-for-the-summer. At frequent and regular intervals I felt the peculiar discomfort of having all my belongings packed out of view in boxes and bags. It seemed impossible that everything I had—a vast emotional cargo, each book or photo or orphaned sock with its own history—fit on top of a twin bed. And the bed wasn't even mine.

But there was a pleasure in it, too, a pleasure in the privilege of transience and in the knowledge that I would later unpack each element of my personal history, turn things over in my hands and mind, and remember why I bothered to bring it all along. When I look around my apartment now I am amazed at what I have carried with me since high school—not only actual objects, but the signs of skills and tastes developed there. The last time I moved, at least a third of my boxes were full of kitchen things, all of which I learned to use through four years of the Putney School's work programs: how to cut an onion so it falls into pieces, how to flip eggs with a flick of the wrist, how to sharpen a knife on a steel, how to scrape a counter clean after kneading bread. What's missing, too, delineates values acquired in those years: no microwave, no electric mixer, no (perish the thought) bread machine.

This same pleasure, pride, and obstinacy in working by hand is evident in many of the objects I've packed and unpacked since high school: bowls thrown on the wheel by friends, quilts made of scraps of well-loved clothes, and the hand-painted diploma each Putney graduate receives—a poignant reminder of the gifted seventeen-year-old who painted it for me with the ardor and generosity of first love, filling it with coded images of our past relationship and the idealized future that never quite arrived. It is almost frightening to realize the extent to which my current life, ideals, hopes, and ethics can be traced transparently to those four intense years. What if something had gone terribly wrong during that vulnerable and exquisitely formative period? But of course some things did go wrong, and others went right in entirely unexpected ways; that's the risk everyone takes in getting through adolescence, and it's intensified by taking on the task far from home. I've been experimenting with the idea of home ever since: how to make my own, and how to dismantle and reconstruct that sense of place with every move.

A rocking chair, it should be noted, is not practical—and it would be a stretch to call this one cheap in the scheme of graduate student life. It's all curves, taking up a lot of space in a small apartment. It's the only piece of furniture I own that can't be dismantled and packed flat. But it was made in Vermont, in the nineteenth century, with hand tools and hand-forged hardware. It draws my mind to the past, but also toward a future in which I might rock on a porch with a view of my garden, maybe, or in a bright window with a view of midtown Manhattan—or even rock a child to sleep. Like every act of packing up for a move, the rocking chair creates a space where I can look back and forward at the same time. And though I came upon it long after high school, the rocking chair more clearly conveys one ideal learned there than anything else I own: it sits facing the window, the light, the outdoors, and the motion of community life.

After graduating from the Putney School, **Kiri Miller** received a B.A. in music from the University of Chicago. She is now a Ph.D. student in ethnomusicology at Harvard University, writing a dissertation on sacred harp singing—a tradition she first encountered at Putney.

Everything But the Kitchen Sink

Kate McCullough '96
Governor Dummer Academy

Every dorm room is the same, at least on opening day. They all have the same basic components, a light oakwood bed set, dresser, chair, and desk with a matching bookcase placed conveniently on top, a mattress which is half the thickness of a geometry book, and four barren white walls. If you are lucky, there might be a couple of windows and a hook for your towel. Basically, it's a clean palette waiting to be splashed with the colors of your personality. There are so many possibilities and so little room. Yet, it's the only place on campus that you can designate as yours. It's your room. It's your space.

When I left my home in California for Governor Dummer, I was assigned my first dorm room. I am an only child, so having my own room to decorate was never a problem. However, having a room which my dorm peers would be constantly walking in and out of was a whole other story.

I had never visited my new school, so I had no idea before my arrival of what a dorm room looked like. A few weeks before the opening of school, I sent boxes full of everything imaginable. I mean everything—from new sheets and a comforter to old tapes I hadn't listened to for years. My friends donated things from every nook and cranny in their cellars to the Kate McCullough Going Away Fund. In fact, as I was sifting through a box in my new dorm room, I found a box of Equal sweetener. How did that

get sent? I really don't have any idea, except that I had accumu-
lated so much junk I could've started my own flea market. When
I was packing, I had the attitude of "Well . . . what if someday I
really need this?" Not only did I collect a storeroom of junk, I also
had a pile of room decorations that didn't resemble my interests
or my personality. I thought the typical preppy would have Van
Gogh posters and big college banners of Ivy League schools. Boy,
was I surprised! The typical female preppy has magazine cutouts
plastered all over her wall, including provocative Calvin Klein
ads. The typical male preppy? Well, let's just imagine what's on
the mind of most teenage males and we'll leave it at that.

Perhaps the biggest difference between having a room at home
and having a dorm room is room inspection. Every school day, a
dorm parent inspects my room. The trash has to be taken out, the
floor vacuumed, the bed made, and the desk straightened. Actually, this policy is very helpful. I can't imagine what my room
would look like after a week of not cleaning it.

Living in a dorm means not only keeping your space tidy, but
also keeping valuable items safe. Usually there is a lock on the
door from the outside, but none on the inside so nobody can lock
themselves in a room. Most students feel comfortable leaving their
doors unlocked, because there isn't really a lot of theft. In general,
however, male dorms have a bigger problem with stealing.

Having people in your dorm room is another important aspect
of dormitory life. In order to have a member of the opposite sex
in my room, my school asks that I get permission from the dorm
parent and sign in my guest. They keep their door open, and I
have to do the same. If opposite sex visitation is okay at your
school, be prepared for rules like these.

After three years of living in a dormitory, I've seen a variety of
room arrangements. They all start out with the basic furniture,
but within a few days they become a gallery of self-expression.
Some people have a cozy room with house plants and curtains,
while others stick to a Spartan decor. Others stack their books up
a wall and display an elaborate computer system with the newest
computerized games. Many students have every Beatle or Pearl
Jam poster available on their wall and a collection of CDs carefully organized in a rack stand.

Never be afraid to express your true interests in decorating your dorm room, whether it's putting up tons of photos or paintings you've made. Your room says a lot about the person you are. Besides, it's the place you'll spend the most time in because it's the place you sleep, study, and talk with friends for hours on end.

Off to Boarding School Checklist

You can't anticipate everything you'll need at boarding school (and we can't either), but this list should give you an idea of what you may need while you are away. Some are obvious, some are not, and clearly the skirts and dresses are not necessary if you're a boy. Check off what you need, and make sure you are supplied when you get to your school. Also, refer to your school's handbook for things that are not allowed at your school.

Clothing

Formal Clothing:

____ Blazer/	____ Socks	____ Dress pants
Sport jacket	____ Suit	____ Blouse
____ Formal dress	____ Skirt	____ Dress shoes
____ Shirts	____ Neckties	

Casual clothing:

___ T-Shirts	___ Bermuda shorts	___ Birkenstocks
___ Dresses	___ Hats/	___ Skirts
___ Underwear	baseball caps	___ Belt
___ Sweaters	___ Athletic shoes	___ Light jacket
___ Underwear	___ Warm jacket	___ Warm hat
___ Jeans	___ Mittens/gloves	___ Jeans (frayed)
(not frayed)	___ Socks	___ Shorts
___ Sandals/Tevas	___ Bathing suit	___ LaCoste shirts

For the Room:

The Essentials:

___ Pillow	___ Desk lamp	___ Pens/pencils
___ Alarm clock	___ Shampoo	___ Deodorant

___ Pencil sharpener   ___ Stri-Dex   ___ Kleenex
___ Conditioner   ___ Calculator   ___ Toothpaste/
___ Tylenol   ___ Razors   toothbrush
___ Shaving cream   ___ Sheets   ___ Brush/comb
___ Comforter   (2 sets)

Heavily Recommended:
___ Extension cord   ___ Hair dryer   ___ Hot pot
___ Cup o' Soup   ___ Vitamins   ___ Tacks
___ Posters   ___ Microwave-safe bowl
___ Mug (for coffee/hot chocolate/soup)
___ Lockable box for valuables
___ Basket or bag to carry your shampoo/
    conditioner/toothpaste, etc.
___ Sports equipment (hockey stick, lacrosse stick,
    baseball glove, football, etc. ad infinitum)

If You've Got 'em, Bring 'em:
___ Computer   ___ Power strip for computer
___ GameBoy/Sega   ___ Monitor   ___ Bicycle
___ Tape player   ___ CD player
___ Printer

At the time of this article (1995), **Kate McCullough** was a Mansion House proctor at Governor Dummer. She was also editor-in-chief of *The Governor*, and a co-director of the Eastern Massachusetts Special Olympics.

Boy, I Miss My Home

Tim Hillman
St. Andrew's-Sewanee School

On a clear and warm September day more than twenty years ago, I stood beneath the arch at St. Mark's School and watched my parents' car pull away. Suddenly they were gone, and I was at school until Thanksgiving, a long three months. Sure, I had been away from home before, but that was for camp. Boarding school seemed horribly frightening by comparison. I had told myself I wouldn't cry, but I felt the tears welling up in my eyes until Mr.

Gaccon, an aging master at St. Mark's, came up from behind, put his arm around me, and said "Off we go, boy." I walked with him toward my new room in a dorm and my new life. Twenty years later, I sit and watch each August as a fresh group of boarding students descends. One by one, they get their keys, move into naked rooms, meet their roommates, and finally say their good-byes. Just as I did, they stand and watch their parents go. There is almost always a tear or two, and always that turn toward the school and the new life.

The weeks that follow move quickly. Classes start, teams form, and friendships develop as each new student constructs life at boarding school. For most students, the transition is fairly smooth. They miss their parents, their brothers and sisters, their friends, their cars; all of those elements that made home special. For a few, however, the sense of loss becomes overpowering, and each day becomes more and more difficult to face. Everything the student left behind becomes a reminder that life is different now, in a different place. The green grass of home looks awfully good. A parade of phone calls and letters home begins. Again and again, the homesick student tries to get Mom or Dad to understand they are unhappy and want to come home. Mom and Dad usually stand firm. Boarding school was chosen for a reason, and parents are awfully good at sticking to their decisions. As time goes by, school becomes more and more dissatisfying. There are loads of complaints: "The food is not as good as home," "I can't take studying when the school wants me to," "The teachers are mean," "Nobody here cares about me," "When I'm home I can go to the beach whenever I want to," "Nobody tells me when to come home on Saturday night at home," "My room is awful," "I don't have a roommate at home," "There are too many rules," "I don't have any friends," "I miss my boyfriend."

Sure it's tough, but there are ways not to let it get the better of you. Let's hit a few of the problems head-on . . .

"I miss my parents."
If this is your first time away from home, you are naturally going to be sad. Don't answer that sadness by calling home every night. Set up weekly phone calls with your parents to share what happened during your week, and hold yourself

to those calls. If you are missing them at other times, see what you can do to help yourself be content. Look for things in the community that make you feel at home. If dorm parents offer to let people sit in the living room, take advantage of the opportunity. While it may not be your home, even other people's homes can produce that feeling of contentment that is so important.

"I don't have any friends."
Hardest of all is the feeling that you have no friends, or no one to talk to and share time with. The only solution is activity. Get out and meet different people. Move around at meals, and sit with people you don't know. Find the things that you've got in common with others (music? art? drama? writing? sports? religion?). Most important of all, don't sit in your room and mope. It'll get you nowhere but lonely fast.

"Nobody here cares about me."
At boarding school, there is always somebody who will care enough to listen. If you need somebody to talk to, try an older student, particularly one that has been identified by the school as a leader. Go knock on his door and tell him: "I'm having a pretty hard time adjusting to being here— could you help me?" Be specific about what's making life hard, and don't be embarrassed. If you miss your parents, let him know. Most boarding students have been in similar positions, and will not look down on you. If you can't find a student, look for a faculty member. Remember, these people have chosen to live at a boarding school and don't mind taking time to listen.

"The food is not as good as home."
Naturally. There's no way that someone cooking for 100–1000 people is going to be able to cook meals that are going to please everyone. Find out how to take advantage of the possibilities in the school menu. Figure out a way to take the school food and turn it into something special. If you're still unhappy with it, try talking to the food service manager. Go to him with a suggestion and see what happens. Ask "Would

it be alright if I made a suggestion or two for different meals?" Be prepared to come up with something, since he usually will do his best to please.

"I like to go to bed late."
Days at boarding schools are long and rigorous, and demand that you get an adequate amount of sleep. That's why so many schools have set lights-out times. If you try to stay up late, chances are that your days are going to be less productive. Sure, it's a sacrifice, but you'll be happier at school if you are successful, and sleeping enough can help.

"Nobody tells me when to come home on Saturday night at home."
Being at boarding school entails a few sacrifices, and this is another. Your school is responsible to your parents to know where you are. So, there are always check-in times. Try starting your weekend days a little earlier so that by the time night rolls around you are ready to settle down to sleep.

"My room is awful."
Sometimes rooms are terrific, and other times they seem like something from a forgotten age. If there are big problems, go to your dorm parent and point them out. Tell him: "There are a few problems with my room, could you help?" Don't sleep on a lumpy mattress just because it's there. I can still remember the 6'6" classmate who asked for (and received) an extra-long bed so he would be more comfortable at night. Bring things from home that make your room feel like home. A comforter for your bed or your favorite pillow will go a long way toward consoling you. Try to find something that will make your room your home. Lots of students sell and trade couches, chairs, and other various items of furniture for low cost. A dorm room is a lot more like home when you can flop down in a big overstuffed chair after dinner.

"I hate my roommate."
Roommates are not always easy to get along with, as even the luckiest administrator cannot always guarantee that

two unfamiliar students will be compatible. Roommates at boarding school often become close friends, however, so do your best to give the relationship a chance to work. If problems continue, try to work it through with your dorm parent and roommate. Sit down with your roommate and try to talk it out. A good start might be: "I wanted to talk to you because I feel like we are not getting along as roommates, and I would like to try and make it work. What can we do?" If that doesn't help the situation, try your dorm parent. As a last resort, schools will usually separate roommates that are having trouble.

The only way out of the homesickness cycle involves time, activity, and acceptance. Give it time to run its course, actively pursue involvement in the community, and accept that there are things about boarding school you just can't change. Once you've got yourself on an even keel, you'll be prepared to both succeed and prosper in your new environment.

The co-editor of the first edition and the fellow who had the idea in the first place, **Tim Hillman** has taught at Phillips Academy, The Buckley School, and St. Andrews-Sewanee School. Most recently he has been writing about education and computer technology, and also teaching.

Family Ties

Joseph Barker
St. Andrew's-Sewanee School

"You've always been great kids ... I'm going to miss you so much!" was one of the last things my mom had said as she and my dad prepared to leave me, my brother, and my sister at boarding school. Panic overtook me and sadness was the only thing I felt. I gave them a tearful hug good-bye and watched them drive off. Did I make the right decision to come to my school as a boarder? I went to my room as soon as my parents left. My roommate from Japan was saying good-bye to his family. I unpacked the rest of my stuff and sat down on my bed, thinking that now I was on my own, and the thought scared me. I did not feel that I was up to the challenge of independence.

For me, the decision to go to boarding school was extremely hard. I came from a very close family and always enjoyed being around my parents and siblings. I had gone to the St. Andrew's-Sewanee School for two years as a day student while my mother finished Seminary at the University of the South (Sewanee). All of my close friends were at SAS, and when my family moved away, my siblings and I faced a tough decision: whether we would stay at SAS as boarders and remain with our friends, or leave for the security of our home and our parents.

I have always done things with my family—trips and vacations, help with homework, laughing around the dinner table, fighting in the living room—I guess what one would call a "normal" family. Coming to boarding school changed all of that. I missed that "normal" life. I missed being able to go to my parents with a problem and talk it out with them. I missed not being able to go home when I was tired of school. I missed the nightly family dinners, even the fighting in the living room.

My relationship with both my brother and my sister changed when we began to board. Before going to school, I was asked if my brother Michael and I would room together. We wouldn't have made it through the first week without killing each other. We had separate rooms at home and were not used to being roommates, so we weren't about to start at school. Besides, he was two years younger than me and I wanted a roommate my own age. So we found ourselves in different rooms in the same small dorm. When our dog died at home, it was good being together so we could talk about it. It was good to see him daily and find out how things were going. Still, before boarding, I would see Michael every day after school and I would see him at length. By boarding, I didn't see him unless I happened to run into him or sought him out. This happened with Amanda, too, because we weren't even in the same building and I had to seek her out to talk to her.

We didn't fight as much either. I guess this came from not being in close contact all the time, but at the same time, I missed talking with Michael and Amanda like we had before going to boarding school. Even so, it was hard being in the same dorm with Michael, because even though I wanted our closeness, I wanted my space, too. Often, I didn't want him to be always in the same place that I lived. When we got in arguments, I didn't want him to be in the same building. Yet, in spite of all of this, my relationship with Michael and Amanda was strengthened because we learned to value our time together. Even though we were often separated, we became better friends.

My relationship with my parents changed even more. I missed them during the first month of school. I missed their just being "there" for me. I hadn't realized how much I had taken for granted. I missed little things like a hug when I came home from school, the way my mom did the laundry, and especially home cooking. I called them often with our personal 800 number, but even this wasn't as good as the real thing. When you leave the people who have cared for you your entire life, you are going to miss them. That's a fact.

You'll change by going to boarding school and you will likely discover that change when you go home for the first time. It was hard to come home on Thanksgiving break my first year as a boarder and do what my parents said. I was already used to making my own decisions and caring for myself. It was good to be home, though, because I had been away two and a half months and I missed my home and my parents. I had my own room and had to follow my parents' rules, not the school's. I found that Mom and Dad treated me more like an adult and trusted me to stay out and drive around to places they wouldn't have before. I still miss my parents, but after being away from home for a year now, I am glad I went to boarding school when I did. I have already started out on my own.

Though coming to boarding school for the first time will be difficult for you no matter what, there are things that you can do to make your life at boarding school enjoyable. Keep in contact with both your parents and siblings; don't lose your family ties. Keep yourself busy enough not to dwell on being in a new situation and on wanting to go home. Even though your relationship with your family will change when you go to boarding school, you will have a new family. No matter if your school has fifty boarders or a thousand, it doesn't matter; you have a new family. Yes, there have been bad days when I didn't want to be here, but the friends I have, the teachers and dorm parents who are my surrogate parents have made me want to stay and be involved with and care for my larger family of many members.

Joe Barker was a class of '96 graduate of St. Andrew's-Sewanee School. He is an award-winning musician and actor.

TIPS FOR KEEPING IN TOUCH

1. Keep your family phone numbers in a convenient place. We've even supplied a mini phone book for you here:

Name: Phone:

_____   _____

_____   _____

_____   _____

_____   _____

_____   _____

_____   _____

2. It's a great idea to have a personal "800" number. Talk with Mom or Dad and your long-distance phone company—it's pretty easy to get set up. Write it down here:

_____

3. Do you have pictures of all your family members? Which ones are missing?

_____

_____

4. If you were to get a "care package" from home, what would it have in it?

_____

_____

_____

Now, when you need one, you'll be able to tell Mom or Dad just what you want.

5. When you feel most distant from your family, give them a call, or write a letter. They are always there. Here are some things that you could write home about.
   • meeting new friends
   • getting a part in a play
   • something special a teacher did
   • goals you've set
   • doing well in a class
   • a great game you played
   • vacation plans
   • special recognition you received
   • almost anything else . . .

Life as It's Lived in C-Dorm

Paul Vickers
Woodberry Forest School

Living in a dorm with thirty-four high school boys, mostly sopho-mores, can be an eye-opening experience for someone who grew up with two sisters. Five years into the experience, I'm still sur-prised by the number of pizza boxes, chip bags, and drink cans that never find their way to the trash. And every September, when the new boys move in, I am amazed at how many of them arrive already equipped with the quintessential boys'-boarding-school posters of scantily-clad women (and then, even more stunningly, put them up right away under their mothers' approving—or at least not objecting—gazes).

There's much more to life on dorm, though, than the never-changing habits, desires, and postures of teenage boys. As trite as it sounds, each boy on Walker Building's C-Dorm is unique, and the 150-odd individuals who have made this their home, a few more than once during my tenure here, have created their share of memorable drama, amusement, and chaos. A few of the happy memories: I remember being called in to do the year-end inspection of Blair Clarke and Matt Donahue's room. Told that there was a hole in the closet wall I needed to check out, I nearly jumped out of my shoes when I opened the door to find a rubber-masked Sandlin Douglas springing out at me. I remember the wild shouts that went up suddenly and throughout the building one weeknight, well after lights out, when some double-overtime Duke-Carolina or Duke-Virginia basketball game finally came to its dramatic conclusion. And I will forever associate the C-Dorm common room with Game 6 of the 1995 World Series, when my Braves finally won it all and Colin Gallahan was there with a celebratory high-five.

That game was on a Saturday night, and the typical Saturday-night activity around here is, too often, watching worthless TV shows or movies the boys have seen so often they can recite all the lines. The same atmosphere that produces a tired, ritualistic response in some boys, though, brings out creativity in others. One night last year, I was lucky enough to be present in Reed Shelger's room for an evening of Shelgerian Theater—a kind of individual freestyle dancing put on by various dorm members to the wildly cheering approval of what seemed like most of the others. This year, I was in my apartment one Saturday night when the sound of acoustic guitars drifted down the hall and under my door. I followed their siren's song to Matt Monson's room, where I was then treated to maybe a half dozen of Joe Harmon's terrifically entertaining original songs. On bad weekends, I am convinced that the boys of this generation are surrendering their minds to Nintendo and "Baywatch." Then, a Fir Tree Open-Mic Night, a well-attended Poetry Club meeting, or the latest edition of the *Talon* (school publication) reminds me that many have not succumbed.

As resident master of C-Dorm, I am most familiar with the cadence of life among the fourth-formers. I love the melting pot that is the whole Walker Building, though, with its mixing of forms and personalities that no other campus dorm building can approach. Beyond that, most of my fondness for the rest of the Walker Building stems from aspects of the building itself. I love the fact that it houses almost 40 percent of the student body. I love the odd system combining numbers and letters which is used to designate the various dorms within the building. I love the quirky shape of C-6 and the fact that it is completely unconnected to the rest of C-Dorm. I love the way wings were patched on and modifications were made to the original main building. I love the high ceilings, the cavernous attic, and the little railed-in perch atop the whole building, offering to the privileged few who have been up there the best view anywhere of campus and the surrounding areas.

Just before dawn on a March morning all is quiet in the Walker Building, but not because of the hour. Almost all my neighbors have departed for spring break. As I walk around the halls, listening to the creak of the floor, I can't help but wonder at the vision of Captain Bob (founder) a century ago. With a student body only about one-seventh the size of today's, he set out to craft the building which would remain the heart and soul of the school into the next millennium, even as new, state-of-the-art facilities spring up around it. I'm sure someday I'll want to move out of C-Dorm and into something a little bigger, but I'm not quite ready yet. I still enjoy my top-floor view out through the columns, down the driveway, and across the golf course to the sunset over the Blue Ridge. It's still a special feeling for me to weave my own thread into the history of this grand old place.

Paul Vickers is a science teacher and dorm master at Woodberry Forest.

Dorm Identity
David and Amy Vachris
Blair Academy

Living in a dormitory is an integral part of any boarding school experience, yet while most private schools highlight their excellence in the academic or athletic arenas, fewer ever cite their strength in residential life. In recent years, however, more and more institutions have placed greater emphasis on the community aspect of their schools, recognizing that the opportunity to learn how to live with others, to manage one's time and commitments, and to interact closely with other students and with adults in a residential setting all make for a very positive and unique educational experience, one that often translates into higher achievement in the classroom and on the playing field. What follows are a few of the ways that we work toward building a strong and positive dorm identity at Blair Academy.

Blair works hard to create dormitory settings that are safe, educational, and structured, as well as comfortable and fun. Each dorm is encouraged to create its own identity (within the framework of the rules, of course) and to build a sense of pride about its living space. The process begins long before the students arrive on campus. In fact, admissions officers and administrators spend many hours over the summer pairing up new students and creating a balance in each dorm of both returning and first time students, athletes and musicians, intellectuals and socialites, and international students and those who live just around the corner.

From a student and parent point of view, the dorm identity process starts on the very first day of school. As families pass through the granite pillars and drive up the front hill of the Blair Academy campus on registration day, they have a difficult time deciding where to look first. In addition to the constant movement of people and belongings, families are often surprised by the display of colors. Dormitory flags are waving outside of the residential halls, and both senior student leaders and adult dorm staff members are decked out in T-shirts representing their dorm's particular color. (Here at Blair we have Insley Red, Davies Purple, East Green, and Annie Royal Blue to name a few.) These helpful folks are ready to assist in the "moving-in" process; they lug boxes and suitcases up the stairs, answer questions from nervous students, and help assuage the fears of the first-time boarding school parent. By the end of registration day, each family knows not only the layout and color choice of the dorm where the student will be living, but they also are acquainted with each of the student leaders and adult dorm staff members associated with the dorm. A "home away from home" is already on its way to being established.

During the first days of school, each dormitory works to establish both individual and dorm goals. At these meetings, housemasters discuss the school's expectations of rules and procedures and solicit adjectives from dorm residents that describe their ideal living situation. Using this student input, the dorm leaders create a framework, or mission statement of sorts, to help guide all members of the dorm throughout a successful year. Often, students will stress that they want a "safe, comfortable, clean, and fun" space. Sometimes a residential hall will form a dorm council, to plan special events and to aid the housemaster with appropriate and effective responses to minor in-dorm infractions. Other dorms will make a commitment to winning the Blair Intramural Games (B.I.G.) trophy by the year's end. Regardless of the goals, student input is a key factor in starting the year off in a positive manner.

Together with their dorm staff and senior prefects, housemasters create a structured environment for academics, but they also create a living experience where students interact socially. Many dorms host events for their residents that have become hallmarks of that dorm's life and reputation. Events such as the Locke Hall talent show, Davies Hall Christmas caroling, Insley Hall end-of-the-year party, and Saturday night "dorm feeds" are a few examples of activities that keep dorm life interesting and lively. In addition, during Peddie Week (the days before the annual autumn matchup against Blair's arch rival, the Peddie School) dorms rally to create a school-spirited week, featuring the occasional small prank, as well as skits and banners for the pep rally and bonfire celebrations.

Dorms also bond by taking on the responsibility of organizing schoolwide weekend activities events. The Mason holiday party in December is a traditional favorite, especially with its annual schoolwide Santa contest. Annie Hall's sponsorship of the Sadie Hawkins dance in January, and Insley's Disco Inferno ('70s–'80s dance) are other examples of how dorms work together to provide the entire school community with fun and interesting activities. These are great opportunities for students to work with each other and with faculty in meaningful ways outside of the class-room.

Yet another builder of dorm pride is the student-sponsored Blair Intramural Games Tournament (B.I.G.) run by the residential life office. Each weekend, some kind of B.I.G. event is organized to add some spice to the weekend activities schedule. Students earn B.I.G. points for their dorm by participating in events such as Frisbee golf, ultimate Frisbee, 3 on 3 basketball, water polo, and volleyball. Contests for B.I.G. points are not limited to athletic events, however; other ways to earn points for one's dorm include dormwide grade point averages, egg toss competitions, chess tournaments, "cash" winnings at Casino Night and participation in community service events. Points are tallied throughout the year, with the winning dorm earning championship T-shirts, a pizza party, and bragging rights until the next year.

Residential life at Blair means more than just having a bed in a room somewhere. Our dorms are places where students can grow socially and emotionally, where they have opportunities to challenge themselves and each other, where they are supported and valued by those working with them, and where they make a difference and a contribution just by being who they are. Our commitment to student life pays off; parents frequently comment that their son or daughter chose Blair because it just "felt right," and that there was a great sense of "belonging" on campus. Senior prefects often choose to serve in the dorm they first lived in, or where they felt the best about themselves, with the commitment to make other students there feel as much a part of both the dorm community and of Blair as they were allowed to feel. Finally, many of the stories shared on Alumni Day and in yearbook entries are based on the community experiences witnessed in the dorms, or as the result of a dorm connection. Given the many opportunities to grow and to share, to learn and to contribute, residential life, centered on a dorm identity, is critical to the boarding school experience.

David and Amy Vachris have been at Blair Academy for ten years. Dave is currently the dean of residential life and Amy serves as the housemaster of Insley Hall, a dorm of freshmen/sophomore boys. They met at Vermont Academy as new faculty, were married at VA, and have three children (Madison, Taylor, and Gunnar)—all born while working at Blair.

Safety, Education, and Fun
Tekakwitha M. Pernambuco-Wise, M.A.
Director, Residential Life
Wilcox Hall Dormitory, Mid-Pacific Institute

From the moment our pupils check into Wilcox Hall, they hear our motto of *Safety, Education, and Fun*. We tell them that for the most part, their parents sent them to us with two eyes, two arms, and two legs and that's how they want them back. They are at Mid-Pacific for a college-preparatory education but since "all work and no play makes Jack a dull boy," they need to have fun every now and then. Most of them think that we have the motto all wrong, though, and that it should be *Fun, Fun, and Fun*. Nevertheless, they try to abide by the official one.

Wilcox Hall is a microcosm of our global society with pupils hailing from South America, Europe, Asia, the Pacific Islands, mainland USA, and Hawai'i. Staff and their spouses are also international and as a result, we resemble the United Nations. With all of these mixtures, one would think that there would be cultural clashes, but we have found that teenagers are pretty much the same the world over. They take the same risks, like the same music, dress the same way and whether they are ESL or not, speak the same adolescent language of me, myself, and I (as we've come to expect at this age).

At the beginning of each year, we have a Family Friday evening, where the boarders are required to stay in (groan) and engage in organized activities that are facilitated by the local YMCA. The object of the exercise is not to punish them by taking away their first Friday night of freedom (as they think), but (as they see by the end of the evening) to help them to bond with their fellow dorm parents, brothers, and sisters.

Our world is divided into smaller dorm families with a dorm

parent as the head. These families meet weekly for meetings or socials and go on monthly outings. Favorites are the cinema, restaurants, horseback riding, parasailing, ice skating, and cosmic bowling. The bigger family of the entire dorm meets fortnightly for meetings where we celebrate birthdays, Residents of the Month, anyone who got all As for the quarter, and recreation awards. Those who attain the president's list or honor roll are treated to supper at the director's home once a quarter.

Because we are at the heart of the Pacific Basin, song, music, and the ocean play a big part in dorm life. Trips to the beach for picnics or surfing are common. We take turns performing at our monthly formal dinners, annual open house and talent shows. The gifted among us sing, dance the hula, make leis, and play the ukulele. The less capable do the same anyway.

We try to expose our teenagers to experiences that some may obtain from home and others might not otherwise get. At times, they are kicking, screaming, and grumbling all the way until they arrive at the event and then they don't want it to end because they're having so much fun. Favorites are dinner-theater shows and dinner boat cruises around the Honolulu harbor. Monthly leadership workshops are offered to help those who are naturally bossy to become more skilled at being domineering, especially if they are interested in applying for one of the elite student leader positions that comes with the perk of a single room.

Adolescents often pay more attention to what an adult other than their parents say, even when their parents use the same words. Our dorm parents experience this same phenomenon and so to countermand this, every Wednesday is guest speaker night. Topics vary from the serious such as safety, substance abuse prevention, fire prevention, and etiquette to the entertaining such as belly, hip-hop, ballroom, and swing dancing. Our myriad of represented countries allows for great variety at our International Nights, where we share clothing, food (always a big hit), music, and stories from our native lands.

Etiquette is practiced daily but is most consciously employed at afternoon teas with the director and monthly formal theme dinners. A favorite theme is the *rose escort,* where the males escort the female boarders into the dining room, with the former offering the latter a rose before taking her to her seat. Chivalry is not yet dead; in fact, it's quite scary to the boys who often prepare for days before to ensure that when it's their turn to attend the young lady, they are doing so with style.

Our annual Valentine fashion show is always enjoyable and we never thought that teenagers still yearn to go trick-or-treating until we saw how seriously ours take their costumes on Halloween night (fake blood is a popular accoutrement for any costume). One of the most pleasurable events of the year is campus caroling, not merely because it's the one night that the pupils get out of study hall so that they can walk with lanterns to the homes of the campus residents, rain or shine, belting out Christmas tunes that most of us don't know the words to, but more because we get goodies at each house and then end at the president's house to exchange Secret Santa gifts and stuff ourselves silly with even more treats.

No one enjoys doing chores, which are done nightly. It takes our pupils about fifteen minutes to complete a chore, such as sweeping the hallway: five minutes to grumble about having to work like a servant even though their parents are paying so much money for them to attend Mid-Pacific, five minutes to actually do the chore, and five minutes to recover from such hardship. For some, there's an extra five minutes because they have to redo the job. This becomes even worse at our all-dorm cleanups, which are done twice per year. The only reward is a dance at the end, when we invite residents from a nearby boarding school. We hear the pupils comparing notes as to which boarding program is crueler and then thank heavens that they actually live at Wilcox Hall because it's worse at the other school since our dorm is coed and theirs is divided by gender.

Senior Farewell is the most emotional night of the year. It is the dorm's equivalent of a graduation. It starts with a formal dinner and then we adjourn to the dorm for a video highlights show of all the events that occurred during the year, after which the seniors each say a few words to the dorm community. We frequently hear apologies for giving the staff a hard time (little do they know that they weren't as bad as they thought). By now, they know the official motto by heart and leave their dorm brothers and sisters with the advice that no matter how hard they think it is to obey all the rules, serve consequences (euphemism for punishment), do scrub down (our way of saying chores), focus during study hall, follow curfew, and pretend to be asleep by lights-out, it's harder still saying good-bye to their home away from home and so much Fun, Fun, and Fun.

Tekakwitha M. Pernambuco-Wise is beginning her fifth year at Mid-Pacific Institute as the director of residential life. She holds a master's degree in education and is the product of a Catholic secondary school, ivy league, and international education, beginning in her homeland in South America and continuing in England, Canada, and USA.

She has over fifteen years experience working with children and youth in the following areas:
- Teacher: mathematics, Spanish ESL, special education
- Coach: as a third-degree black belt judo competitor, she has coached at the high school and university levels
- Administrator: education, substance abuse and violence prevention, and human services

She and Dr. Paul Pernambuco-Wise have been married for thirteen years. She counts among her hobbies hula, writing, and American Indian crafts.

Slumber

Hallie Gordon '97
The Thacher School

When I left home to attend a boarding school on the East coast three years ago I had a hard time describing my new life to my friends back home in Wyoming. One of the things that shocked them the most was the idea that not only did I spend the night at school (which to them was a fate worse than death) but I also had to spend the weekends there. How could I survive? I was asked again and again. In one letter home my freshman year I tried to explain the weekends at prep school by describing it as a big slumber party with all your friends and some teachers. But they really didn't buy that; they wanted to know what I did on Friday night.

As I mentioned before this is my third year at boarding school. I attended one on the East Coast and now am at one in California. I figure that is two and a half years so far, each with eight months, with four weekends to a month, coming to eighty weekends (more or less) that I have spent at school. And, as with all things, if you observe something enough you will inevitably begin to see patterns. This is no different for the weekend experience at a boarding school. Through careful observation and analysis (which stems from boredom) I find that there are several different stages that one goes through as the weekend begins. First there is relief. Finally all that work and running around from place to place has once again temporarily ceased. The hardworking student takes a deep breath, maybe even two.

Next, hypermotivation strikes. The student, having relaxed for a split second, realizes that now there is plenty of time to get everything done that needs to be done. To catch up on work, sleep, and all the other important things that tend to get neglected during the academic week. She will immediately set ridiculously unreasonable goals for herself. For instance, Friday afternoon the student will smile and say to herself: "Finally it's Friday and I have the whole weekend. And this weekend won't be like last weekend: I am going to make a list, accomplish something, organize my life. This weekend I am going to clean my room, do my homework, do my laundry, go to town, read a book, write a letter, edit the yearbook, call my sister, go running, go hiking, read ahead in history, and finish my term paper."

Calmly she will head back to her dorm room and instantly fall asleep to make up for the previous night when she had been up until two with a paper on political parties during the Federal era. After an appropriate length of time (four to six hours) she will wake up and her brain (which is highly skilled at defending itself from becoming overworked) will have automatically erased all those silly notions of productivity and organization. This leaves our student free to spend the remainder of her Friday night hanging out with her friends talking about how they wished there was something better to do on the weekends. Perhaps one of them will mention homework, but she will instantly be silenced by the unanimous protest of her classmates who remind her that the subject is taboo.

So curfew arrives (all too early) and everyone makes their way back to his or her respective dorm where their dormmates are preparing a feast of foods with high sugar content. They stay up very late talking about other people's love lives and complaining that there is never anything to do on the weekend. Saturday morning arrives and the sun streams through the window onto the cluttered desk. Something clicks and our student realizes that it would be wise to do a little homework before she heads for the basketball game.

So in response to the question regarding how boarding school students spend their weekends, I would answer that it is not so different from what we would be doing at home except we don't have to drive anywhere to complain to our friends about boredom—they are right across the hall. In Wyoming, you might have to go twenty miles.

Hallie Gordon began her boarding school career at Deerfield Academy. At Thacher, her main interests were poetry and writing.

SOME WAYS TO LEARN THE LANDSCAPE

Make a map of those places at your school that you most often frequent. Then, compare that map to a real map of your school. What are the differences? What part(s) of the campus are covered by your daily route? Are the places that you frequent clustered together? Are they related in any way? What is outside your loop? Are there places you have never been to?

Try these simple goals:

- once a week, for three weeks, visit at least one building/ place on campus you've never seen
- without missing classes, alter the route you take every day
- spend at least an hour in the library and/or art gallery just exploring
- eat in a different dining hall with different people
- visit an administrative office that oversees some aspect of the school unrelated to your daily experience: the business office, the admissions office, the treasurer's office

- find out how something about the school's physical plant works, like the electricity

Consider the following map made by a tenth-grader at Phillips Academy. She scaled the buildings according to their importance in her daily life. The arrow represents her direction, the numbers the sequence of stops.

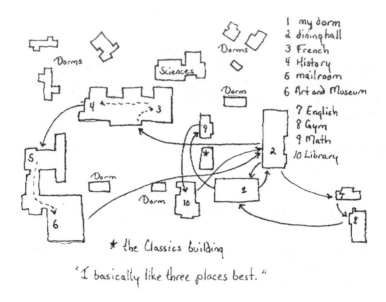

What does this map tell you about her?

SETTLING INTO RELATIONSHIPS

Packing Your Cultural Knapsack

Nadine Abraham-Thompson
Phillips Exeter Academy

It is August 15th and you are deciding what to pack in your bags and boxes for Exeter. You know that you definitely want to take your favorite things—books, games, computer, stuffed toys, CDs, cassettes, your favorite blanket—all of the things you need so your room will look like home. If you don't want it to look like home, at least you'll make a statement about who you are.

So, who are you anyway? What are the things and events up until now that describe who you are? You have read all of Exeter's publications, visited the campus, and no doubt you have heard about multiculturalism and diversity. The students at Exeter take a lot of pride in being a richly diverse school. Next to academic excellence, diversity is the second most important reason to attend our school. So, the question is, what do you have to offer culturally? What does it mean to be culturally diverse? At Exeter and other schools it means students from many countries and states, boys and girls, teachers, administrators, staff, and custodians, all living and working together in a community. The student body is the most diverse population in this equation.

So you ask again—what makes me special? What do I have to add to this diverse community? This is a good opportunity to take inventory.

- What state or country do you live in?
- Do you live in a city or rural area?
- What about your family—where do they spend most of their time? What language do you speak?
- What places have you visited?
- How many brothers and sisters do you have?
- Who do you consider to be part of your family? What religion are you?
- What holidays do you celebrate?
- What are your favorite foods?
- What musical interests do you have?
- Do you do volunteer work? If so, where? Do you belong to any organizations at school or in your community?

Which of these things are important to you? Do you want to share this information with others? Do you want these things to be a part of your life at school?

If the answer is "Yes" to any of the above, maybe you need to make room in your "cultural knapsack" so you can take appropriate things with you. Let me correct myself here. There are two knapsacks: One is real, a place where you can put important objects that may help you to remember those significant things that are important to you and are part of your cultural identity. The other knapsack is invisible, a place where you can store all of that cultural information about you that makes you special. So, now let's rethink this packing thing. You may want to take that new CD with the great Indian music, that quilt that your grandmother gave you, your chopsticks, Indian jewelry, posters, music, your harp, your favorite carving from the Ivory Coast, a supply of dried noodles, a crocheted afghan, a six-pack of your favorite soda from Trinidad, or your Thai costume and dance ensemble.

Great! Now you have decided what to take. Isn't it interesting to find out what is important to you? I bet some of your next questions will be: Do I want to show or tell any of my new friends about these things? Will they like me? Will they like my things? Will they respect me? My initial response is that none or any of that is guaranteed, but part of living in a diverse culture means having to learn tolerance and respect. Feeling good about yourself, your ethnic nationality, religion, and cultural icons are part of what makes these communities so exciting and rich.

Another idea may be to talk to your parents about what their cultural icons may be. They may be ethnic or religious, like the legacy of Martin Luther King or Sojourner Truth, or a statue of Buddha, or the Bible. You often bring this type of diversity with you whenever you leave home and will begin a journey of self-discovery when trying to explore its significance in the development of your identity.

Once you have arrived at school, there will be numerous student organizations and clubs to join. You will be bombarded with requests from your new friends to join their special-interest groups but you may also want to join a club that connects you to your cultural and religious upbringing. You may want to join the Jewish Student Organization which meets once a week, to share a meal and worship together. The event is called "Shabbat." The Exeter Social Service Organization (ESSO) provides community services such as knitting hats for the homeless or planning the homeless vigil or volunteering at the local hospice or child-care center. You may want to join the Afro Latin Exonian Society or P.I.P. (People Interested in Poetry). At Exeter we have approximately forty student organizations and musical groups that a student can belong to. All of them are an expression and celebration of the rich diversity that each of our students bring when they attend our school.

It is important to remember that even though Exeter is described as diverse and multicultural, it is only so because of the rich cultural diversity of the individuals who attend. So what you bring with you, what you pack in your "cultural knapsack," comprises our school's culture and defines as well as redefines it over time. Culture and diversity is inclusive of gender, race, ethnicity, nationality, sexual orientation, music, politics, art, literature, beauty, athletics, and individual taste and preference. So, go ahead and pack the merengue tapes, Korean noodles, your favorite sari, or African carving. You may be surprised how good it looks and feels to have it close at hand.

Some Ways to Celebrate Your Cultural Knapsack

First, consider where you come from . . . specifically, consider what place most closely defines what you consider the essence of your personality. Here are some choices:

- a neighborhood
- a landscape
- a room

- a nation
- a region
- a family

- a house
- a social class
- a favorite haunt

Some of the "places" are small; some are huge. Some are geographical; some are political or economic. What is your place of origin?

_____

_____

_____

Second, imagine that hundreds of years from now, an archeologist is excavating the site where you spent much of your childhood. Imagine the archeologist asking herself, "Who were these people?" She wants to know what you cared about, what kind of language you used, what you worshiped, what you feared, what entertained you, what saddened you, what you loved, and what you hated. What clues might she uncover which would help her to answer these questions?

_____

_____

_____

_____

What information might the excavation yield about the family, home, neighborhood, local community, region, racial culture, or nation?

_____

_____

_____

_____

Perhaps she finds your knapsack. What's in it?

_____

_____

_____

_____

Third, think about these things that influence who you are . . .

- schools
- homes
- friends
- culture
- genetics

- media
- community
- economics
- family history
- race/ethnicity

- politics
- groups (athletic, social, religious, extracurricular)
- personal and physical characteristics

Do you think of yourself as more heavily influenced by your environment or your family and your upbringing?

_____

_____

_____

_____

Do the two overlap in your personality? _____ _____

How might the new school you are attending change your sense of who you are?

_____

_____

_____

_____

What new forces might influence who you are?

_____

_____

_____

_____

Fourth, find groups at your school that celebrate your cultural background. If you can't find any that do, then try to organize one that reflects your cultural background, however you define it.

Fifth, think about the stereotypes—racial, social, religious, cultural—you see people use. What stereotypes might people use to describe you?

_____

_____

_____

Would they be fair? Do you fit a stereotype perfectly?

_____

_____

_____

If you do not (and of course you do not), then does anyone?

_____

_____

List all your personal characteristics.

_____

_____

_____

Now, consider how many stereotypes some group of those characteristics might belong to. What groups can you think of?

_____

_____

_____

Nadine Abraham-Thompson is the associate dean of multicultural affairs at Phillips Exeter Academy. She is originally from Trinidad.

What Do I Bring to This Place?
What Does This Place Bring to Me?
What Is Culture Shock and How Do I Deal with It?

Michaela Pavlisova '96
St. Andrews-Sewanee

I looked behind me and saw my mother crying and my father just standing there as if he were hoping that I was not going to leave. There in the distance was one of the paths I could travel, the one

I had known for years, the one I could take almost without looking where I was going. There were my little sister, my friends, my favorite bakery, stores and houses I passed every day on my way to school, my school and teachers . . . my life. All of that was left behind as I slowly disappeared from my parents' sight in the airport crowds trying to find the right way around. Rain was falling and far away, where the planes could not be seen anymore, the sun was trying to find its way through the clouds.

I didn't know. Finding my way in the ant mound called Letiste Ruzyne, sitting surrounded by the screaming jet engines and looking out of the small round window, I didn't know. I didn't know and maybe I didn't even want to know right then. It was early . . . early to say how the day would turn out or what it would be like there, behind the big ocean, on the other side of the planet. Nobody could say. As one Spanish proverb says "What will be, will be." And choosing a path that I wouldn't even have dreamed of a year ago promised a lot of excitement and something that not everyone has a chance to experience. And here I am. . . .

Coming from a city of more than 1.5 million people to a community of less than 350 people might itself be considered a shock. Yet the beginning seems to be the best of all—at least for a time. Call it "the honeymoon." Trading rainy weather and a cold summer for a hot southern environment seemed to be the best thing I ever did. Just like a newlywed bride, I was in love . . . literally. Everything was new and I was excited about so many things. Meeting new people, learning new things, eating different kinds of food—all that was like a dream, not because it was necessarily that great but because it was different. But there comes a time when things fall into a routine and nothing is as exciting as it is supposed to be. After a while the husband doesn't bring flowers anymore and instead of going out for dinner the bride has to learn how to cook. Staying in a different country works very similarly. The food that was once new and interesting becomes old and almost the same every day. School gets started and the schedule and daily routines aren't always our best friends. People who at the beginning seemed to be funny, or at least tried to be, become tiring. Then the time for culture shock comes. And together with it thoughts like "What was I thinking? This is a better life? Fun? Good joke. . . . What am I doing here?"

"So where are you from?" That was the most common question I had to answer the first couple of days while staying here in the United States. It wasn't very surprising. I expected the question. What was surprising, and maybe a bit annoying once asked too many times, were questions like: "Is your country still part of Russia?" "Have you ever seen a television before?" "Do you want me to teach you how to use a calculator?" Well, one might think that it is not a big deal but it is not that easy to accept someone else's ignorance and just keep quiet. My mother brought me up to respect others and try to understand them. I remember her talking to me just a couple of hours before my departure for the U.S.A.: "Remember that no matter what you achieve in your life, you are no more than anyone else. Also don't forget that just because you are from such a small country, which the Czech Republic is, it doesn't mean that you are any worse than those Americans." I don't think that I'm naive but I must admit that being brought up that way and suddenly finding myself among people who seem to consider themselves the best and the fittest was shocking. Slowly I was starting to think, over and over again, "What was it I was going to bring home from here?"

I never really thought about what culture shock was. Whenever I heard about it from people who tried to prepare us, the potential students abroad, I kind of joked about it. "Inevitable reaction to the absence of familiar patterns in social interaction, and to the differences between the 'hidden dimensions' of the home and host cultures." That, according to one of several brochures, is how to define culture shock. It sounds unreal, but during those first couple of weeks, as time went on, small events stacked on top of one another and I finally came to a decision that culture shock was real.

I will never forget my friend's expression when she came into the laundry room and saw me ironing almost every piece of clothing I owned. "Michaela," I heard, "you know, we don't really iron things here." I didn't stop but I was listening. I later found out it is very common for Americans to take things out of the dryer and just put them into the closet. In my house everything has to be neat, clothes even more than anything else. "Clothes are the first thing you always notice on a person," says my mother. "Everyone looks at you differently when you are nice and clean compared to wearing not neat or dirty clothes." For some time I kept my habit of ironing. Later on as I started becoming more and more part of the community I lived in, I started ironing less and less often until I finally stopped. It wasn't one of those "everyone is doing it that way so why shouldn't I" things but simply one of the things that I absorbed as part of the adaptation process to a different environment, lifestyle, and culture.

Living in a dorm and attending school brings many opportunities to encounter and absorb a different way of life. Even one single history class was an experience for me that I will not forget for a long time. I remember how surprised I was not to have to stand up when the teacher entered the class, or that we were allowed to drink a Coke in the classroom. Raising my hand was sometimes considered funny by my classmates and my display of respect for the teacher was said to be strange. "Not a big deal," I would say now and I wouldn't be far from the truth. It is much easier to absorb things that you like than the other way around. And so not long after I started going to school I was enjoying the habit of bringing a Coke to class as a means of staying awake after a sleepless night, or just "shouting out" my answer to a question.

Yet there was one aspect of me being a part of the class that was not as easy to become familiar with. There was a discussion going on in my U.S. history class which I was not really included in—simply because I wasn't used to expressing my own views and supporting them and maybe even getting into an argument without fear of punishment. In my native school the teacher has such authority that if he or she says that two and two is five then it is true even if it obviously is not. "Whatever," I said quietly to myself, not agreeing with one of my classmate's points. Unfortunately or maybe fortunately, it was loud enough for the teacher to pick up and tell me to say what I thought about it. "Oh God," I thought, "now I'm in trouble. I say something the teacher doesn't like and I can say good-bye to an A in this class." To my surprise my idea seemed to make sense to the teacher and I was encouraged to express myself. Many times did I say things that were wrong or stupid and look! Nothing happened.

Now, already thinking about my departure for home and adapting to my old life, I am saying to myself, "Girl, you'll have to put tape over your mouth when you get back or you'll get in trouble." On the other hand, I have also experienced students being more disrespectful and taking advantage of being treated as adults by the teachers, which is not anything that I would like to bring back home with me. Adapting is not the only possible way of dealing with culture shock and one of the things I became aware of even more after having this experience is that it is not only important to be adaptable but also to be able to set limits and be oneself.

"The capital of Spain is Paris and London is in France . . ." "I live in the U.S.A., what else do I need to see?" "Why would I learn another language when almost everyone can speak English? . . ." I couldn't believe my ears when I heard these statements come out of the mouths of my classmates. Strangely, these statements made me feel very proud of who I am and where I am from. It seemed to me that a great majority of American teenagers were brought up to believe that America's the best and to have almost no interest in what is going on outside of their country. "Wow," I thought when I first got to talk about this with a couple of my friends, "this is unbelievable." I felt as if I were coming from outer space. We talked about what it is like in my country and Europe. I got really absorbed in talking about traveling and different cultures which one can see there. I related this to Tennessee, a place known well by the majority of my friends. Even after driving for two hours in almost any direction one is still in one state, with almost the same culture and the same language. This is very different in my case. Driving two hours from where I live can take me to Germany, Poland, or Austria, countries with different cultures and languages. My friends were looking at me with amazement. I don't believe that I changed the way these people are looking at the world around them or the world outside of the U.S.A., but at least I was able to give them a picture of what it really is like where I live as opposed to what they thought before. In their eyes I lived in a place with lack of food and water, where people have never seen a calculator, TV, or a cellular phone. That was what made me at times a bit upset and disappointed, but I was also happy because I knew then that my mother was right. No matter how my friends thought of themselves they are no more than me nor I better than them.

I'll return to my culture with knowledge of my own values, pride, and self-confidence, but different in many ways. Culture shock is often viewed as a negative experience leading to homesickness and an inability to become part of a "new" community. I don't agree. It is a set of events that forms your personality, lets you grow, and expands your knowledge of others. Life is indeed like a boat on the sea, bobbing up and down, and the sailor remembers a storm better than a normal voyage. I will leave with a great number of memories, filled not only with the simple things I have learned, but richer for going through those "harsh" and shocking moments.

Michaela Pavlisova graduated from St. Andrews-Sewanee School in 1996. At the time of publication, the school's alumni office did not have an address for her.

It's in Your Hands

Denise Crews
Northfield-Mt. Hermon School

Stop for a moment and look at the back of your hands. They may explain a great deal about your past and tell you a great deal about your future—not by their size or how many wrinkles, but by their color. In today's society we are still preoccupied by one's color. Besides the gender issue, there is no other physical feature that has such an impact on our society. *Webster's 21st Century Dictionary of the English Language* offers this definition of race: a group of persons with a common origin. To me this is a simple definition for such a complex and powerful word.

Racism has been around since the beginning of time. It has been woven into our culture as an acceptable way of treating one another. Racism is learned behavior and anything that is learned can be unlearned. You may be asking what all this has to do with boarding schools and the experience you will have. Think of a boarding school as a microscopic idea of the real world, people coming from all over, living and working in one place.

Let me give you some ideas as to what I mean:

Just imagine that you are a thirteen-year-old white youth and are going away to boarding school for the first time. Up until now you have been living in an environment where people looked very similar to you. You now must break out of that comfort zone. It's the first day of school and you can't wait to meet your roommate. As you are unpacking your things the door opens and in walks your roommate. You are surprised to see that this person and his or her parents are nothing like what you had pictured. They are from Korea and your roommate can speak very little English. This is a person who will spend the next nine to ten months in your living space. What do you do?

_____

_____

_____

_____

_____

_____

_____

_____

_____

Perhaps you and your roommate are on your way to dinner. Your roommate just happens to be a Native American. You see your "homies" gathered at one end of the dining room. They motion you to come join them. As you sit down you notice that your roommate is not behind you. Instead he has decided to sit by himself at another table. What do you do?

_____

_____

_____

_____

_____

_____

_____

_____

_____

_____

It's time for history class. The teacher announces that the topic for today will be "the O.J. trial" and the issues surrounding the race factor in the case. Someone makes the statement that the only reason that he got off was because the jury was mostly black and unable to make an intelligent decision. Everyone turns to look at you because you are the only person of color. What do you do?

_____

_____

_____

_____

_____

_____

_____

_____

_____

Finally, consider this situation. You have been dating this really great guy. Things seem to be getting serious. But you haven't told any of your friends that you are dating because he happens to be from a different ethnic group and you are not quite sure how they will respond. So you decide to keep it a secret. One night you and the girls are sitting around just chatting about different issues. TLC is playing in the background and the subject of interracial dating comes up. Your best friend makes the statement that she would never date anyone outside of her race because it's not natural. You are shocked because you never knew that she felt this way. As the discussion continues more comments are made about being an "Oreo" or "lost and confused." The more you hear these things the more you start to have second thoughts about the relationship that you are in. What do you do?

I am not raising these situations to make you think that boarding school life is horrible but I want to raise issues that nine times out of ten you will face. You can see each of these situations in a negative way or you can see the positive in each one.

One solution to the first example that I offered is to view this as an opportunity to help someone out who doesn't know English very well, while at the same time allowing yourself to learn a new language and culture. The dining room example is the most common situation and you will definitely see this happen. Instead of having your roommate sit by himself, ask him to join you, or encourage the people at your table to move and sit with him; again an opportunity to learn about another culture. At Northfield-Mount Hermon School we have roundtable discussions over dinner. The topics vary but the idea behind the round table is to get people from different cultures to come together to learn from one another. The third situation is also a very common one. Frequently, you may be one or two people of color in a class. Take this opportunity to enlighten your fellow classmates that there is no one spokesperson for a race and participate in the class so as to educate them about another perspective, yours.

Interracial dating is a challenge that human beings have dealt with since the beginning of time. The only advice that I would give in a situation like this is to know yourself. If you are happy, it should not matter what color someone is. Here is a chance to enjoy companionship, while setting an example that people of different cultural or ethnic backgrounds can get along.

In closing I would also like to share with you some ways to celebrate your culture while educating those around you. There are many support vehicles that can help make your experience a pleasant one. At Northfield-Mount Hermon School we have several organizations that are geared to meet the needs of our students of color. JAMAA, our organization for students of African decent, serves as a vehicle for those students to have issues addressed that they may face as a group. JAMAA also celebrates the rich heritage of its people by holding special events on campus such as dances, guest speakers, and campus meeting presentations for special holidays in the Black community such as Martin Luther King, Jr. Day and Kwanzaa. Our Latin American students also have their support system in a group called COLAS (Coalition of Latin American Students). Many of our Latino students attend plays and dances at neighboring schools and similar to JAMAA address the issues that affect their community. For our Native American students we have the Native American Student Alliance which tries to support their special needs. My job at the school involves bringing all of these groups together under one organization to help educate everyone about the cultures that we have at our school and the issues that each one faces. The organization, AIMS, the Association in the Interest of a Multicultural School, has seventy-five members from all cultures. It includes faculty and students. Some of the ways that we address these issues are: hosting multicultural student conferences, dances, regular meetings, faculty forums, campus meetings, and special events that involve the entire community. The school also offers many religious organizations, as well as gender and sexuality organizations that serve as support systems.

I hope that I have given you some insight into the opportunities that diversity can offer at schools. Remember to be yourself and proud of where you come from while open to the idea of learning from others. Now, look at your hands again. Do they look any different? They should. You should now be able, with one hand, to take hold of your culture and the richness that it has to offer and share it with someone, and with your other hand grab on to what someone who may be different from you has to offer. Remember that we are all the same. Although we might not like everyone, we must respect one another. I leave you with a quote that I like to encourage my students to live by. "Judge me not by the color of my skin but by the content of my character."

As the time of this piece (1995), **Denise Crews** was the director of multicultural affairs at Northfield-Mt. Hermon. She majored in African-American studies in college and has always been interested in promoting diversity.

SOME WAYS OF UNDERSTANDING RACE RELATIONS

A dilemma begins any discussion of your relationships with people who represent different racial backgrounds: How do we and when do we think of people in terms of their racial backgrounds? On the one hand, you do not want to judge people by or think of them solely in terms of the color of their skin. On the other hand, you do want to acknowledge, understand, and even celebrate the racial backgrounds of people whom you befriend. This may seem like a minor distinction, but there are subtle racial stereotypes all around us and often we are exposed to equally subtle forms of insensitivity. So here are some simple exercises that demonstrate the importance of paying attention to what you are doing, saying, and even thinking:

Pick up any magazine and flip through the advertisements, thinking about the assumptions the advertisers make about your habit of stereotyping. Who are the advertisements directed at?

List the friends you have who represent another race. What features do these friends have that might be called racial, in your opinion? What features do these friends have that are clearly personal?

Friend	Racial Features	Personal Features

Write down an incident in which you were exposed to and/or witnessed some kind of racial prejudice.

Write down some features of your own culture, i.e., beliefs, behavior, food traditions, modes of expression in language, music, and celebrations. (Culture is not the sole property of nonwhite races. Everyone has a cultural background, mixed or not.)

Consider the following situations:

A boy in the dorm has a room filled with paraphernalia from the Deep South: Confederate flags, license plates that read "The War's Not Over Yet!" and "Bring Back the Good Ole Boys!" You know that some of the material bothers a black boy in the dorm. What could you do?

_____

_____

_____

_____

_____

A Pakistani girl lives in your dorm. Some of your friends decide not to include her in a slumber party because "she always wears the same robes." What could you do?

_____

_____

_____

_____

_____

You want to play a game of pickup at the school's basketball court, but when you arrive, a game involving all white players is already in progress. You notice that the two teams argue over who gets you even though no one there knows you that well, and to tell the truth you're not that good. You are black. What could you do?

_____

_____

_____

_____

You're bemoaning your performance on the first math exam when your roommate offers this advice: "Just ask Suyuan. She's got to be a math geek. They're all intense." What could you do?

_____

_____

_____

_____

As an Hispanic student, you notice that there are no Hispanic adults in the local community save for the guy who collects the soda cans every Thursday. In fact, the only Hispanic faculty member is the assistant dean of community affairs at your school. What could you do?

_____

_____

_____

_____

You are an African-American woman from Los Angeles. When you arrive on campus, you notice that there are twenty-five tennis courts but not one outdoor basketball court. When you ask someone about it, the response is "we're worried that basketball games tend to get too rough and loud." What could you do?

_____

_____

_____

There are hundreds of situations like this cropping up every day and no one expects you to have a right answer for them. If and when you speak up, you should remember some basic guidelines: stereotypes tend to twist reality, allowing people to accentuate differences between groups, ignore individual traits, and assume therefore that certain kinds of people are exactly the same; prejudices are unwarranted, and possibly demeaning, attitudes about a group, type of people, or cultural practice; and racism occurs when someone uses a stereotype to defend the belief that one race is inferior to another.

Just being aware of both a person's racial background and those features that make her a unique person represents the starting point for good relations.

Navigating Relationships

Craig Thorn
Phillips Academy

Several years ago, an eighteen-year-old boy in my dormitory walked into my study, looked me right in the eye, and said, "Craig, tell me all you know about sex." I was far more embarrassed than he, and to this day I think I learned more from that conversation than he did. Needless to say, no one knows everything there is to know about sex or sexuality. In fact, the first rule about relations between men and women is that you do not know everything, nor will you ever. Therefore, we have a second and more important rule: Listen, pay attention, and pay attention with all the empathy you can muster. And we have a third: Always respect the feelings of others unless those feelings are deliberately hurtful to someone else. And a fourth: Never let anyone else speak for you unless you've asked someone to speak for you and you're happy with what he or she says on your behalf. They are simple rules to remember, hard to follow sometimes. They inform almost every aspect of your experience in a boarding school involving issues of gender, and nearly every possible situation. Consider just a few . . .

———————

You live in a boys' dormitory. A tenth-grader has received permission to have a female visitor. On the way up to his room, she's aware of the posters of nude and nearly-nude women on the walls of several rooms and even on the doors. How does that make her feel? How does it make you feel? N.W.A. is blaring from another room; the song is explicit about women and unflattering to say the least. As you find the key for your door, you notice that some of the guys are scoping your friend. Furthermore, you notice that she's aware of the undisguised appraisal as well. When you walk into your room, you see the St. Pauli girl poster, the SI swimsuit issue on your desk, the car poster with the shape of a naked woman hidden in it. You are seeing these things for the first time because you're seeing them through your friend's eyes.

Your best friend seems to be very easygoing and friendly with girls. However, one night you and he are with a bunch of guys in the dorm and he is saying things about women which are disturbing. He's playing off the older boys in the dorm who, much to your surprise, are egging him on. You're sure that they don't feel this way about women. Then, it gets really ugly; they start to talk about specific girls on campus. You're thinking that these guys just moved effortlessly from talking about their exploits with lots of girls, stories you know are not true, to bad-mouthing girls for the very same exploits. They're criticizing girls who are too short, too heavy, too skinny, too this or that. Meanwhile, they themselves are short, tall, thin, and stocky. Furthermore, one of the girls your friend is "disrespecting" is someone you like. You catch yourself wondering whether you should like this girl or not, and you are ashamed of yourself for wondering. But this guy is your friend. What happened to him in this stuffy room filled with other guys and half-empty pizza boxes?

You are a ninth-grade girl in a dormitory and your roommate is acting strange. You are no expert, but you're sure she has an eating disorder. Her side of the room is crowded with junk food and fashion magazines. She's rail thin. You've seen a picture of her when she played field hockey in eighth grade. She looked healthy, athletic. Now she spends more time in the bathroom than on the playing field. So what is happening? There are other girls on campus like her. You don't see too many overweight people on campus. At the dining hall, the guys look slovenly and they heap their plates with food. Rows of glasses with brightly colored juices line their trays. You realize that many of your girlfriends eat next to nothing for lunch—a couple of broccoli florets, some saltines with peanut butter, a salad with a little balsamic vinegar. You hear about boys' dorms keeping the local pizza stores in business at night with endless deliveries. The girls in your dorm slice up apples. Now you're thinking that maybe you should change your eating habits, perhaps cut out that luxurious breakfast of cantaloupe and a bowl of your favorite cereal, Frosted Flakes.

You are with a girl you've been seeing since midway through fall term. Now it is the beginning of spring term, and your school allows ninth graders to have room visitations after the first six months of school. This is not your first "girlfriend," but you find yourself somewhat overwhelmed by the opportunities that present themselves because you can visit with your girlfriend in the relative privacy of her room or your own. The two of you like each other very much, but you haven't talked about any kind of involved relations. Whatever happens just sort of happens and things have never gone very far because you're usually in relatively public situations and you're not really ready anyway. Suddenly, you're having room visitations. It's a Saturday night. You're listening to your favorite bands—DMB, Dashboard Confessional, Green Day, Smashing Pumpkins—and you've had an excellent day outside hanging out with your friends. The speakers are in the windows for your dormmates who are still playing hacky sack outside. All your peers are impressed with how together you and your girlfriend are. After all, you've been going out for quite awhile. Some of the older guys, the senior proctors in your dorm, have asked you if you've "hooked up" with your girlfriend. You don't know if they're curious or worried. You're hanging out on the couch you bought at a junk shop in a room that is the most popular simply because girls and guys comfortably hang out in it. And the two of you are suddenly well beyond kissing. Is this what you want? You don't think so, not really. Is this what she wants? Have you ever talked about it? Are you protected? Is she? Would it be incredibly uncool to stop? And how would you stop this anyway? Do you even want to?

Every time you walk past a certain boy's dorm, the comments you hear are inflammatory. They do not seem to be directed at you personally. No one in the dorm seems to know your name. In fact, the comments are directed at your appearance: the clothes you wear, your figure, your willingness or unwillingness to participate in sexual activity. Whenever this happens, you look around at your peers who clearly are within earshot. They're playing Frisbee; they're walking by with their heads down; they're pretending not to notice. Does this mean that you should laugh it off even though you dread these moments? After a week or so, you're taking a different route from your French class to your math class and you feel resentful and manipulated. A few days later in the lunch line, you actually run into one of the boys whom you've seen in the dorm windows. He nods and smiles at you, and you smile back unwittingly. You feel ashamed of yourself. Why did you smile? The guy's a jerk. You feel like you may have allowed him to feel that his behavior was no big deal. But it was. How do you respond to the boys in that dormitory? If you report their behavior, will you be the laughing stock of the school? Should you follow this boy to his table and chew him out? You watch him weave his way through the dining hall until he reaches a table filled with guys from his dorm. They're all wearing lacrosse baseball caps from schools like Duke and UNC and Harvard. They all seem to be wearing the same flannel shirt, the same worn jeans and sneakers. It's like they have a uniform, a team, and you're one against all of them.

You've been going out with a popular guy on campus for about three weeks. The scene at your school doesn't really support serious relationships, you've noticed. Guys and girls get together for parties, but no one seems to stay together. In your old school, guys and girls would actually hold hands. At this school, no one would be caught dead holding hands. By the same token, plenty of guys and girls seem to be comfortable with each other as friends.

However, you're getting signals from your boyfriend that make you uncomfortable. You hear rumors, that you've been sleeping with him. You haven't. Worse, you think that he's been promoting those rumors, because they seem to be coming from his friends. Furthermore, he doesn't want to go to school dances or the snack bar. He just wants to hang out in your room. And once you're there, he presses you to go all the way with him. He has all kinds of lines. He says that he's going to come off as a jerk if you don't. He says that no one has to know. He says that you're not serious about the relationship. He says that the two of you will just do a little bit. He says that he has a condom. When he talks like this, he feels like a stranger. You don't even want him to kiss you when he talks like this. You don't have any trouble telling him no. He always backs off. Unfortunately, when you do say no, it's like saying no to everything. He suddenly wants to take off. He's angry and he's not interested in doing anything at all. You like him very much. He's really nice, funny, and clever most of the time. When you tell them, some of the girls in the dorm think that you're a jerk for going out with him. Other girls, however, ask you if you are teasing him. That thought never occurred to you. Thinking about it that way is like looking into a deep well. Now you don't know what kind of message you are sending. If you sigh happily when he kisses you, does that mean that you want to go all the way? Are you leading him on?

There are no easy answers to any of these situations. There are, however, appropriate and acceptable ways to look for answers. Be honest and direct. The very same young people who make the crude jokes, show insensitivity, pick on their peers about matters sexual, or brag about sexual exploits are the ones who are not ready for real relationships. Furthermore, there are rules that go beyond the "rules" of a dorm, a campus, even a community. There is the law to consider. In Massachusetts, the law is pretty clear. Here is how it is presented to students in our *Blue Book*, or book of rules and guidelines for appropriate behavior at the school:

> In accordance with Massachusetts's law, the dean of students is required to report all instances of sexual abuse or statutory rape to the Department of Social Services (DSS). Because the age of legal consent in Massachusetts is 16 years, the dean of students must report even consensual sexual activity involving a student under 16 years of age.

So if you are under the age of sixteen and you are involved in sexual relations, you should definitely seek counsel from your family or family doctor. However, if these adults are not viable options, you should of course turn to a responsible, trusted adult, whether it is a house counselor or coach, teacher or school counselor. Just understand that these adults are responsible to your parents and are professionals themselves. Understand that in cases of consensual sex, the law is designed for your health and safety, not your harm and humiliation. In cases of nonconsensual sex, however, the law, your boarding school, and your family must act responsibly and so should you.

I was embarrassed, surprised, and amused when the boy—we'll call him Alan—asked me about sex. Most of all, I was impressed. Alan wasn't simply curious; on the contrary, he recognized the importance of the commitment inherent in romantic relationships that involve sex. He knew that I knew he'd been seeing the same girl, a senior also, for two years. He did not know what I would say to him. Would I tell him not to have sex? Would I warn him that I might deny him visitations if I knew sexual relations were imminent? I think Alan cared more about being safe, sensitive, and smart than he did about "hooking up." He showed his respect and love for his girlfriend when he knocked on my door. I was his house counselor.

As it turned out, we talked about much more than sex because, as we both knew without having to say it, there is much, much more to good relationships than sex. So Alan learned about protection, virginity, honoring a woman's needs, taking your time, and remembering that two people's feelings are involved in sexual relations. I urged him not to be afraid to say or hear "let's wait," or just plain "no," but I also told him as well as I could what to do if they were both absolutely sure they wanted to have sex. After all, at your age, holding off on sexual relations is the best advice, but not having safe sex is just plain stupid, and not advising Alan about honest and safe sex would have been morally irresponsible on my part. I learned how a senior at Phillips had discovered on his own how to find his best friend in his girlfriend, and I saw how he learned much about himself by listening to what a wonderful, smart young woman had to say about him. Mutual respect and affection informed their relationship as it did our conversation that night.

Did they have sex? If that is the question you are asking yourself, then you have already forgotten the rules.

Craig Thorn is an instructor in English at Phillips Academy, where he has been a house counselor, adviser, administrator, and coach for twenty-one years. In addition to writing and editing books about education, he writes essays about literature and reviews of alternative rock music.

Falling into Place

Ellie Griffin
Milton Academy

Adolescence is a time when we wonder about who we are. Why am I here? What is my purpose in life? Who am I? How do I define myself? Am I a good student? A great athlete? An artist? A musician? These are some of the ways in which we might describe ourselves to others. Most of us are usually already pretty clear about what it means to us to be male/female, black/white, American/Chinese, Christian/Jew, English speaking/French speaking . . . other ways we define ourselves. And although we're learning daily more about what it means to be male or female, the issue which seems to cause much more reflection and questioning is that of our sexual identity. Now, if we are quite clear that our attraction is and always has been exclusively toward the opposite sex, we tend to spend much less time contemplating our sexual orientation. We are comfortably in the majority in this culture.

If, on the other hand, we have been questioning our sexual orientation for a while, or at least since we encountered puberty, adolescence can be a very difficult time. Prep schools are, for the most part, no different from other schools when it comes to how it feels to be gay or lesbian on campus. Because the teenage years are the time when people come to terms with all of these questions of identity, there is often a greater intolerance in young people toward those who don't fit a particular norm. We've all seen instances of the kind of teasing banter that occurs daily on a campus. Anyone who, as a result of having grown up in the Boston area, acquired that "Boston accent," (broad a's, with which we take a "baath," rather than a bath, and an "ah" sound instead of "r," so that we "paak ouwa caah," rather than "park our car") knows how it feels to be made fun of for something which seemed perfectly natural in our previous environment. Ah, the delight in exaggerating the accent to get a laugh at another's expense! Or we can imagine the student who arrives from the Midwest with a brand-new jacket to wear to chapel, only to discover that "jacket" on the East coast means a blue blazer, not a new nylon windbreaker!

But being gay or lesbian may invoke much meaner ridicule among members of the adolescent population. Males seem to be even less tolerant than females toward people who are gay, assigning feminine (and therefore derogatory!) attributes to boys whom they believe to be gay. You've heard the terms—faggot, queer, fairy, and many others—applied generally and intolerantly to anyone who doesn't fit a person's view of masculinity. These demeaning remarks usually cover fear and uncertainty in kids who worry that they will be "tainted" if they don't take a strong stand against homosexuality. Although many kids are truly kind, sensitive, and accepting of others, there are always those who will make the life of a student who is different in any way quite miserable. What makes the difference?

We have many examples at our school of students who chose to come out, and of those who chose not to. In fact, much to their surprise, those who, after a great deal of thought decided to tell a few close friends usually found their friends to be very kind and sympathetic. (When you know someone well and love him, you're far more apt to be tolerant of differences and accepting of whoever he is.) After the first shock of finding out that he was not who they assumed he was, they realized that it really didn't make any difference to them. They still loved him and considered him a very good friend. In another instance, a student was quite hurt and disappointed when he decided to tell his friend that he was gay, and also admitted that he was in love with him. For the friend who was not gay, his friend's announcements felt threatening at first, and they had to talk it out and work out how to keep on being friends when one friend wanted a relationship more than that . . . which sounds very much like a common theme in heterosexual friendships! Many students have decided not to come out until they were in college. They just didn't feel ready while they were still in high school.

Most people in prep schools are understanding about these issues. But, when prejudice and harassment does occur, how do prep schools combat sexism, promote acceptance of differences, and support students who may be gay or lesbian? Many schools have gay or lesbian faculty who are open about their orientation and who make themselves available to students who are searching and seeking answers, as well as those who already are clear about their orientation. A faculty member who is much loved and esteemed in the community and who is also openly gay or lesbian makes a strong statement about a school's acceptance of differences in people.

Some schools have anonymous and confidential support groups for gay and lesbian students, and some have support groups which are openly publicized. Some schools focus on political causes, seeking equity and civil rights for people who are gay or lesbian. Many schools have gay/straight alliances which promote understanding and support of gay and lesbian issues. A good number of schools now have policies on sexual harassment which make it a punishable offense to act in a prejudicial or harassing manner toward a person because of his or her sexual orientation. Almost all schools now have counseling services where a student can talk confidentially about his or her sexual orientation and get help in determining how best to live in the particular culture of that school.

If you are gay or lesbian, should you come out at your school? This really needs to be answered person by person, school by school. My advice is to take your time, understand the climate of your school, talk with someone confidentially about the pros and cons and about what coming out entails in your school, your family, with your friends. Talk with your parents before you talk to anyone at the school who cannot promise confidentiality, because if people at your school know, it's likely that your parents will hear it . . . and better from you than someone else. Most people will be understanding and accepting; some will be intolerant and unkind. You may find yourself in a position of having to educate others about what it means to be gay or lesbian, at a time when you're still trying to figure that out yourself. It's best to move slowly and thoughtfully, seeking help and support from caring adults. In boarding schools, as in most small communities, little is totally private. Once you tell someone anything (outside the counseling office), often word quickly spreads. People know and mind each other's business, which can be a good thing . . . but just be certain that you are prepared for the consequences before you disclose personal information to others at your school.

Boarding schools are fun, happy, exciting places. The years one spends at a boarding school are rewarding, full of growth, and challenging, a time to try out new things, engage in adventures, and learn about one's self. Make the most of it, and work at being yourself . . . the rest will fall into place.

Ellie Griffin is director of health and counseling services at Milton Academy where she has worked for nearly three decades. She has written about issues of women, Hispanic students, sexual preference, and relationships for numerous publications.

BEYOND THE FIRST FRIENDS

Closer Than I Ever Imagined

Rudi Alvey
The Hill School

"So I have no friends, I don't want to be here, my room makes me feel like an inpatient at a mental ward and it's hot out, very, very, hot!" That was thought number one on day number one at boarding school. Soon after, within the next couple of days, I got used to my room and accepted my attendance at boarding school but I couldn't handle not having any close friends. How was I supposed to know how to make friends? Last time I did that was in kindergarten. And about that heat. Wow, it was hot, you know, like 99 and so humid you swam down the sidewalk as opposed to walking. But amazingly, when my new roommate walked through our door with a two foot by two foot high-powered, turbocharged fan, my friend-making skills came right back to me.

"Hi, what's your name? That's great. Oh yeah, it's nice to meet you and I'm sure we'll be best friends in a day or two. Uh, can I help you with that fan?"

"No thanks, I . . ."

"Here, I got it, all right I'll just put it here by my bed."

If my roommate had been an average guy, I would probably have needed reconstructive surgery on my face from the pounding I would have received, but this guy was different.

"No problem, set the fan down wherever. Do you want anything to drink? I'm gonna run and grab some lemonade."

His name was Dave. He had been at this school for a year already and he must have known how hard an adjustment it was. He tolerated me, even began to like me. He gave out well-needed information on how to get girls and how to sneak them through the window and into our room. He also taught me how to tie a tie that was required by our dress code. He took me around campus, showed me what restaurant to eat at, and he introduced me to people.

But just as quickly as we became friends, our relationship was on the verge of abruptly ending. What Dave never told me was that he was on scholarship. His family had little or no money but they somehow got Dave enrolled in our school. Now in his second year, his parents could not scrape up the minimal funds the scholarship required. So Dave had to pack up his things and head back home. Surprisingly, the last thing I cared about was his fan.

I guess I wasn't the only person Dave extended a hand to, because before I knew it, thirty other kids started collecting money for Dave's tuition. Being a new boy, I had an outsider's perspective and I couldn't believe how these guys came together like a family, yeah, like thirty brothers and one was just ripped away from them.

These guys frantically collected all the money they could, but in the end, it just wasn't enough. And so, accordingly, I believed Dave would not return.

But I miscalculated. My error was that I thought the family only consisted of siblings. I learned from firsthand experience that boarding school atmospheres are even more like a family than I expected.

I knew all the guys acted like brothers, and that in itself was foreign to me, but what really astonished me was that the faculty, yes, even the teachers, old and young, male and female, acted as parents and it hurt them equally as much to lose Dave.

It's still a mystery to us students, but the next thing we knew, Dave was back at school. We know his family didn't pay because they had no money. So, we've come to agree that either the faculty waived his tuition or someone paid it for him. Now that's a family. And although I've only been at boarding school for a short time now, I feel a part of this family. Among boarding school students, there is one thing we all have in common: We no longer live at home. Boarding school does not replace our family, but rather becomes another one. Our school is our home, and our home is our family.

Rudy Alvey was a 1996 graduate of The Hill School, where he was the head of the peer counseling group, and captain of the hockey team. Rudi also played football and lacrosse at The Hill School.

Going Home

John Green
Indian Springs School

When people ask me where I'm from, I tell them Birmingham, Alabama. I was raised in Florida, where my parents still live, but it hasn't been home to me in a long time. Nowadays, when I go back to visit my parents, the palm trees and strip malls of suburban Florida seem utterly foreign to me.

I know now that allowing me to leave home and board at Indian Springs School in Birmingham, Alabama, was one of the hardest things my parents ever did. I'd like to say I wanted to go to Springs because I was excited by the chance to attend school in an environment that valued learning above all else, but really I mostly wanted to go because I was bored. My friends, my classes, my neighborhood—I found it all horribly mind-numbing. Boarding school promised—if nothing else—a dramatic change.

Dramatic, indeed. I arrived as a sophomore, and my roommate, Danny, was a Korean exchange student with a passion for

Korean pop music that I, to put it mildly, did not share. For the first few months, I struggled to find a place on campus. Danny appreciated it when I copyedited his research papers, but he despised my complete disinterest in ever cleaning our room. I met other people, of course, but I couldn't seem to connect with them. They weren't like me. Most of the students at Springs were either wealthy or on full scholarships, and I was neither. Most of them were from the South or some faraway foreign country, and I was from Florida, a northern state situated below the Mason-Dixon line. But most of all, they already *knew* one another, and their witty banter and inside jokes only made me feel left out.

And then I met Todd Cartee. Todd was poor beyond my wildest imagination. He lived in a trailer park before getting a scholarship to Springs as an eighth grader. Todd had long ago made Indian Springs his home, and for some reason, he took it upon himself to make it mine, too. We met in the laundry room one night, and while he tossed lights and darks into the same washing machine with impunity, he entertained me by listing the nations of the world. In alphabetical order. His talent for memorization was matched by a brutal, biting wit, and by the time our clothes were dry, I had met my first real friend.

Todd and I came from different worlds, of course. I was a good student, but he didn't miss a single question on the S.A.T. I grew up in a nice suburban neighborhood with parents who loved me and loved one another. Todd grew up in a poor, violent, and dysfunctional family. But though our pasts were different, we shared the present. Together, we explored the spots on campus you don't see on the campus tour. We trudged up a muddy hill in late autumn to an old graveyard overrun by kudzu and littered with cigarette butts. Once, we even borrowed a canoe from Dr. Cooper, our European history teacher, and braved the fast and shallow water of Bishop's Creek, paddling until we were surprised to find ourselves at the Waffle House a mile off campus. We shared interests, too. We both loved William Faulkner and both had a weakness for petite brunettes. And despite our disparate upbringings, Todd and I shared a profound fear. We feared failing, and so we studied hard. I couldn't bear the thought of disappointing my parents and Todd wanted more than anything to make enough money to buy his mom a house, "a house you don't

have to jack up on cinder blocks," as he often put it. Our friendship taught me that it is more important for me to find friends
who share my hopes and fears than it is to find friends who share
my upper-middle-class background.

Through my friendship with Todd, I met more students. I was
surprised how well I related to them. The laid-back approach to
coed living at Springs even made it possible for me to have close
female friends (I wish I could call them girlfriends, but there were
precious few of those). Most of my best friends, though, were
guys. Masa, a Japanese student, and his eccentric sidekick Sid became two of my best pals, even though Masa didn't speak English very well when I first met him and Sid honestly believed
that certain members of the student body were aliens. Masa and
Sid didn't come from the same world I did anymore than Todd
did, so we made a world we could share. We stayed up late
studying and playing computer games and talking about girls.
There were serious times, too, but like with any family, the quality of the time didn't matter near so much as the quantity of it.
Friendship at boarding school is pretty much like friendship in
kindergarten: it's all about sharing. I shared everything with
them, from soap to heartbreak, and through that sharing came a
profound and unconditional loyalty. I would never have called it
"love" then, but that's precisely what it was.

Of course, I never got into Korean pop music and my roommate Danny never learned to appreciate my clutter. Springs is a
small place, with eighty boarders at the most, but there is still
plenty of room for dislike. But the wonderful thing about having
an extended family of eighty siblings is that it's okay if you don't
get along with all of them.

It *was* a family, but it wasn't my only family. I never missed
Florida, but I did miss my parents. In Florida over spring break
that first year, I reveled in having a room of my own and home-
cooked meals. And I actually enjoyed spending time with my
parents. Although we still bickered plenty about curfews and the
like, I had missed them without knowing it. When the time came
to leave, however, I was more than ready.

The night before I went back to school that spring, my mom
cooked my favorite—smoked salmon. Halfway through the
meal, I slipped up and said, "I'll miss this food when I go back

home." But what's most amazing is not that I came to see Indian Springs as home, but that I still think of it as home. I still answer that ubiquitous question—"Where are you from?"—with the God's honest truth, that I grew up at a little school outside of Birmingham.

John Green works for *Booklist* magazine, where he reviews literary fiction and books about the Islamic world. He is also a regular contributor to Chicago's NPR affiliate, WBEZ. His web site is *http://www.sparksflyup.com*.

Outside the Classroom

As you might expect, what goes on outside the classroom is as important as what goes on inside the classroom at a typical independent boarding school. In fact, many of you will remember what you learned outside the classroom long after you have forgotten the details of what happened in particular courses. Broadly speaking, the school's official residential life includes sports, extracurricular activities, off-campus programs, community agencies, and the school's relationship to the world beyond the campus.

So, this section is divided into three subsections—"Athletics and the Outdoors," "Extracurricular Life," and "Citizenship, On and Off Campus." Though the section suggests that residential life may not be part of your formal education, you will find that students and teachers alike describe these experiences as great opportunities to learn all kinds of things about your skills and limitations, and the remarkable talents of your peers. In addition, you will notice repeated references to the rewards of taking chances, of stretching yourself.

As you will see in these stories, you can almost always find a way to express your developing interests. One student raises a python. Another builds a canoe. Still another tries the gospel choir, and yet another goes white-water rafting. Along the way, many of these students and teachers will tell you about teamwork, and our shared responsibility for the well-being of others, whether it be demonstrated in a campus work duty or a campus-wide observance of a national tragedy. You will also hear about setting tough goals for yourself and meeting them, sometimes entirely on your own.

If you get just one thing from reading this section, it should be this: Do not fear mistakes. Schools love honest mistakes. Students will tell you that "succeeding" is not as important as the effort. No one in this section emphasizes the success of the enterprise. In fact, your peers seem to dwell on the humorous disasters that befall them along the way or the fatigued sense of accomplishment they enjoy just from finishing whatever it was they started. Enthusiasm, energy, and a genuine desire to try anything worthwhile at least once will get you a long way in boarding school, and you will have some strange and wonderful experiences along the way.

ATHLETICS AND THE OUTDOORS

Getting in the Game

Chuck Timlin
Choate Rosemary Hall

Oh sure, Evan has had a full day of classes. But it's a brilliant day in early May, and he hasn't been able to concentrate very well in classes today. All he can think about is 3:00 P.M. at Hotchkiss. Evan is a middie on Choate's varsity lacrosse team. Yes, there are two more games to play after Hotchkiss, but the winner of this game will win the Founder's League and be able to lay claim to being the premier lax team in western Massachusetts and Connecticut. From the first day of the team's spring break trip to Florida, these two teams have been moving inexorably toward each other, like the *Titanic* and the iceberg. And Choate, to Evan's thinking, is the iceberg.

After sixth period ends, Evan eats exactly one bowl of Cheerios followed by one bowl of Fruit Loops, and chases that with two bananas. It's been his pregame meal for every sport he has played since he came to Choate. Because Hotchkiss is an hour-and-a-half bus ride away, his team must be excused from seventh and eighth periods. Evan is an honor roll student who loves his classes (especially Mr. Cobbett's humanities elective on modernism), but it's sweet to get out of classes early for the occasional long road trip—it makes him feel like he's in college.

Walking down the hill toward the gym, he thinks back over his three years, athletically, at Choate. He arrived as a fourth former (a sophomore). He first considered going to prep school as he grew up playing in the youth hockey program in his New Jersey hometown. He went to a summer hockey camp at Avon Old Farms school in Connecticut and learned that Avon was where New York Rangers' star defenseman Brian Leetch had played his prep school hockey. Then he heard of Craig Janney at Deerfield, Jeremy Roenick and Tony Amonte, linemates now on the Chicago Blackhawks, who were linemates at Thayer Academy as well. Even Choate had Dave Williams, now playing for the San Jose Sharks. So he loved Choate's big-time hockey schedule and tradition. And it was a great place academically.

Evan smiles as he remembers that in the summer before he began at Choate he received a letter from the varsity football coach asking him if he would be interested in trying his hand at football. The letter said not to worry about his lack of prior experience. The coach had lost count of the number of kids who learned football for the first time as freshmen and sophomores and ended up playing one or two years on the varsity, some even going on to play at schools like Williams, Amherst, even Yale and Harvard. Evan went to that preseason and ended up starting at outside linebacker for the JVs. In his junior year he had gotten some quality playing time on the varsity, and then this past season on a team that went 7–2 and lost the New England championship to Andover in overtime. All of that bruising checking in hockey had helped him to make a smooth transition into football. And then one winter day in the dining hall during hockey season Mr. Hutchinson, the lacrosse coach, approached him at the Cheerios dispenser and asked him if he'd ever played lacrosse. When Evan said no, Hutch (as all of his players called him) smiled and said, "Hockey and lacrosse have a lot in common. Transition, speed, and hitting. I saw some of the hits you laid on the Deerfield forwards last Saturday."

So Evan learned to play lacrosse for the first time at Choate as well. And while he came to like football, he found that his passion (and talent) for lacrosse almost equaled that of his love for hockey. In fact, this year he was recruited by both the Bowdoin hockey and lacrosse coaches. Evan has every intention of playing both up there.

The bus ride to Hotchkiss seems to last longer than an hour and a half should, but that is because Evan is so wired for the game. By the time the bus pulls onto the campus Evan has listened to Guns 'n Roses' "Patience" and "November Rain" countless times on his Walkman.

The game itself is indeed a titanic struggle. Hotchkiss, in front of a charged-up home-field crowd, takes a 3–1 lead after the first period. But Choate owns them in the second quarter, scoring four unanswered goals to take a 5–3 lead into halftime. Evan is playing well. He has two assists and a hit on Tommie Lind, the wicked fast Hotchkiss attack, that he can't wait to see on the videotape. It was a particularly sweet hit because Evan and Tommie have lined up against each other for three years on the ice and on the lax field. In fact, Tommie had tried the land version of the hockey move he faked out Evan with at Choate this year for the game-winning goal against them. This time Evan didn't bite, but jarred Tommie completely off his feet, so that he lost the ball. Even the Hotchkiss crowd *ooooo*ed.

The second half is truly seesaw action, Hotchkiss scoring and Choate answering to preserve the two-goal lead. But with 1:39 remaining Lind scores on a beautiful breakaway: 10–9, Choate. Hotchkiss wins the face-off, works the ball around on offense, and with 24 seconds on the clock looks to score. Evan's rival takes a pass from the left wing and tries a spin move, but Evan is there. He bumps Lind off the ball and the game is over.

As the teams exchange handshakes, Lind approaches Evan and says with a wink, "I owe you one. We'll see you when you come to Amherst next winter."

Evan shakes his head. "We're even. Remember hockey season? But I'll see you when you come to Bowdoin next winter."

The bus ride home takes no time. Evan has some reading for his law and social change course, but he knows he's not going to crack the book. Last spring as a junior he would have been poring over his pre-cal. He's about to graduate in three weeks. It's been a long and at the same time incredibly fast three years. He reflects upon how widely he can think about things now. Going away to prep school was the best decision he (and his parents!) has made so far in his life. He can't imagine how college is going to live up to this. Especially the good athletic times. Evan looks around the bus at his friends, good guys with whom he will keep in touch for a long, long time. He opens the bagged lunch that the dining hall prepared for his team to eat on the ride back. He pops "Patience" into the Walkman, leans back in his seat, closes his eyes, and smiles.

Chuck Timlin served as athletic director at Choate Rosemary Hall and has taught English and Latin there for over two decades.

On and Off the Court

Ashley Mudge '02
Brewster Academy

Before coming to Brewster, I went to another school where girls had few opportunities to participate in team sports. Girls were generally found on the sidelines as spectators or cheerleaders. From the third to six grades I had played a sport every season: soccer in the fall, basketball in the winter, and softball in the spring. I no longer continued to play any of these team sports when I reached my new school. It was as if there was an unwritten rule that girls could not contribute to sports. For two years I was absent from sports. I missed being on a team, being competitive, and the feeling of winning. When I came to Brewster that all changed. Brewster encouraged girls to be involved in sports. You were able to try out for a varsity or junior varsity team, and no one was excluded even if you had never played before.

As a sophomore, I tried out for the varsity basketball team. I never expected to make the varsity team since I was a sophomore. In my previous school the varsity teams were mainly made up of seniors. Sometimes, freshmen, even though they were good enough to make the varsity team, were not picked just because they were freshmen. This was not the case at Brewster. There were three freshmen that made the team with me.

Once tryouts were over and the team was selected, we had hour-and-a-half to two-hour practices every day. Quickly, the team became very close. We would hang out together in the dorm and invite the day students on the team to join us. Before games we all ate breakfast together. Essentially, we did typical family stuff—eating together, hanging out with each other, and playing together. We were away from home, but we became each other's families during the season. The seniors were never cruel to the underclassmen like you find in many other schools. If anything, the seniors were like big sisters to us especially on Wednesdays and Saturdays, which were game days. I felt great pride wearing my warm-ups to school and having everyone know that I was on the varsity team. In the halls people would pass by and wish you good luck.

When our games were away, we usually had a two-hour bus ride ahead of us. This gave us more time to get to know each other. Watching movies, talking about friends and school, doing homework together were great bonding experiences. The real excitement occurred when we had home games. Countless times we would make posters to hang in the gym before a game. We would hang them up in the empty gym and then before every game we would meet with our coach to get focused and review the strategy for the game ahead. The next time we would go back in the gym for warm-ups, the stands would be packed with teachers and friends cheering us on. The bigger the crowds, the better we played. I think my fondest memory of the Brewster gym is playing under a banner that I had helped put there (the Lakes Region Championship).

Our time together wasn't only limited to the court. Sometimes, the team didn't play well together as a team and communication failed. When this happened, our coach would make us do team building activities off the court. One time after it had snowed, Coach Thomas told us to wear warm clothes and our winter boots. When we showed up in front of the gym, she told us our mission was to build an igloo as a team that could fit at least one person. Despite our doubts, we completed this mission by working together. Then, we were split into two teams and had a race to see which team could build the tallest snowman the fastest. Another time, we did trust falls (following backward into the arms of teammates, trusting that they would catch you) to come together as a team. These exercises of teamwork and trust that we learned off the court carried over when we played on the court.

I don't always remember which games we won and lost, but

when I look back, I do remember the friends I made and the fun times we had together as a team. For many of us, high school will be the last time we play competitive sports but our friendships will go onward. We all learned the lesson that people who work together as a team can accomplish much more together than as individuals. I hope that we carry this message with us and apply it to our college experiences, our business careers, and our family lives.

Ashley Mudge is a 2002 graduate of Brewster Academy in Wolfeboro, New Hampshire. While at Brewster she played three years of varsity basketball, two years of varsity soccer, and one year of junior varsity soccer, for which she was named Most Valuable Player. In 2000 and 2001, she helped her team capture the Lakes Region league title in soccer. Ashley is currently a student at American University in Washington, D.C.

The Athletic Life

Heather Lindman '95
Choate Rosemary Hall

It was the summer of 1989. It was my first introduction to boarding school life. My older brother was touring many different schools and I was along for the ride. As all of the teachers, buildings, and campuses blended into one, the only things that distinguished one school from another, in my mind, were the swimming pools and the conversations with the swim coaches. I had been a competitive swimmer, swimming year-round since the age of five. Athletics had become one of the most important things in my life, and I was quite eager to learn how each school and coach would help develop a serious athlete amidst the academic pressures and numerous other demands on time. I wondered if I could be a serious student and still improve as an athlete. Most of all, I questioned my goals as an athlete, and if I could accomplish them at boarding school.

It was the sixth of six tours. It had rained, and my shoes had been biting into my heels as we walked. I had decided that I would never attend Choate . . . but that was before I met my future coach. I met him on the track on that rainy summer day. He was a very pleasant man and I was excited with what he shared about the Choate swim team. I liked his training style, the team spirit he seemed to encourage, and the fact that he had coached some great swimmers. At that point in time, Mr. Burns stood above and beyond the many things and people who had impressed me.

Three years later, I found myself telling Choate that I would be coming in the fall. Since each student must do a different sport each term, I chose to run cross-country. Running in New England in the fall was a great experience, but to my disappointment I seemed to spend more time in the training room that fall than I did on the cross-country trail. An injury to my foot forced me back into the pool to do my aerobic training in the water.

To my delight, swim season approached quickly, and I finally had a team with which I felt really connected. Practices were challenging, and I began to feel strong in the water again. Swimming is very much an individual sport. As a swimmer you spend most of the time with your head under the water. You are alone when you step up on the block, as well as when you race. This is what I had always felt about swimming. On my club team back home, everyone had been out to improve himself. At Choate, however, Mr. Burns taught the team a new philosophy. Though it required an individual effort, he helped us to value our collective efforts. I never felt alone in practice, on the block, or in a race, once I became a Choate Dolphin.

The swim meets began quickly. When we swam against our rival Deerfield during my first year at Choate, I was shocked to find the stands packed with people as I came out of the locker room. No one came to the swim meets my freshmen year in public school. But now, the Choate Dolphins had a crowd cheering for them. I found throughout my years at Choate that this was common at most of the sporting events. The support for each team by those at the school was extraordinary.

The fall of my junior year I chose to do water polo instead of cross-country. I had never seen the sport played before I went to Choate. It was one of the best decisions that I could have made, however. I was glad to stay in shape for swimming and enjoyed learning a new sport with a team, rather than an individual focus.

I loved these things about athletics in boarding school: I was encouraged to try new sports, I did not have to give up my intensity as an athlete, and I was able to improve in my favorite sport, swimming.

Boarding School Life as an Athlete

When I came into boarding school as a highly competitive athlete, I found many temptations which I needed to address. I had to decide how important my athletics were to me and how important it was for me to excel. The first thing that I found challenging was that during the off-season for my sport I was nearly on my own for training. The spring of my sophomore year I attempted track, but after stress fractures in my shins, I swam in the spring of my junior and senior years. No one else swam in the spring. I had to motivate myself. On many gorgeous sunny days I dragged myself down to the weight room. Then I would go to the pool on my own, occasionally coercing another swimmer to come with me. The hardest thing was to train in an indoor pool as the spring sunshine was beckoning outside. Many days this did not seem very appealing. With no threat of a coach questioning me if I did not show up for practice, it was a definite challenge to keep up the intensity of training.

Another great temptation that I found in my daily life at boarding school was the number of opportunities to get in endless conversations with a variety of people. Many nights I had hours of homework, and yet the sound of friends laughing in the dorm was hard to ignore, and the conversations around the dining room tables were enticing. I struggled often with the fact that I had to get my work done, so that I could get plenty of rest and stay healthy. Through my three years at boarding school I learned my limits, sometimes painfully. I learned that if I wanted to compete with the best, I would have to forego a few laughs with friends.

Another concern was diet. At home, eating right was easy. Mom would make healthy meals and there would not be much junk food in the house. But, I must say that at boarding school there is a plethora of unhealthy options. The cookies, cakes, and doughnuts stared at me from the dining hall lines. The "Tuck Shop" offered an array of unhealthy options as well: milkshakes, candy, fried this and fried that. At 9:30 P.M. everyone piled out of their dorm after study hours to get ice cream, pizza, or Chinese food from the vendors in front of Memorial House, and someone always had food in the dorm from a care package sent from a concerned parent at home. But the biggest temptation, however, was the homemade "mug nights," when the house adviser would make delicious desserts for everyone in the dorm. It is fairly easy to start eating in an unhealthy way in an environment like this, and an athlete has to be self-disciplined to eat right.

The Overall Athletic Perspective

Perhaps you can tell from what I have said so far that being a highly competitive athlete at a boarding school is not easy. Studies and other extracurricular activities make great demands on time, and most of us still want time to enjoy life. I often wondered if boarding school would reduce my chances of being recruited by a college coach, and if I could have gone further with my sport if I had remained at home. These are legitimate questions, and undoubtedly the difficulty in being able to have a single focus on swimming while at Choate did reflect a certain compromise, but I would not trade my experience for another. I realize now that I am much more than a swimmer. I am a young woman with a number of interests, one who has been challenged to grow in many ways. I have been exposed to other sports, to cultural opportunities, to leadership opportunities, and to an academic community that have all brought a great balance to my high school years.

To the question, "Was boarding school the right decision overall?" I am able to let out, without hesitation, a resounding "YES!" At Choate, I learned to love athletics again. I had a team and a school that supported me. Though I trained less than I would have at home, each New England championship brought improvement in the pool and a greater love for the sport. Yes, my performance as a swimmer may have been compromised somewhat, but there were benefits in going to Choate that I could not have anticipated, understood, or valued before I made the decision to attend. The system at boarding school resulted in swimming being integrated into the rest of my life, and as I developed as a whole person, I discovered a balance that will help me maintain my love and excitement for the sport for years to come.

Editor's Note: Heather graciously agreed to write a follow-up to the piece she wrote in 1995.

Now five years removed from my life as a competitive athlete, I am able to approach the topic with more objectivity. The interesting thing, however, is how similar I feel to my concluding paragraph written seven years ago. In fact, I am all the more convinced that my decision to attend Choate was a positive one. Boarding school did indeed enable athletic success, while also preparing me for life in college and beyond.

Following graduation from Choate Rosemary Hall, I went on to swim for two years at Harvard University. I would be fooling you to make you think that in college I struck the perfect balance, that being a student-athlete was easy, or that there were not trade-offs. Nevertheless, I believe that boarding school prepared me better than any other experience might have for the rigors of being a student athlete in college. I continued to wrestle with the great balancing act between academics, athletics, and my commitments to church and friends; however, the study skills, work ethic, and discipline Choate engendered aided tremendously in my efforts. Furthermore, the challenging classes in high school that taught me how to write, think, and debate prepared me for the demands of college syllabi, thus enabling me to have time to focus on sports and other aspects of college life.

Athletics played an integral role in molding me, and I would not trade my years as an athlete for anything. Athletics developed my character through the ups and downs, taught me the value of hard work and dedication, and helped me develop lasting friendships and memories. Swimming was very important to me, but as an athlete it was also necessary to remember that except for the rare few, competitive athletics would cease to be a focal point after college. In the midst of competition it was often hard to understand this and see beyond the upcoming season and immediate goals, but it was crucial to contemplate the ramifications of present decisions on future goals apart from athletics. For me, a balanced life would have been harder to achieve with the demands of my club swim team at home, and yet at Choate and at Harvard I was able to continue to grow and be challenged as a swimmer while being exposed to many other facets of life. Although athletics were a large part of my life, I have seen that many of my other interests and experiences have shaped much of my future and led to a richer life in college and beyond.

As you may be debating the merits and demerits of athletics at boarding school, I urge you to look at the larger picture. Notice how various schools approach athletics and find out if there are opportunities to excel and be challenged, but also consider how these same schools seek to nurture you as a student-athlete with an array of talents and interests.

Heather Wolbert graduated from Harvard in '99 with a BA in government. After teaching third grade for one year, she spent this last year at home and volunteered at her church and with a Christian organization at Yale University. Following her retirement from competitive swimming she has enjoyed competing in a triathlon and running races, and continues to swim as she expects her first child.

The Canoe

Evan Lichtenstein '03
Dublin Academy

I strapped my canoe to the roof of the Toyota and tightened the knots, realizing that the long process was over. While this realization came to me as somewhat of a joy, I had a nagging feeling that something important was about to disappear from my life. For the past six months I had been working for hours every week in my school's workshop. Instead of going out for Chinese with my friends, or sledding down the hill below the dorm, I worked on my canoe. The musty old building became an integral part of my life, perhaps more so than I would like to admit. For many grueling afternoons and evenings, I hunched over the sawhorses, my back aching as I forced thousands of staples into the wood, and later applied countless layers of epoxy to the hull. Through the dreary winter on into the bug-infested spring, my canoe slowly began to take shape, emerging into what would soon become a boat.

During the fall of my junior year, my crew coach, Caleb Davis, announced that he would teach two students how to construct wooden canoes. With crew season in full swing, I could easily imagine myself in a handmade vessel, cruising along the water in the crisp fall air. I approached Mr. Davis along with Tom, a senior at my school and a guy who genuinely loved the great outdoors. Although Tom was not on the crew team, he sailed on the lake, so we always passed each other on the water. Mr. Davis appeared eager at our interest and readily accepted us as his pupils, yet warned us about what we were getting into. Little did I know the intense work it would require. His estimation of 150 labor hours simply did not sink into my naive teenage mind. Only after the wood was purchased and the work began did I comprehend the grand scale of the undertaking.

The boats we aimed to construct were to be fashioned from pine with thin cedar accents. They were designed to be spacious enough for two people, yet light enough to be portaged upon one's back. Having canoed quite a bit, Tom and I knew the copious details that had to be incorporated in order for the boats to float and travel in a straight line. Our trio traveled to Belletetes, the local hardware store, where we picked out the high quality pine to be used in the majority of the hull. Once the wood was run through the noisy table saw, and later through a router, Tom and I were ready to begin the formation of our canoes. We were excited at the prospect of the construction, yet we each had some doubts about the level of craftsmanship required. Luckily, we managed fine, and with the help of Mr. Davis were able to successfully structure two seventeen-foot wooden canoes.

The opportunity to build a boat is one of the advantages of a small independent school. I attend such a school, a small prep school located in southern New Hampshire. The region is home to Mount Monadnock, and little else. While I am a day student, and am not confined to the campus, I often feel that we are isolated from the world, enclosed in a private bubble in which nothing enters and even less escapes. While Dublin School succeeds in its academic program and athletic endeavors, it also triumphantly succeeds in a lesser-known aspect of education: experiential learning. Dublin provided me a rare chance to engage in an independent study, not only to build a boat, but work alongside people in such a manner that would provide personal growth as an individual.

The key component in my experience was Caleb Davis. As a faculty member at my school, he coached as well as taught. During the crew season I discovered that while he enjoyed teaching at Dublin, his true passion lay in boat building. Luckily for Tom and me, he was able to combine his two interests to provide us with a valuable experience. Although the only relationship I had with him was as a coach, I knew that he was a comical yet stern instructor. Mr. Davis is an outwardly jovial man, and integrates his humor into everything he does. When he laid out the steps of the construction, I envisioned that he would be there each step of the way, making sure there were no missteps. However, while he showed us how to accomplish key elements in the construction of the boat, he often allowed us to learn by trial and error for the rest of the process, a process I am sure he watched with amusement sometimes. What at once felt like an absence on his part, I quickly realized was simply his teaching style, methods which would ultimately aid us as the student. Through Mr. Davis's instruction and intentional neglect we were able to do the work ourselves, and be accountable for our mistakes as well as triumphs.

A particular event epitomizes our boat-building journey. One day in the winter trimester, Tom and I were approached by Mr. Davis and informed that we were falling behind and had to complete a portion of the boat by the end of the week. What should have been a relatively easy undertaking turned into a burden, as Tom and I had conflicting responsibilities which prevented work from being accomplished on the boats. Due to the nature of the project, Tom and I were receiving art credit for our endeavor, yet owning to the fact that we did not share a common free block, the bulk of the work had to be completed during lunch or outside of school. Factor in time-consuming sports such as skiing and lacrosse, and it was a wonder we found any time at all. We finally found a day when we were both free, and began working after dinner, applying fiberglass to the exterior of the hull. Now, we are both competent individuals, yet this was a new experience for us, and things went slower then they should have. We were quickly covered in the gluelike epoxy, the thick molasses mess sticking to our cloths and skin. By nine, we had just finished one layer, upon which a second layer must be applied that evening. Tom and I worked hard that night, all the while cursing Mr. Davis and the school for burdening us with such a difficult life. At ten, one of our friends snuck out of his dorm and helped us. We toiled for hours in the dimly lit shop, the toxic fumes filling the air. By the middle of the night we had completed our task. Both exhausted and fatigued, we cleaned up and headed for our cars. The simple good-bye sparked in my mind the reason I chose this school. Had I attended a large institution, there would be no opportunity for such growth and challenge. However, at Dublin, with its small classes and devoted faculty, Tom and I were able to work together in relative freedom to complete a project. Through the course of the year Tom and I deepened our friendship, and through the help and guidance of Mr. Davis, learned not only how to build a boat, but learned that education could happen outside of the classroom. Dublin provided me the opportunity to do what I was interested in, and thus aided me in learning about myself, which will not only help me in school and work, but ultimately in the rest of my life.

It was many weeks later when I finally stepped in the boat for the first time. I must admit I was nervous. I had a troublesome thought that perhaps the boat would sink. While the canoe soon proved otherwise, I could not help tightening my life vest as I headed away from the shore into the small pond behind my house. To my delight and pleasure, the boat not only floated, but also cruised gracefully over the water on that magnificent summer afternoon. As I paddled, the boat traveled effortlessly, allowing me to focus on nature, rather than on the more physical side of canoeing. During my time on the water, the entire experience came together: I had completed a loop, starting on the water in crew season, and ending many months later once again on the water, this time in my handmade vessel. I contemplated what I had learned and what the final product had entailed. What I discovered was that while the thrill of owning such a boat was incredible, the journey I took along the way was perhaps an even greater thrill, something I could not have understood at the beginning of the year.

Evan Lichtenstein was born in Chicago, Illinois, and currently lives with his family in Marlborough, New Hampshire. In addition to rowing, skiing, and lacrosse, Evan will serve as the student body president for the 2002–2003 school year at Dublin School.

The Outdoor Advantage

Sami Boyle '02
Colorado Rocky Mountain School

My education at the Colorado Rocky Mountain School was shaped and molded by the wilderness's impact on my life. Honestly I can't describe only one outdoor experience: starting with my wilderness orientation in the Frying Pan Wilderness Area and concluding with my final spring trip out along the Escalante River, there is no one particular instance or outdoor experience that defines my learning experience at the Colorado Rocky Mountain School. There just is not one single story or defining moment in all of the time I have spent in the wilderness that could possible convey the importance of the outdoors and the significance it has had on not only my education at Colorado Rocky Mountain School, but also my entire life.

I didn't reach some overwhelming moment of enlightenment one day out on a backpacking trip; no, for me it just didn't happen that way. The realization that the outdoors has played such a defining role in my education came through years of wilderness excursions and traveling hundreds of miles with a pack strapped to my back and blisters bubbling up on my feet. My entire education has been defined by my love for the outdoors, as well as a desire to never stop exploring new horizons.

Each backpacking, climbing, and river trip left lasting impressions on both my mind as well as my soul, further developing my affection for the wilderness and this engaging "outdoor classroom." Through the course of my education at CRMS I have learned more about myself from my time spent sitting on a rock in some alpine meadow with the sun beating down on me, compared to the amount of time I have put in crunched over at a desk under fluorescent lights with my nose buried deep into some book.

The wilderness is bold, beautiful, and free. It demands your attention; you can't ignore it. The wilderness isn't just some elaborate description in a textbook, outlined by historical events; the wilderness is real. It lives, it breathes, and it grabs you. It forces you to define your limits or perhaps just realize them for the first time. But more important, the wilderness has the power to show you just how far beyond your perceived physical and emotional limits you can go. Yes, you are capable of reaching the top of that 5–11 route; yes, you can summit that 14,000' peak in the distance; yes, you are capable of surviving a seventy-two-hour solo; and yes, you can run sixteen miles over a pristine mountain pass. The wilderness forces you to look at and examine yourself in order for you to realize or redefine what you are truly capable of doing.

The wilderness shaped my education at CRMS because it was my best teacher. It taught, or rather demanded, that I pursue my own learning; I choose whether or not to further my own knowledge. The wilderness was such an impressionable teacher because, when I would reach that next level, it not only invited me to push farther, it encouraged me to. The wilderness has never heard of a grading scale; my parents were not going to receive any teacher comments or my grades marked on a report card. Out there it was simply a matter of pass or fail, and my teacher comments came in the form of cuts, bruises, and scratches on my body.

What also made nature such an impressionable teacher is that it never let me forget about the previous lessons I had learned. The wilderness first tested and continuously retested my skills, to sharpen my memory and my awareness. Outside there was no way to cheat; no one can do your homework for you, and there is no looking over your friend's shoulder for the correct answer. You are on your own out there, allowing for the wilderness to challenge your personal knowledge, soon to make sure you know everything by heart, and by the end of my time at Colorado Rocky Mountain School I did.

The wilderness's method of teaching forces you to learn about yourself, and the wild untamable beauty of nature. The wilderness teaches you about respect, responsibility, humbleness, and compassion. Yet, unlike the traditional classroom, where learning occurs through homework assignments, readings, videos, slideshows, and lectures, learning with nature is much more interactive. My wilderness education came from treks to mountain summits, the serenity of alpine lakes, the relentless power of sandstone cliffs, the currents of the river, the delicacy of a wildflower, the vast views of the valley floor laid out before me, and the untamed and unparalleled beauty of the rocks, trees, animals, and the soil. I was taught through the limitless expanses of the sky, unveiling where my next adventure lies awaiting me on the horizon. And as a result of my time spent in the outdoors and at Colorado Rocky Mountain School, I am eager to embrace it.

Sami Boyle graduated from Colorado Rocky Mountain School in 2002, when she received the school's highest academic honor, the Academic Excellence Award. An honor student at CRMS, she was a key member of the Nordic ski team (going to state finals and the Junior Olympics) as well as soccer, cross-country running, and rock-climbing teams. She also was a student leader on backcountry trips. For her independent senior project she volunteered with Food for the Hungry in the Dominican Republic. She is attending the University of California at Santa Cruz.

Getting Your Hands Dirty

Lissa Pabst '02
Colorado Rocky Mountain School

I attended for four years the Colorado Rocky Mountain School, a small college preparatory school that encourages faculty and students to work in collaboration in and outside of the classroom. One activity that takes place at our school that sums up our mission statement and core values is Scholarship Work Day, a program that I helped organize for the past three years.

During my sophomore through senior years, I was given the opportunity to help the director of special events organize six Scholarship Work Days. In the fall and spring of each year our student body and faculty spend an entire day working for people and businesses in the greater local community to raise money that goes toward our scholarship fund. We are hired to garden, work in fields picking rocks, paint, clear brush, clean windows, and the like. Engagement and compassion are two core values of Colorado Rocky Mountain School, and it is demonstrated in this day, when we are empowered to earn money that contributes to the diversity of our student body.

Having an opportunity to help organize Scholarship Work Day was a true gift in my eyes: I was able to see all sides of my high school; I was able to get to know the student body through matching personalities on crews with their assignments; and perhaps most important, I was able to not only give back to my school, but I was also able to give back to my community.

The mission statement of our school states that the "Colorado Rocky Mountain School challenges students to excel in a college preparatory academic curriculum balanced within a program of the arts, athletics, physical work, service to the community, and enriching wilderness experience " This philosophy of physical work as a valuable learning experience is an integral part of the Colorado Rocky Mountain School curriculum. While Scholarship Work Day happens twice a year, other physical work activities are planned into each student's schedule, at least twice a week. This means that students help with campus upkeep in work crews that do everything from vehicle maintenance to cooking, electrical wiring to gardening, and irrigation ditch clearing to childcare in the preschool.

You get a sense of accomplishment and fulfillment that comes in handy in the "real world," by doing something that you might not have previously viewed as compelling. No matter what type of school you choose to go to, boarding or day, don't be afraid to jump in and get your hands dirty (no pun intended)! If you put yourself out there, doing something that you might not otherwise choose to do, you will get some of the biggest rewards of your life.

Lissa Pabst graduated from Colorado Rocky Mountain School in 2002, when she received the school's highest honor, the Community Service Award. She was on the honor roll and soccer team, active in school plays and on outdoor trips, and for several years organized the school's community work program in support of student financial aid. For her independent senior project she volunteered at a primate research center. On a merit-based scholarship, she is attending Edgewood College in Wisconsin.

Editor's Note: The following three pieces are journal entries about programs at Proctor Academy which typify the kinds of off-campus opportunities many boarding schools offer. But first, here are the course catalog entries describing the programs involved:

Each fall term, twenty students sail the 130-foot topsail schooner *The Spirit of Massachusetts* from Boston to San Juan, Puerto Rico, while gaining full academic credit in literature, history, navigational math, and marine biology. Director: David Pilla, dave_pilla@proctornet.com

Each winter and spring trimester, ten students join two instructors to participate in the Mountain Classroom program. Living in a separate dorm on the eastern edge of Proctor's forestlands, they prepare for a western field trip by studying Western American authors, geology, desert ecology, and Native American history and culture. Three weeks into the term, the group begins its western travels where they will eventually experience rock-climbing, canyoneering, backpacking, river rafting, sea kayaking, and Native American culture while camping and living out of their minibus and trailer. Each student earns a full trimester of academic credit in english, history, science and expedition skills. Director: Patty Pond, patty_pond@proctornet.com

Brothers

Zachary Zimmerman '03
Proctor Academy

As I came above deck, the bright sun flashed into my eyes. Ahead of me stood tremendous cliffs and mountains. As we sailed into the bay, my nose caught an unfamiliar odor: the smell of stagnant garbage, of human waste. As the schooner sailed closer to shore, an enormous mountain of garbage caught my eye. Worn tires, crumpled-up plastic, broken glass, and remnants of metal were being pushed into the ocean. I was looking at and smelling Haiti for the first time. I understood that Haiti was the poorest country in the western hemisphere, but I had never imagined what I was about to experience.

I was aboard *The Spirit of Massachusetts*, a 130-foot schooner with twenty other classmates. As we stepped ashore, forlorn, starving children ran up to us: "Do you have any money?" The open-air marketplace was filled with malnourished mothers selling foul-looking fruits and vegetables. Unrefrigerated, bloody beef hung out in the hot market while flies swarmed and people urinated in the streets. Discarded plastic and paper lay everywhere about us. Children with armfuls of necklaces ran up to us begging, "You want to buy?" For some families, this was their only means of income.

One boy, who had tagged alongside me for the entire afternoon, begged for anything I could give him. It bothered me that the T-shirts and money I gave him would only be a temporary fix in his tragic circumstances. I can still remember his puffy cheeks and bright, wide-eyed expectancy. I finally had to leave him and get back on the ship. The boy stayed alongside *The Spirit* for the rest of the day, but the next morning he was gone.

Haiti seems far away as I walk into Bucky's eighth-grade classroom at Andover Middle School and see his face light up with excitement. We sit at a desk and review vocabulary words. I encourage Bucky to try harder, knowing that he has the potential to do well. After he finishes his work, we go outside and play basketball. I am Bucky's official "Big Brother." While I felt powerless to help the young boy in Haiti, I am fortunate enough to have the opportunity in my own community to be a mentor to Bucky; working with him is incredibly rewarding.

In Haiti, I experienced a culture that has caused me to view the world differently. So much of life's circumstances are a result of where one is born and one's family of origin. I have a new appreciation of just how lucky I am to have been born into circumstances where I have choices, and I am moved to make a difference where I can.

Zachary Zimmerman is a four-year senior from Hopkinton, New Hampshire, who participated in Ocean Classroom during the fall of his junior year. He chose that experience as one of the subjects of this college essay.

On the Boat

Gwenn Fairall '03
Proctor Academy

Ocean Classroom was such a great experience! It challenged me in so many ways; being part of a crew, setting and striking sails while I was seasick and at the same time, I had classes to attend and papers to write. After this experience, I feel as though I can get anything done no matter how many things I have to do, or how hard they are.

The hands-on aspect of Ocean Classroom taught me so much more than I would have learned if I had been in a classroom. I will never forget the class about the pirates on Cape Hatteras that we had as we were sailed past the Cape Hatteras lighthouse, or how dynamic the root system of mangroves are because we had class and played "capture the flag" in mangroves down in the Dominican Republic. By contrast, if someone were to ask me about a class I had a month ago I probably would not remember it and if someone asked me about something I supposedly learned in a classroom, I might not be able to tell them nearly as much.

Being on the ship taught me how to live with other people and how to work well together as a team. At the same time it taught me to be independent and to be my own person. It taught all of us that hard work, late nights, and early mornings pay off. For me it was seeing many different cultures, learning to live together and work together, which in turn created a lifelong memory of sailing down the eastern coast of the United States to Puerto Rico.

Looking back, I am so proud to have been able to accomplish that great feat with nineteen other students with whom I shared this amazing adventure.

Gwenn Fairall is a five-year senior from Andover, New Hampshire, who participated in Ocean Classroom during the fall of her junior year. She also attended the Proctor French program in Aix en Provence during her senior year and has chosen to attend Proctor for an additional year in order to participate in the Mountain Classroom program this winter.

On the River

Rebecca Barker '03
Proctor Academy

I do not think there is any way possible to describe in words how much Mountain Classroom affected me. Besides learning skills for living in the wilderness, working with a group, and being a leader, what Mountain really taught me was who I am. I learned that it is not always about reaching the top; it is about the climb that got you there. All those little things combined are what help you to overcome an obstacle. Most important, however, Mountain Classroom taught me that no matter what the circumstances are, you can make anything fun.

We started our adventure with four days driving sixteen hours to get down to Redford, Texas. Our first expedition was a seven-day paddling trip down the Rio Grande, directly followed by a two-day canyoneering trip in Bruja Canyon. There was definitely no better way to start our trip. The weather was perfect and the sky was unlike anything I had ever seen. The beauty of the environment surrounding me in Big Bend National Park was astonishing. I had never realized how vast and extraordinary the sky was. We saw shooting stars every night, and never a cloud in the sky during the day. Although I had been canoeing before the trip, I was far from an experienced paddler. The river was very low, but the twelve of us still managed to make every minute of it the best ever. Even the scorpion in my sleeping bag did not bother me!

The canyoneering trip was much more out of my comfort zone. Even though I had been rock climbing many times before, I had never been rappelling until Mountain Classroom, and it was not something I enjoyed very much. After climbing into the base of the canyon, we had to climb down into the center of it, which involved rappelling down a fifty-foot wall into a large pool of freezing cold water. I was not sure I would be able to complete this, but I knew I had to. I wanted to. I gathered as much courage as possible, locked myself in, and began the descent. With each slow step, I could hear the other members of my group encouraging me, telling me I could do it. Even through all my fear, it was so reassuring to know that everyone was here for me, wanting me to get beyond this obstacle just as much as I did. Relieved, I made it to the bottom, and then realized I had to jump into the freezing water. The fear came back and I did not think I could do it. One of the guys in my group came over to the other side and told me not to worry; just a quick swim and I would be there. I jumped in, but, shocked by the coldness of the water, my brain forgot how to swim! Luckily, my body remembered, and I was on the other side, and my friend was pulling me out. This expedition showed me that no matter how difficult something seems to be, or extreme the circumstances are, you can always do something if you just set your mind to it and have caring people around to encourage you.

Our second expedition was a four-day backpacking trip and a three-day, three-night solo in Joshua Tree National Park. I don't believe my body has ever been in so much pain as it was after the first day of backpacking. I had swollen hips and my back felt like someone had taken a sledgehammer to it. However, even with all this pain, I still went to bed with a smile on my face. I couldn't believe all that the group had accomplished in just one day. We had climbed up 400 feet in elevation over large boulders, and then another few miles through the barren desert.

The next three days were long hikes through the desert. We

would tell jokes while hiking to keep everyone from thinking of the pain and forgetting about what lay ahead of us. I learned that as long as you can still laugh, you are fine. Four days later, with swollen hips and chafed shoulders, it was time for our solo. I was much more excited than nervous for solo, although I still wondered if I would survive. The impact of a solo is something that cannot be fully explained; it is something that a person has to experience on his or her own. The things one discovers about oneself are priceless. I think back to sitting in my small site, in the sweltering heat, and remembering how all I wanted to do was see people and be back in civilization. When I was attacked by bees, I ran around like a maniac and cried my eyes out. However, I managed to see that the bees were just a distraction to allow me to prove to myself that I could survive solo, no matter what obstacles came along. I think back to solo and sometimes I wish I could be back in that solitude. There is something so special about spending seventy-two hours alone and surviving.

Every day on Mountain was an adventure. Every day I woke knowing I would do something new; see something I had never seen. There was something about that unfamiliarity that was so exhilarating. Most of the expeditions were very much out of my comfort zone; however, that was part of the fulfillment of going on, and completing, Mountain Classroom.

Rebecca Barker is a four-year senior from Hopkinton, New Hampshire, who participated in the Mountain Classroom program during the winter term of her junior year.

EXTRACURRICULAR LIFE

A Python Story

Lizzie Kay '03
Cate School

Slowly the python positioned himself for the kill. The unsuspecting rat had lowered his head for a sip of water, unable to find shelter from the sweltering heat. In the blink of an eye, it was over. The powerful jaws of the three-and-one-half-foot ball python locked onto the flesh of the silky gray rodent, holding the stunned animal, helpless, while the heavy coils of the snake. . . .

This scene plays out every day and is seen as the natural order of things. Watching what happens in the cage of my pet python, Monty, some animal activists might consider this cruel. I consider it an unfortunate necessity. Monty is a wonderful pet in a loving home, and even if others may not want to give homes to such animals, there are many people who would. In the real world, there are many Good Samaritans who love animals and have set up shelters for homeless animals not as fortunate as Monty. Unfortunately, keeping these shelters in business requires money.

As a student at boarding school, it would be easy to stay isolated within the confines of the campus. There is a lot of work to do for each class. And, there are also traditional high school extracurricular activities such as school plays and varsity sports. While I enjoy participating in these types of activities, I did not see any reason I could not also make the time to help support the efforts of someone helping homeless animals. A visit to one particular animal shelter, the Lange Foundation, inspired me to help. In Los Angeles, one woman, Gillian Lange, has been caring for homeless animals for years, and through my efforts at Cate School, I have raised thousands of dollars to support her cause. Who would even have guessed one student body could ingest so many brownies and Krispy Kreme doughnuts in just two years?

Bake sales on a boarding school campus made perfect sense as fresh late-night snacks are always in demand. But, the success of my project had much more to do with the wholehearted support of our Cate family. In the beginning, many people were skeptical about Animal Allies, and they did not believe that my program could make a difference. But, after a little while with lots of effort, money started rolling in and the community became supportive. Many kids bought baked goods, but quite a few simply donated their money to the cause. And, many faculty members not only bought goods, but also baked goods in their spare time. It was not long before I was known as "the head ally" and "the animal lover girl."

The result has been gratifying. Not only did we raise money for a good cause, but also becoming the spokesperson for that cause has helped me grow as a person. We were so successful that we raised thousands of dollars. Being responsible for that much money was a very sobering thought. By helping me grow as a person, Animal Allies has probably been as beneficial to me as to the animals.

Animal Allies held bake sales every Wednesday evening in the Community Center (on campus) at 9:30 P.M. to raise money for the Lange Foundation, a nonprofit organization dedicated to saving the lives of animals that would otherwise have to be euthanized by pounds. The money raised by Animal Allies was donated to this foundation to help pay for veterinary bills, shelters, food, and blankets. Participants within the program did at least one of the following: baked for the weekly bake sales, sold the baked goods, or bought the baked products. As the head of the program, I made weekly announcements for three main reasons: to thank the community for its support, to keep the community updated on the program, and to raise awareness regarding the harm inflicted upon domestic animals.

As a senior, this year will be my last at Cate. But two younger students, already heavily involved in the program, are planning to take it over when I leave.

No wonder Monty is smiling.

A senior this year, **Lizzie Kay** '03 is the varsity volleyball captain, a member of the Santa Barbara Volleyball Club, the leader and founder of the Animal Allies program, a dormitory prefect, and a tour guide. As well, she will be taking challenging courses such as AP government, AP Calculus, and AP English literature.

Spectating Is a Team Sport

Caroline Bates '06
The Andrews School

"Caroline, hurry up!" my mother yelled up the staircase. I was searching for any meaningful belongings I might have forgotten to pack. I stood in my square room and tried to make a mental picture of how it looked. After one more very loud call from my mother, I decided to leave and make my way toward the car. I got into the silver minivan, with all my belongings packed, and my family and I made our way out of Mansfield and toward Willoughby. While in the car, I was encouraged by my family to have positive thoughts about my new boarding school.

I remember walking out of the dining hall, after having breakfast on the first day of school, into the auditorium where announcements were being held. I found my section and assigned seat number and sat down. I heard shrieks and many names being called out. Friends were obviously being reunited. I introduced myself to some girls sitting next to me. Then I heard three bells and everyone suddenly became quiet. I focused my eyes to the front and I heard one tiny girl yell cheerfully, "Welcome back returning students and welcome new students to The Andrews School. My name is Gabrielle Armfelt-Llamerino and I'm president of student council." As morning announcements continued, I learned more about the school and its small community qualities. When announcements were over, I went to my classes, met some of my new classmates, and became familiar with my new surroundings. Later on that week, I was in the student center after class, socializing with a classmate and my big sister, Lindsay, when Gabby approached us. Gabby asked if my new friend Katie and I would like to join field hockey. (Both Gabby and Lindsay were forwards on the varsity squad.) Katie and I had never played field hockey before, but since neither of us was involved in any activities at the time, we figured that it would be a good opportunity to meet new friends, so we joined.

As we began to attend practices, I noticed how Gabby and Lindsay had a certain zeal toward field hockey. As we continued with practice each day, I realized that our invitation by Gabby to participate in field hockey was made without any "outward expectations." We had been able to join a sport without knowledge of our abilities, but it was assumed we would play hard and challenge ourselves as we did in the classroom. This sense of community and competition "without boundaries" was something I had never experienced at my public school. Lindsay and Gabby practiced each day as if it were the last time they would ever play. I found myself respecting the two girls because they had been engrossed in this sport for four years, yet still were enthusiastic players.

I was convinced to stay at The Andrews School because there was such dedication present in how my peers performed in the academic classroom, as well as the playing field. Then suddenly it occurred to me that this boarding school was a small community in itself. We celebrate our academic and athletic successes together without any inhibitions. When we played our last game of the season, the whole team worked tremendously hard and we all felt a sense of ownership. That described how my school educates students to go on in life to become self-reliant women. We didn't sit and watch the drama go by, we took part.

I have a new outlook on my boarding school. My attitude is positive because I'm more aware of what The Andrews School has to offer young women. The most superb quality about my school is that girls have the opportunity to express themselves freely and explore many opportunities. I find that I benefit from not only my personal success but also the successes of my classmates in my Andrews School community.

Caroline Bates is a ninth-grade student at The Andrews School, an all-girls boarding school in Willoughby, Ohio. Since her older brother and sister have attended boarding schools, Caroline wanted to share in the same experience. Caroline is involved in Blue Key Club, Community Service Club, and participates in field hockey.

Getting Active

Craig Thorn
Phillips Academy

Imagine that at ten o'clock at night, Eric Older and I are on our backs looking into the guts of an eighteen-channel McGurdy console, trying to figure out why we can't get any pickup on the Tascam 40–40 (a four-channel reel-to-reel) from the microphones in Studio B. I am handling all the wires with large rubber gloves, testing each one with a voltage meter in the hopes that we'll find a dead line. Eric is shining a flashlight into the patch bay, looking for loose connections. Or Jessica Rosenberg and Nadia Sarkis are considering the layout of *Backtracks*, a student magazine that features reviews of the arts and commentary on current events and general interests. Does the book review work better with the political commentary or the essay about cycling? Can we get an artist to come up with something nice for the cycling essay so that the piece will fill a page? I'm reading the articles while they move text from one page to another. Or Nikki Bilwakesh and Parris Bowe are trying to decide how to advertise a panel discussion featuring black journalists sponsored by S.A.R.C., Students for an Anti-Racist Community. Do they present the evening as a discussion of minority issues in a big city, the responsibilities of minority writers to bring untold stories to light, or the experiences of black reporters in the workplace? They decide on all of the above.

Later that same night, I notice that Julian Davis has shaved his spectacular hair, until now a cross between Kate Pierson of the B-52s and Buckwheat, down to a fine mat. He's in character for the lead of senior Luca Borhese's student-directed *Six Degrees of Separation*. Right now, he's arguing with close friend Eve Bradford, the patron saint of dramaturgy on campus, about the set design for the production. He is waving his arms furiously at a crowded table in the dining hall. Various compatriots dressed in countless varieties of black are peering at the two intently. Eve has a big smile on her face. Although I can't hear Julian above the din, I catch a few words: "focus," "turn it around on the audience," "light, light, light."

"Extracurricular activities" fails to capture what these events mean to students and faculty. The term has a formal ring to it which belies the thrill, the visceral charge a student gets when she makes something happen: a magazine, a radio show, a film, speaker, scene . . . a change in the way your peers look at a thing, whether it is *Bless Me, Ultima* by Rudolfo Anaya, the wetlands along the Northeast corridor, political prisoners in Chile, or the Mississippi Delta blues. In a boarding school environment, connections are everything.

I treasure my time with students in extracurricular activities because we are colleagues creating something together. The focus isn't on something to be produced by one person and judged by another; we're in it together. Not surprisingly, my closest friends among students are those with whom I work on the radio station, the magazine, or the panel discussion. Side by side, we end up talking about everything, making connections that having nothing to do with the matter at hand, a nest of wires or a screen filled with text blocks. The phrase "extracurricular activities" deceives.

What you do in a student organization should be more than an activity; it should be an absorbing avocation. You make your own world of ideas when you seriously engage in a political magazine or the drama club. When you work hard with the rest of a radio newsstaff on a profile of a local politician, the resulting ideas belong to you. They have not been introduced to you by a teacher nor have you arrived at them via a class discussion. You have initiated them, coaxed them into being. Along the way, you have learned how to work with your peers, how to lead and how to follow. You have learned how to win an argument by persuasion, how to lose an argument gracefully, and how to compromise. You've honored a deadline, a budget, a policy, a tacit contract with an audience, whether it be in a theater, at an art show, on the printed page, or through a stereo system. When you pursue an interest with others in the form of an extracurricular activity, you connect yourself to the intellectual and cultural life of a school, the life that exists outside the structured environments of the school: the classroom, the playing field, the dorm.

When you find yourself in a boarding school environment, know this about extracurricular activities. They are not about getting into college. If that's your take on them, you're not going to find yourself under the console or at the dining hall table. You're not going to be a part of a smaller community that respects and nurtures your genuine enthusiasm. In other words, your peers will find you out, and so will your college counselors. Extracurricular activities are not about numbers. Getting involved in half a dozen activities is not getting involved in any at all. Look for the quality of the experience, not the quantity. If you're overloaded, the experiences are not outlets for your imagination; on the contrary, they are drains on your energy and creativity.

The real words for "extracurricular activities" are "passionate interests." If what interests you is not at your boarding school, either make it happen or find something like it. If you're curious about a hobby, project, cause, or organization, join it. Don't worry about fitting in. Your genuine curiosity is the only price of admission. Sometimes boarding schools can feel like big, complex places where everything is passing you by and everyone seems to have a purpose you cannot apprehend. The Asian American society, the radio station, the school newspaper, Amnesty International, the poetry group, a chamber orchestra or hardcore rock band . . . these are the smaller communities where the real connections are made, where you can make a home for yourself in your own image.

Craig Thorn is an instructor in English at Phillips Academy, where he has been a house counselor, adviser, administrator, and coach for twenty-one years. In addition to writing and editing books about education, he writes essays about literature and reviews of alternative rock music.

The World of Theater at Thomas Jefferson School

Karen Fairbank
Thomas Jefferson School

It's Friday night at The Rep, and students are either dressing up and secretly excited, or moaning and groaning about another Friday night at the theater. Six times a year, the entire student body of Thomas Jefferson School (this year seventy-four strong), along with numerous faculty, staff, and parents attend the full subscription of plays at the Repertory Theatre of St. Louis. We have eighty-nine season tickets, and sometimes we have to buy additional tickets for the more popular shows.

Thomas Jefferson School, a college preparatory, coed day/boarding school for grades 7–12, was founded in St. Louis in 1946, in part because of its access to a wide range of cultural institutions. It also provides a strong classical education, requiring both Latin and Greek. For a number of years, we had taken students to two plays a year at The Rep, but we decided that going for the full season (six plays), in good seats, would give us a more rewarding experience. In 1992 TJ got a full-season subscription for all faculty and students. That year the plays included *Six De-*

grees of Separation and *M Butterfly*, two rather sophisticated and daring (some nudity) plays for students that were as young as seventh grade. The other plays that year were *Pygmalion*, *Dracula*, *Woman in Mind*, and *A Funny Thing Happened on the Way to the Forum*. It was a very good first year for TJ at The Rep. Perhaps the all-time favorite play was a production of the musical *Sweeney Todd*.

We've observed over the years that like all theatergoers, the students have a wide range of opinions about which plays they like and don't like. We've been surprised at some of their reactions. They loved *Avenue X*, a doo-wop musical about clashes between ethnic groups—in fact, the student who writes the reviews for our school newspaper, *The Declaration*, went back to see it two more times! The students were more critical, however, of some plays that were "popular" with the public, feeling they did not have the same "weight" of the customary Rep fare.

Some years the schedule included plays that were already included in the TJ curriculum (*Inherit the Wind*, *Julius Caesar*, *The Brothers Karamazov*, to name just a few); other times a play that was included in The Rep's season was added to the TJ curriculum (*Death of a Salesman*, for instance); and on another occasion, TJ's eighth grade performed a play that had been put on by The Rep (*Black Coffee*, by Agatha Christie). When the students have already read a play, they are sometimes disappointed that The Rep production edited out parts that they considered critical to the work.

Study guides prepared by The Rep have added to the educational experience and are used regularly in the eighth-grade English class and occasionally in other classes. We also have post-Rep discussions with actors, directors, and production staff (sometimes the next week at TJ and other times we stay after the play). These discussions can be boring for the more sophisticated students when curious seventh graders ask "obvious" questions, but also produce mature and insightful comments that even some of the adults hadn't considered. As with any required activity, we get the negative "do we have to do this?" response from many students; however, a recent article in *The Declaration*, written by a sophomore who has been at TJ for four years, criticized her classmates for not going into performances and other events with an open mind. At the last performance we attended, the hugely popular Cole Porter's *Anything Goes*, one junior boy hid in the bathroom for the second act. His classmates laughed at him for missing out on one of the funniest plays they had seen in a long time.

In addition to novels and short stories, the eighth-grade English class (which I teach) also studies theater throughout the year, covering acting as well as production aspects of the play, along with a discussion of themes and other content. The fourth quarter of English 8 is devoted to a producing a play that is presented to the entire school (and proud family members) at the end of the year. While we do not have a theater (we have a wooden stage that is set up in our Common Room), we've actually become quite sophisticated in our production. The popularity of "doing" theater at TJ is attested to by the requests of older students to be in the eighth-grade play. Even if they don't want to act, some older students have also helped with other aspects of the production, from makeup, to set design, to sound and lighting.

This year for the first time, an all-school play will be staged at the end of February. The impetus for this production came in large part from last year's eighth grade, who had so much fun with their show that they wanted to do another. A junior who had starred in *Black Coffee* as Hercule Poirot is co-directing the play with a second-year teacher who, like me, has a theater background. The cast is made up of ninth to twelfth graders, most of whom are veterans of the eighth grade, some of whom are acting in their third play. While special accommodations in homework, study hall, and athletics attendance are given to the eighth grade during the last few weeks of rehearsal, and no evenings, weekends, or vacation time is used for the play, this all-school production of Woody Allen's *Don't Drink the Water* requires the students to squeeze out rehearsal time whenever they can. No school money has been budgeted, although we will probably find some way to assist the production. For instance, a fund-raiser that the yearbook no longer depends upon is being used for the play.

Other theater opportunities for students include theater classes that are part of the fine arts curriculum. Seventh and eighth graders take one required eight-week drama course over two years, and in grades 9–12, a theater class is offered every other year. We also get tickets to other theatrical events throughout the year that are optional, including such popular events as The Reduced Shakespeare productions, as well as a wide variety of plays at theaters around St. Louis. Sometimes as few as two students attend, while others attract a much wider audience, and teachers often offer extra credit in a relevant class (attendance at a production of *Copenhagen* earned extra credit for physics students, for example).

What about the future of theater at TJ? When the board of trustees seeks requests for capital projects, a theater is always mentioned. In fact, the admissions department has noted that we lose some female enrollees in part because we don't offer more theater. Perhaps in the next capital campaign, building a facility for both theater and other fine arts will be part of the package. Until then, we will continue to educate theatergoers and to provide opportunities for both the Greek scholar *and* the thespians.

Graduated from Washington University B.A. '71 (political science), J.D. Washington U '75, M.A.T. Wash U, '84, **Karen Fairbank** is a teacher of seventh-grade social studies, eighth-grade english and twelfth-grade AP U.S. history at Thomas Jefferson School since 1984. She is also a member of the board of trustees and the director of student activities, adviser to the school newspaper, coordinator of the fine arts program, and director of the community service program.

The Active Life

Justin Steil '96
Phillips Academy

Shocking though it may sound, of all the aspects of a boarding school education, I think that it was hobbies that had the most profound effect on my life. The interests I found at school changed my outlook on the world and on my future. Surprisingly, the hobbies in which I became most involved were not ones in which I had previous experience or interest, yet they became integral parts of my school career.

As a freshman, away from home, thrust into an alien environ-

ment, I clung to old, familiar activities. Too intimidated to inves-
tigate new clubs or hobbies, I tried to force my favorite sports
onto an unreceptive athletic director. I presented him with detailed plans for a climbing wall and later a proposal for a sailing
team; the highlight of my fruitless efforts was the exasperated
athletic director's description of me as "a nightmare that just
won't go away." Undeterred, I tried to keep in good sailing shape
by building a large wooden contraption that ended up taking up
most of the space in my closet. Some thought it was a sled, others,
just a heap of garbage, but as I became engrossed in my schoolwork, it did little more than decorate my room and entertain in-
quisitive and amused guests.

Though I have yet to give up my two favorite sports, I accepted that sailing would have to be limited to the summer. My
climbing, however, improved measurably through a combination
of practice at school and away. I took advantage of the outdoor
program the school offered and did rock climbing as a sport. I
found friends who climbed and on afternoons we biked or drove
with day students to the local cliffs to practice and relax. Requiring complete focus from body and mind, climbing cleared away
all the stresses cluttering my head and let me strive for excellence
in an arena completely free from outside pressures. It was always
a relief to spend two hours where, for my own safety and that of
those around me, I could not be distracted by the thoughts of
school that so often dominate my life. Using my experience from
school, I diversified into other aspects of the sport such as ice
climbing during the vacations. As I plan for my senior winter, I
hope to spend several weekends relaxing by hanging hundreds
of feet off the ground from two or three sharp points stuck in a
frozen waterfall (it really is fun). I learned from the disparate
paths my sailing and climbing followed that one has to choose
what interests one truly wants to pursue at boarding school. Do
not be discouraged if a school doesn't offer the activity you want
to pursue; you can certainly practice it outside of school and
maybe be more successful than I at starting a new sport or club.

During my sophomore year, when I was more comfortable
with boarding school, I tried some new hobbies. For the first time
in my life, I started running and joined the cross-country team.

Discovering that many other aspects of my life benefited from improved fitness, I have continued running both during the cross-country season and on my own. Deciding to try singing, I joined chorus and narrowly passed the auditions for the cantata concert choir; though I never became a great singer, I have enjoyed it immensely. At the urging of several friends, I also began to attend bible study sessions and church services. Unexpectedly, I had added three new and different elements to my life that I plan to continue well into the future.

In my junior year, though I was already busy with the school's difficult course load, I started even more hobbies. A friend suggested that I go to gospel choir; so, armed with the singing experience I had gained from chorus and cantata, I decided to give it a try. It has become the activity that is most important to me. All week I look forward to the rehearsals where I can absorb the music and be absorbed by it. The songs are always in my head and it is often their beat that provides the rhythm for my life.

Photography has always been one of my hobbies and at the start of my eleventh-grade year I tried to start a photography club. Three other students and I collected names of interested students and planned meetings and field trips. As the term continued, however, the rigors of school work eroded our initiative and exposed our inexperience, eventually causing the club to flounder miserably. We learned the hard way that one shouldn't try to start a new club or hobby unless one is extraordinarily devoted, organized, and energetic.

Toward the middle of the year I found myself getting involved in more new hobbies. I began writing articles for the *Phillipian,* the school's weekly newspaper, and was asked to be the news editor. Little knowing what the job entailed, I happily accepted and began work. I soon discovered that it took me at least sixteen hours every week to fulfill the responsibilities. Though I would not do anything differently now, it is important to understand what responsibilities accompany a leadership position. I made great friends working at the *Phillipian* and learned more than I thought there was to know about newspapers and journalism. The position challenged my physical stamina, my time management skills, and my ability to work quickly, and the vast experience gained certainly made up for any difficulties it caused. No other activity or class on campus could have taught me all the lessons I learned in my late nights at the *Phillipian* room.

At the same time that I was beginning to work with the newspaper, my house counselor asked me to be the environment editor of a nonfiction literary magazine. Though this did not require nearly as much time as the *Phillipian,* it led me to focus much more on my writing, and the combination of the two positions transformed my understanding of literature and journalism. By my senior year, I diversified my writing hobby and, in addition to writing and editing nonfiction for these two publications, I submitted poetry to a fiction magazine.

Worried about my health and academic performance, my parents constantly asked if I was overcommitted and if I could really handle all that I had taken on. I thought I could. At first, I struggled to stay awake in classes and out, but with practice, the *Phillipian* went more smoothly and my body adjusted to a little less sleep. I decided, however, to put rock climbing on hold for my senior fall so that I could continue my other hobbies and focus on academics and college applications. A wide range of activities can broaden your education and provide invaluable diversions; overcommitment, though, can do just the opposite, exacerbating stress and leading to poor performance both academically and extracurricularly. Don't be discouraged by parents or advisers who think you may be unable to handle a difficult workload, but also don't be afraid to admit that you have spread yourself too thin and might be better off concentrating your interests more narrowly. Some people thrive under pressure and do their best when they have the most to do, while others need more time and sleep. You must recognize your limits and discover what is most important to you. If, however, you see your health deteriorating and your grades falling and you find yourself sleeping through classes, either in your bed or at a desk, don't be stubborn; cut back on your activities before serious damage is done. There are many other activities that I wished I had tried, but I knew that I could not manage more.

Self-made opportunities, hobbies provide much of the student-faculty interaction and peer education that make boarding schools unique. When you get to school, you don't have to abandon your old hobbies and become a new person, but part of an education is experimenting and discovering what interests you most. Whatever you choose to pursue, if your experience is anything like mine, you will find valuable friends and lessons.

Justin Steil graduated from Phillips Academy in 1996. After college he has become very active in community-service related jobs, most recently working with prisoners.

Appalachian Spring:
A Passionate Interest Becomes an Intellectual Endeavor
adapted from a speech by J. W. Bonner
Asheville School

When I have read the *Little House on the Prairie* series to my three children, I find that in Wilder's day students were obligated to demonstrate to the entire town community mastery of their subjects: history, geography, math, literature. This demonstration took place in public and was a great civic celebration and cause for pride. The stakes, consequently, were elevated for both the student and the teacher. The students were evaluated in front of friend and family, neighbor and mentor; implicit in the success of the student's demonstration was the student's commitment to and passion for the subjects and the effectiveness of the teacher's own passion and commitment.

A special graduation requirement of Asheville School holds its students accountable to a similar culminating experience: the Senior Demonstration. The Senior Demonstration, or Demo, is a rite of passage that allows students the opportunity to demonstrate their mastery of written, oral, analytical, and research skills— skills essential for college (and work or life) success. Students explore a topic of particular interest, whether chosen from a provided list of over 150 topics, or a self-designed project. To fulfill the requirements of the Demo, students write two analytical papers, the second of which requires the use of secondary sources, and maintain a reading journal. The project culminates with an oral defense of the work before a panel of faculty.

Topics in recent years have ranged from study of such traditional writers as Dante, Shakespeare, Austen, and Lawrence to more contemporary authors such as Anne Tyler, Eudora Welty, Allan Gurganus, and Gabriel García Marquez. Several students have designed interdisciplinary projects combining interests in, for example, literature and medicine or illness and death. Other topics have ranged from the Manhattan Project to relativity, from medieval music to the blues and even punk music.

Given the range of possible topics, the self-directed aspect of this program, and the rigorous, collaborative work with the faculty sponsor, the school's truly gifted students generally enjoy the Demo process the most. Although the Demo challenges all of the school's college prep students to meet a high standard of achievement, those students with the strongest passions and academic interests working in conjunction with curious and engaging faculty members often enjoy the greatest degree of intellectual growth and exchange.

The expansiveness of the topics allows a student an opportunity to become something of an authority or "expert" in an area. Students have interviewed writers for their papers incorporating secondary materials and have been able to send their papers to current writers for feedback and constructive criticism. For example, a few years back one student of mine with a particular interest in punk music had used several works by Greil Marcus as part of his readings. I had asked him to look at the writings of Marcus because of my own enthusiasm for Marcus's ability to limn the connections between the Sex Pistols, dada poetry, and the '68 French student and worker uprisings. Indeed, I had interviewed Marcus when his collected essays (*Ranters and Crowd Pleasers*) on punk music appeared, so I was eager to have my student's reactions to Marcus's writing inform his thinking about punk music. My student sent his first paper directly to Marcus, who responded that he found the paper "very fine," although he did suggest the paper "could be better if [the student] trusted himself more and quoted others less."

Two years ago I worked with a student with an interest in both literature and science, so we developed a topic that explored literary connections to disease in such pieces as, for examples, Defoe's *A Journal of the Plague Year* and Sontag's work on illness and metaphor. I had also suggested that the student include Allan Gurganus's novel, *Plays Well With Others*, an artistic coming-of-age novel set in New York City in the midst of the AIDS crisis in the '80s, knowing that she might have an opportunity to interview Gurganus as a source. We sent Gurganus a copy of the student's analysis of *Plays Well*'s use of metaphor in the context of her other readings, and, after reading the student's paper and after her interview with him at his Hillsborough home, Gurganus gave her in appreciation an as yet unpublished story he had written about a doctor treating a Midwestern town during the cholera epidemic of 1850. Thus, Asheville School students are provided an opportunity to develop unique, interdisciplinary, and personal approaches to topics.

The Demo creates an intellectually charged environment until year's end, allowing students the freedom and latitude to explore a topic of interest throughout the spring semester. The Demo also fosters close intellectual partnerships between students and faculty. Most students enjoy the process of discussing the readings with their faculty sponsors. A student often works through multiple drafts of a paper with the sponsor before submitting the final copy. This connection with the faculty member as a fellow "investigator" creates a collaborative approach to education and to learning that will serve students well in college and in life.

Finally, students engage in a public discussion of their topics in a year-end colloquy. Interested seniors join faculty, as well as younger students, to share with other classmates and with faculty their work from their final months at Asheville School. Students question peers who have studied Freud and Jung or the poetry of Pablo Neruda. This give-and-take session is often one of the most exciting aspects of the semester's work, a chance for the pure intellectual excitement to play out without the need for assessment or evaluation.

The Demo has engaged students even beyond their time here. A student's examination of disease served her at a personal level when she suffered Hodgkin's disease later in college. After successful treatment, she returned to college and undertook an independent, interdisciplinary course of study following the same topic explored in her senior Demo. Her work on the Demo provided a stable framework for dealing with her own personal health, served as a course of academic inquiry in her undergraduate major, and led her to her current career interest in pediatric oncology as she finishes medical school—high stakes, indeed. No stronger public statement or example is possible. She is one exemplary demonstration of what such a program may entail for curious and committed students. Even the citizens of Laura Ingalls Wilder's famous town would be proud.

Jay Bonner received his A.B. at Duke University and A.M. at Brown University. The associate head of school, Bonner has been an English and humanities instructor at Asheville School for more than seventeen years. Mr. Bonner also owns a publishing company, writes for various periodicals, inspires students, and listens to punk rock music.

Some Ways to Explore and Develop Your Hobbies and Extracurricular Interests

How do you decide what to sample of your school's opportunities? Here are some simple exercises to work through that will help you make informed choices:

1. Make two lists:

    All the things you do or   All the things you
    wish you had done   might want to try
    at your present school   at your new school

    _____   _____

    _____   _____

    _____   _____

    _____   _____

    _____   _____

    _____   _____

    _____   _____

    _____   _____

What would you be willing to give up in order to try something new if you were limited by available time?

_____

_____

Are the activities you've selected varied? For example, are some private, social, indoor, and outdoor activities?

_____

_____

Have you made most of your friends as a result of the activities you participated in at your old school?

_____

_____

If one of the activities you would like to pursue is not offered at your new school, who can you go to about starting the activity?

_____

_____

What are the names of the student leaders involved in the activities that interest you at the new school?

_____

_____

2. Make a day-to-day weekly calendar. Find an hour a day during which you engage in a hobby or extracurricular activity. Remember what Craig Thorn and Justin Steil said about hobbies and activities. They are an important part of your boarding school life.

3. At the end of the first term, create a narrative of your experiences thus far and put it in a medium that appeals to you:

- a story
- an opera
- a play

- a TV drama
- an album
- a musical

- a film
- a poem
- a dance

- a symphony
- a mural
- a monologue

What do you think of it? Why did you choose the form you did?

_____

_____

Keeping Your Balance

Ed Kowalchick
The Hill School

My first experience in contemplating the art of balancing occurred several years ago before my immersion into the sea of secondary boarding schools. While my wife and I were both completing our undergraduate degrees, she came upon a very inexpensive artwork which she wisely placed before me after an unusually grueling evening of study. At the time the object was just what I needed for a diversion from the academic world. Since then, it has reminded me too many times that remaining balanced is essential to living a centered life in a topsy-turvy world.

The "objet d'art" consists of two separate pieces. The base is a rectangular block of wood which stands approximately six inches in height. The other piece is a silver stick figure. Its arms are outstretched and bear an arc much like the apparatus a tightrope walker might use to keep from tumbling down. Battered by external forces, the figure rocks back and forth. Sometimes, pivoted on only one "leg," it seems likely to topple headfirst from its base, but because of its symmetrical design, after frantic swaying and swinging it returns to a calm stillness, poised and steadfast, all motion ceased.

It would be unrealistic to proclaim that during the past eighteen years I have never lost my balance, that I have always felt my feet were planted firmly on the base of Mother Earth, and that my steps never faltered or stumbled. As with all the members in a boarding school community, it is the very struggle of balancing that keeps me aware of the need to organize, reorganize, and evaluate my priorities, responsibilities, and duties. On any given day, the balancing of my time and energies determines my accomplishments and sense of purpose.

Over the years I have spent residing in boarding schools, I have had numerous occasions to reflect on the need for balance in my life and in the lives of the faculty and students who choose, for whatever reasons, to participate in a residential life community. For all of us, the choice to participate in an inclusive environment has also presented a challenge to keep centered in time when, faced with an overwhelming number of duties and responsibilities, we might unwittingly lose our balance and topple from terra firma.

Accepting this challenge is the first step we take when we decide to reside in a boarding school community. But accepting the challenge is only the beginning. We all need to plan our strategies in order to set goals that we can successfully attain.

I encourage you to take some time to reflect on your life in boarding school. The following recommendations and questions will be helpful guides as you determine exactly how you are going to go about swaying on your own little platform without toppling over. Fill in the blanks, and get started . . .

Some Ways to Keep Balanced

Priorities

Goals are best made by you rather than established by others. Your strongest commitment will be to the priorities you make.

Why are you coming to a boarding school?

_____

_____

_____

What short-term goals do you expect to achieve at boarding school?

_____

_____

What long-term goals do you expect to achieve at boarding school?

_____

_____

How will completion of your short-term goals lead to the completion of your long-term goals?

_____

_____

What grades do you wish to get? (It's not enough to say "I want good grades.")

English	_____	History	_____
Math	_____	Language	_____
Science	_____	Other	_____

What will you give up in return for getting higher grades?

_____

_____

Time Management

You can increase the opportunities to do the things you want to do and need to do by improving how you manage your time. People who manage their time effectively have the same twenty-four hours in the day as everyone else. They plan and schedule time so that they can achieve a balance and be successful in all parts of their lives. If you take the time to organize your efforts, you can easily save one-quarter to one-third of your time. The trick is to develop a concrete plan.

What's your prime time?

When are you the freshest? _____

Do your most difficult studying when you are at your best. Do the most interesting things last as a kind of reward for doing the most difficult work first.

Plan your study time realistically.

In an hour of study time, how much time do actually spend studying? _____

How much on study breaks?

A one-hour study block should really be fifty minutes with a ten-minute break, or thirty minutes with a five-minute break.

How much time do you allow for sleep each day?

Meals? _____

Exercise? _____

Relaxation? _____

Relaxation and exercise are very important to good studying. Don't sacrifice them for long hours of study. Allow for periodic breaks between study sessions.

Which subjects are going to require the most work?

_____   _____

_____   _____

Allow yourself more time on these subjects, not less.

Plan your average day on this hourly schedule.

AM		PM	
1:00	7:00	1:00	7:00
1:30	7:30	1:30	7:30
2:00	8:00	2:00	8:00
2:30	8:30	2:30	8:30
3:00	9:00	3:00	9:00
3:30	9:30	3:30	9:30
4:00	10:00	4:00	10:00
4:30	10:30	4:30	10:30
5:00	11:00	5:00	11:00
5:30	11:30	5:30	11:30
6:00	12:00	6:00	12:00
6:30	12:30	6:30	12:30

Now, look at your time management plan. Have you allowed yourself enough time to do all the things you need to do? What changes can you make to arrange your time better?

In 1995 when this piece was written, **Ed Kowalchick** was assistant head-master for residential life at The Hill School, where he had worked for over twenty years. He has been a house counselor and a consultant with the Harvard-Milton study skills series.

CITIZENSHIP, ON AND OFF CAMPUS

Try Something New! May Program at Oldfields School

Katrina Murphy
Oldfields School

Every year, during the last two weeks of May, everything changes in our school. Half of us disappear—to France, Italy, Peru, Quebec, the canyons of Utah, or the hills of Appalachia. The other half of us stay on campus, and do everything from learning to cook *paella* and restore old Corvettes, to improvisational comedy workshops and rock climbing expeditions. A few seniors design independent projects, sometimes art or photography-based, often internships in hospitals, veterinary clinics, and other businesses. We call these weeks May Program, and for many students, May Program is one of the most important and memorable aspects of their time here.

Oldfields School offers May Program as a way to provide learning opportunities in areas not easily offered in a traditional school schedule. Language immersion, time-intensive sports and arts, film, travel, and field trips are all made possible by the program. Oldfields believes that this type of experiential education can help our students deepen current passions, develop both specialized academic and nonacademic skills, and explore new fields of study.

Teachers and administrators develop off-campus trips and on-campus courses in the preceding summer and fall, offering them in a catalog which parents and students usually receive during

Thanksgiving break. A sign-up assembly follows in December. Students who have gone on the overseas trips say things like, "We learned so much in our two weeks (in Italy)—the culture, the history, the art, the food! I am now so much more excited about studying European history next year." And from a student who went to Costa Rica: "The highlight of our trip was learning about all the different flora and fauna. I love animals and to see new ones was awesome!"

Community service experiences are increasingly in demand. We work with Habitat for Humanity, inner-city elementary schools, and hospitals, shelters, and soup kitchens to provide a variety of service programs. For fifteen years, a group of our students have traveled to a remote settlement in Kentucky, where they paint porches, help renovate houses, and spend time visiting with the residents. Our girls come home full of passion, often feeling transformed by their experience, saying, "The people you meet are so amazing. To see the improvements your work brings to their lives is so rewarding," and "It may sound cliché, but I really did learn that material things are not what's important and that friends and family are what really matter."

Students often combine the best of both off- and on-campus programs by traveling for one week (a theater trip to New York City or a river-rafting trip in West Virginia, for instance) and then spending a week doing things like pottery, golf, sailing, photography, cooking, and film courses here at school. Or they stay on-campus the whole two weeks, and enjoy the pace of one six-hour or two three-hour daily courses, late afternoons around the pool, picnic dinners, and optional evening outings and activities. It is a time to make new friends around shared interests, and especially to see the faculty in a new light. (Who knew your chemistry teacher had a secret passion for flamenco dancing?) No matter where they go and what they do, our students say their May Program was mostly about getting to know themselves a little better: "My course was about getting to know new people and discovering who you really are," and "I learned to step out of my comfort zone and be myself."

At the end of the two weeks, just a few days before graduation, the travelers return, and we all come together for a day called May Sharing, where every course or trip gives a brief talk, skit, slide show, or performance. We applaud and laugh our way through presentations from three overseas trips, six U.S. trips, and twenty-three different on-campus courses. As we walk down the theater steps at the end of the day, teachers and students both find themselves musing, "What should we do next year for May Program?"

Katrina Murphy has degrees in English and creative writing from Stanford University and the University of New Mexico. A longtime English teacher, she now runs the May Program at Oldfields School and keeps busy with her two toddlers, Helen, three, and Jacob, two.

The Student Beyond the Classroom

Nicole Weyer
Brewster Academy

As I walked across campus last spring, a freshman approached me—all smiles, a lacrosse stick in his hand, and an excited look in his eyes. I said hello and asked how he was. He replied, "Can you believe that I just got three hours of community service for teaching a group of fourth graders how to throw lacrosse balls? Isn't that cool?"

A proctor began the year more interested and capable of "fixing" problems among his housemates rather than helping his peers work toward their own solutions. Throughout the year, I watched a transformation take place. The proctor began to understand that it takes patience and listening skills—especially when you are the designated person to whom students go to with problems—to mediate conflict and help find a compromise solution. Later in the year he commented, "I've learned that it takes a lot of patience to listen to both sides of an argument and then try to arrive at an acceptable compromise." The proctor had learned through this leadership opportunity how to work *with* his friends in the dorm to solve problems rather than solve them *for* his friends—an invaluable skill to have mastered for future endeavors.

After a student dismissal occurred, I logged onto e-mail and read the announcements folder to check the pulse of the student community. The announcements folder is an open e-mail forum for all members of the school community to post messages or respond to daily events on campus and around the globe. Some students sent brief messages blaming the school for punishing the student who was dismissed; however, others wrote that the student had made a poor decision and that this was an inevitable outcome because students know what is acceptable and appropriate behavior at the school. I was impressed with those who understood that each student is responsible for his or her behavior and must be prepared to accept both the positive and negative consequences of their decisions.

These are just a few examples of how our community-life program impacts students. At Brewster Academy the community is grounded in a policy that drives the development of each component of the school: academics, athletics, and community life. As a foundation, Brewster seeks to "maximize achievement and personal development" in each student in our community.

The community-life program encompasses weekend activities, the health and counseling centers, the community-service program, student leadership programs, and student life in the dorms that includes dorm activities and weekly group meetings. Our mission is to support each student in becoming an independent and responsible young person who communicates clearly and makes healthy choices.

As with students who live at home with their families during high school, dedicating time for regular family meetings is an essential component to developing a safe and healthy living environment. This forum at Brewster is a weekly group meeting where each member of the house with his or her community-life parent sits together to discuss upcoming events, check in with each other about their days, and find solutions to dorm or interpersonal conflicts. During the group meeting, emphasis is placed on finding solutions to dorm issues, whether they are among a few people or dormwide. During this time, students also plan social functions and other fun activities. The focus of weekly meetings is for each student to gain listening skills, develop effective communication skills, and allow an opportunity for each student to participate fully as a member of the dorm. Meetings are not solely facilitated and directed by the community-life parent. Students are encouraged to bring issues to each meeting and must actively participate in discussions that result in solutions. In this way, students are actively engaged in managing their home and become invested in what the group accomplishes in weekly meetings and throughout the year.

Dedicating time to community-service projects on and off campus is an opportunity for students to give of themselves while building both the campus community and surrounding communities. At Brewster, community service is an expectation and some students are initially reluctant to give their time but most students end up gaining from this experience. I've watched students develop new interests, discover new passions, unselfishly give back to people or a cause in which they believe while contributing and strengthening the bonds of the community. Community-service projects also facilitate relationship building among students who may not have other opportunities to interact. Students often do not realize that community service can be fun, allowing for the students to benefit as much as the person or group to whom they are giving.

Whether a student is part of student government, a dorm proctor, head of a club, or member of the judicial board, finding balance in a boarding school environment means dedicating time to the campus beyond academics and athletics. Student leadership roles enable students to develop self-confidence, strengthen communication skills, and to grow and challenge themselves outside of the classroom and off the playing fields. Students who participate in student leadership opportunities on campus invest time to develop themselves comprehensively.

Boarding school is demanding and faculty know that providing social programs and events as outlets for students, faculty, and families is an important part of learning to balance school demands. Whether it is a weekly activity such as meeting friends at the snack bar or going to an off-campus dance, students must designate time in their lives for healthy fun. Attending athletic events, helping plan a movie trip, working with a campus club to bring a band to campus, participating in a talent show, or trying out for a school theater performance are all outlets for students that strengthen the entire campus by creating an active and energetic community.

Fundamental to balancing life beyond the intensity of boarding school life are the faculty who support each student and maximize opportunities for students to gain life skills. This means capitalizing on "teachable" moments—mediating a roommate conflict, supporting students in generating ideas for dorm activities and community-service projects, or supporting students in resolving dorm issues. Rather than provide answers for students, community-life parents support each student in discovering the answers for themselves. Faculty will consistently support the student while addressing behavior, which may need adjustment. Similar to parents whose children come home at the end of their school day, most boarding schools offer compassionate, responsible, and dedicated teams of community-life professionals who willingly accept the role of surrogate parent to boarding students. Faculty work collaboratively with students and support their growth beyond the classroom.

We know that building a campus culture where students and faculty function as respectful, independent, caring individuals is one of the most important vehicles to teaching balance within the boarding school environment. We also know that the hallmark of success comes in observing a change in behavior and witnessing the development of an independent student who is responsible and an advocate for him or herself. And, that's what can happen when a school has an intentional community-living curriculum in place.

Nicole Weyer is the dean of community life at Brewster Academy in Wolfeboro, New Hampshire. She has a bachelor's degree in political science from the University of Minnesota and a master's degree in international and intercultural management with an international education and training concentration from the School for International Training in Brattleboro, Vermont.

Where Is the School? How Does It Adjust to Its Cultural and Physical Landscape?

Tim Hillman
St. Andrews-Sewanee School

Years ago, when I first moved to St. Andrew's-Sewanee, I experienced what was probably the most severe case of culture shock I could have ever imagined. After seven years of living and commuting in Los Angeles, where every street corner was a reminder of the diverse ethnic makeup of the city, I moved with my family to a small boarding school on a mountaintop in Tennessee. Gone were the variety of ethnic foods, the possibilities for cross-cultural exchange, my Lebanese friends, my Iranian students, my English and Spanish colleagues, and a large quantity of smog. In its place was a student body and town that seemed at first glance to be remarkably homogeneous, and certainly lacking in the cultural richness Los Angeles had to offer. Of course, the air was much cleaner, the noise at night was from crickets and cicadas, not sirens, and the bars on my windows were replaced by deadbolts that grew dusty from purposeful neglect. I think it's called a "trade-off."

As that first year passed, however, I slowly but surely became aware that diversity is not solely the property of diverse ethnic communities, and grew to realize that even places as isolated as St. Andrew's, Tennessee, had its own cultural life lurking beneath the surface. Day by day, I started to see the subtle differences and cues. The fact that "y'all" didn't roll off my tongue with ease. This curious food called "grits" that didn't appeal to me one bit. The remarkable volume of deep-fried food that seemed to fill so many menus. The way that the Confederate battle flag seemed to find its way into life. The almost maniacal worship of University of Tennessee football (a disease that I fear I've caught). Adoration of grown men in fast cars going around and around a paved track at breakneck speed (a disease I know I've caught). The occasional display of ugly racism that bubbles out. The quiet veneration of God and family that is part of the texture of life. The poverty that still pervades Appalachian life. The Anglican traditions of the local university, replete with professors in gowns. The hedonistic remains of the sixties found in the people who have come from afar to call the mountain home. The remnants of the old South in the literary figures that have long congregated in Sewanee. The initial site of the University of the South, burned long ago by Union troops pressing the battle on toward Chattanooga and Atlanta. Each day passing seemed to bring with it a new awareness of something that made this place unique, and our presence here special.

This "sense of place" becomes central to the education of students who attend St. Andrew's-Sewanee. Like so many boarding schools, our student body has grown increasingly diverse, but the relatively small size of the group forces a different manner of acclimation to the environment. Where a larger school might have a substantial representation of ethnic groups, in most cases we have fewer than five students whose ethnic background identifies them as a group. In any given year, the international boarding group might include two Germans, a Hungarian, a Russian, three Japanese students, two Koreans, a Thai, a Vietnamese, and a Swede, while the American boarders are predominantly white, with a sprinkling of African Americans, Latinos, and a few naturalized citizens from other countries. We do not have what you could call a "critical mass" of any one group. This lack of distinct cultural groupings could easily be a disadvantage, but instead the school has devised a fascinating way to take the students and ground them in the substance of the mountain and the community of which they are a part, thereby allowing their cultural heritage to become an important feature in their individual growth.

Our mountain is located at the far western edge of the Cumberland Plateau, flat on the top, and rimmed by precipitous bluffs that offer spectacular views of the land below. Between these bluffs, in forested coves, run the streams that give life to the farmers below, and to the remarkable flora and fauna that populate the forests. Each year, the senior class is introduced to both the phenomenal reality of the mountain, and also to the people that populate the place. Through the year, the seniors have a number of "senior days" devoted to exploration of a specific element of the world they live in. They listen to the oral history of the mountain told by the people whose lives have been played out here. They hear stories of a different age in Sewanee. They hear stories of war, of famine, and of birth. Artists tell them how the mountain has influenced their work, and writers speak of similar inspiration. Biologists tell them of the fragile ecosystem supported on the mountain. A geologist explains both how the mountain came to be, and how the passage of time has affected the land. Collectively, they attend local churches, from Episcopal to primitive Christian, to understand better the faith and beliefs of the people with whom they live. After an initial lecture on a given topic, the students travel off to visit with people, hear the stories, and walk the land. An afternoon of reflection follows, then they come together for a dinner where they respond, in small groups, to the experience they have shared.

An example of this exploration is the yearly hike through Lost Cave. The mountain is comprised of sandstone and limestone, with a resulting network of caves formed by the dissolution of limestone. Their names are descriptive: Wet Cave, Dry Cave, Solomon's Temple, and many others. On a Senior Day, students are grouped together and walk a long trail deep into "Lost Cove," a desolate but glorious example of a Tennessee cove forest that culminates at a cave carved through the mountain over thousands of years. After entering the cave, they follow a labyrinth through to where the cave actually opens on the other side of the mountain. Muddy and exhausted, they tromp back to campus for dinner and reflection on the events of the day. Quite literally, they travel through the structure of the land that they walk on every day. Their minds are etched with the knowledge that they know not only that which occurs on top of the land they stand on, but also what happens beneath their feet, and how strong yet fragile their environment remains.

While the "sense of place" program serves to give the students an extraordinary experience of the world around them, it is the culmination of their senior year that becomes their defining cultural moment. In coordination with their senior religion class, the students are asked to take the knowledge that they have gained from their study of world religion, their experiences in the "sense of place" program, their cultural heritage, and the body of knowledge they have gained through the years at St. Andrew's-Sewanee and create a "credal statement," a statement of who they are and what they believe. In addition, they choose a symbol that they identify with themselves. The credal statements are presented at the end of the year to the student's adviser, a member of the administration, and any other guests that the student wishes to have along. Over the years, I've been present at many, and none are forgettable. The boy who, after years of academic struggle, likened himself to a hickory tree, strong and resilient. The young woman whose symbol reflected her closeness to the earth, and a different god. The student whose symbol was a handmade chalice that she used to give us a symbolic communion. The dark confession of a girl whose symbol was the belt her father had used to whip her when she was young. The actor who used the theater as the location for his statement, but placed me on the stage, along with the headmaster, surrounded us with the artifacts from his gypsy-like existence, and played his own music for us. The girl who sat us down in a field and talked of her love for God, her symbol a wreath of flowers.

As I reflect on the "sense of place" program and what it means to the students of St. Andrew's-Sewanee, I am drawn to the cultural differences celebrated. The mission of our school is grounded in the idea that we are not solely a school, but also a church, a place where we celebrate spirituality and belief. The mission is achieved when a student leaves the mountain knowing that what she takes from the mountain in a practical sense is no more or less important than the intangible elements she has assimilated. Equally important is the knowledge that when she leaves, her presence does not fade away, and her actions and beliefs will echo for years to come in the lives of people she touched, and those who touched her. The student comes to know that while the time spent at school is small, the school and the people whose lives were touched are changed forever by that contact.

Culture is, after all, the accumulation of belief and knowledge, and the way in which those elements combine to create a whole being. The school's answer to its location and physical surroundings is to use those elements to steep the students in the culture of their world, thereby helping the students to better understand and define their own cultural heritage. They go out into their worlds stronger for their brush with a school on a mountain, and we are richer for the elements of their lives left with us to guard.

The co-editor of the first edition and the fellow who had the idea in the first place, **Tim Hillman** has taught at Phillips Academy, The Buckley School, and St. Andrew's-Sewanee School. Most recently he has been writing about education and computer technology, and also teaching.

You Mean I Have to Do What???

Tim Hillman
St. Andrew's-Sewanee School

One of the rude surprises that may confront you at boarding school is the manual labor that you may have to perform as a part of school life. Schools have different names for it, and some schools don't have it all, but for now, we'll call it "work duty." It goes like this—your school has a list of tasks that students will perform on campus. You may have to sweep the halls, empty the garbage cans, serve as a waiter for meals, wash dishes, rake leaves, clean bathrooms. Each and every day, you will have to perform one of these tasks under the supervision of a faculty member, staff member, or older student. Any way you look at it, the tasks are menial, and not a whole lot of fun.

The most frequent complaint from students is "My mom and dad are paying a lot of money for me to go this school, and I shouldn't have to work like this!" Certainly, that feeling is understandable. The reasons that work duties exist are varied. In some older schools, work duties came into being during either World War I or II. Schools were suddenly faced with a lack of local labor and were forced to institute work duties for their students to make up for the loss of labor to the war. Other schools have work duties as an integral part of their concept of the important things taught at the school. Still other schools use work duties primarily as punishment for students. Any way you look at it, however, it's still work and not a whole lot of fun.

So how do you deal with one of the not-so-fun parts of boarding school? Simple. You do the job, and try to have as much fun with it as you can. Remember, if you were at home, you would probably have chores to do as a part of day-to-day living, and work duties are really no different. It's all part of taking care of your surroundings.

The worst thing you can do? Treat it like it's some awful thing that you have to do every day, something to be avoided at all costs. If you go that route, you are likely to end up with more and more work, and less and less freedom to do what you want to do when you want to do it. Even worse, you won't make any friends with your peers if you try to shirk the responsibility. They don't like doing it much either, but they are giving an effort.

So, grin and bear it. Get there on time, do your job well, and get on with the rest of the day. And remember, if you do your job well, consistently, you just might end up in the position of supervising others carrying out their duties. One former boarder I know remembers it being kind of fun to walk around the school in the morning checking to see if the wastebaskets had been properly emptied. He remembered emptying the bins himself, and wishing he could be the inspector. Once that day arrived, life seemed just a bit sweeter. I also remember the grim expression on the face of a four-year boarder who spent all of those years loathing work duty, skipping it again and again, and not understanding why he wasn't chosen as a supervisor.

Work duties are chores, and chores are a pain in the neck, but they are a part of life at boarding school. You'll get through them, and they'll seem like nothing when it's all done.

The co-editor of the first edition and the fellow who had the idea in the first place, **Tim Hillman** has taught at Phillips Academy, The Buckley School, and St. Andrew's-Sewanee School. Most recently he has been writing about education and computer technology, and also teaching.

School Year Abroad

Sarah LaBrie
St. John's School

After the initial airport nervousness where I met the sixty other students who would attend my school, and repeated the words

"Hi, my name is Sarah, I'm from Texas" until they had lost all meaning; after that first terrifying car ride with my French host mother prattling away while I tried and failed to understand a single word she was saying; after the first few nights of waking up at 2 A.M. wondering where I was and what the heck I was doing there; I finally settled into my new life and realized that my decision to move to Rennes, France, as part of the School Year Abroad program was the smartest one I had ever made.

The first month of school was mainly about learning to adapt. Habituating myself to a school day that started at 8:00 and ended at 5:30 every day was difficult at first. But I soon discovered that although the work was hard, it was worth the effort.

I took an advanced placement French literature course. As I grew more and more skilled in the language, the works of Voltaire and Baudelaire gained new meaning. When I didn't have to struggle to understand the words, I could focus on interpreting their message. School in France was different from anything I had ever experienced. Where else could I spend a month learning about the castles of the sixteenth-century Renaissance and then take a three-day field trip to the Loire valley to see the castles we had discussed? Living in Brittany gave me access to places I would otherwise never have gotten the chance to see. On the school trip to Paris, I spent whole days exploring the Louvre, deciphering the symbols in the baroque paintings with the skills I'd gained from my art history class. We studied Shakespeare in depth in English class, so over February break, my friends and I decided to go to London where we were utterly blown away by the Royal Shakespeare Company's production of *Hamlet*. In the spring, we coordinated a trip to a tiny island off the coast of Provence. Porquerolles was about five miles wide with a single town that was smaller than a city block. We spent a week biking mapless through forests and vineyards, living in a sort of perpetual wonder at the impossibly blue sky and the white beaches that no one besides us seemed to have discovered.

I lived in a suburb called Chartres de Bretagne, with a family of four. My host father, Claude, was a retired chef. He and his wife, Jacqueline, delighted in cooking huge gourmet meals made with vegetables and herbs they cultivated in Claude's prize-winning garden. I spent much of my free time bonding with my host sister, Morgane, over a mutual addiction to homemade crepes and nutella.

My host family was the most important part of my year in Rennes. Upon arriving, I was nervous. I come from a small family, and I was daunted by the idea of a house full of people speaking a language I had hardly mastered. Over the course of the first few weeks, my fears dissipated. My family was amused by my relentless questioning: "*Je ne comprends pas . . . qu'est-ce que ça veut dire?*" and patient with my minor cultural gaffes (word of advice: no matter how much you hate mayonnaise, if your host father concocts a batch completely from scratch, accept it when he offers you some, then ask for seconds. It's a small price to pay for your family's unconditional adoration).

When I left Rennes at the end of the year, it was like leaving home all over again. I knew the shortcuts to all the best cafés, where the owners didn't mind if you stayed all day and only ordered one cup of coffee. I knew where to go to watch the kids with dirty hair playing Frisbee and sharing sandwiches with their dogs. Near my school, there was a huge garden made up of infinite rows of roses and rare flowers interrupted sporadically by stone fountains and koi ponds. I went there when I wanted to get lost.

The summer before I went to France, I was repeatedly asked what made me decide to leave. I had several answers. I wanted to be able to speak French, I mean really speak it, to the point where no one in France would ever mistake me for a tourist. I also thought it was important to take advantage of the opportunity to experience life somewhere outside of Houston, Texas. I wanted to do something I had never done before to prove to myself that I could withstand a complete shift away from my familiar environment, that I could adapt to anything and come out of it stronger. I wanted to leave France tough and sure, ready to take on the rest of my life without insecurity or fear. Instead, I spent my time in France coming to know my limits and my strengths. Now I know how much I am capable of achieving, and I feel confident in my ability to make the decisions that will affect my future. The School Year Abroad experience is different for everyone, but it invariably leaves its mark. Once you've done it, your mind-set is forever widened, and you can't see yourself or your home in the same way again.

Sarah LaBrie is currently a senior at St. John's School in Houston, Texas. She plans to pursue a writing career in France after she graduates from college.

9/11

John Strudwick
Lake Forest Academy

On the morning of September 11, 2001, I was in my office, teaching an independent study course in economics. News began to reach us of the events in New York and Washington, and I was faced with my first real crisis as the head of school at Lake Forest Academy. I realized that it was vital for the students to be made fully aware immediately of what was unfolding in the world around them and, most important, to bring the students, faculty, and staff of the academy together as a community.

After consulting with the dean's council, I gathered the LFA family together in the chapel to inform them of the terrible tragedy and to allow them to reflect on the events together. The dean's office identified students and faculty with relatives living or working in the New York and Washington areas and shepherded them to phones so that they could try to contact their families. In the chapel, we placed a large-screen TV to allow the students to watch the events live and to catch up on what had transpired earlier in the morning. As we grieved together, our information technology (IT) office sent out an e-mail to all parents letting them know what we were doing and how LFA was responding to the crisis. We also posted up-to-date information on our web site, with constant updates. After an hour of watching together, I addressed our students in the chapel with words of sorrow and a call for reflection. We invited students to meet in their dorms where faculty would be available to talk about what had happened and to gather in other central points on campus. We also allowed day students to call their parents to get permission to go home to be with their families.

That evening, the cultural diversity club sponsored a discussion for students and faculty to speak openly about their thoughts and fears. Our Muslim students spoke eloquently about their disgust of what had transpired and there was a clear call for an understanding from everyone that what had occurred was the work of terrorists and murderers and not something in the name of a religion. There was emotional support for all of our students of all faiths and backgrounds, a strength apparent at LFA throughout the ordeal. Three days later, we gathered again and listened to the soothing yet inspiring words of our dean of students, Kate Parker-Burgard, who read from the Koran and spoke of the importance of love and faith. I delivered a poem by Shelley, which speaks of the power of hope in erasing the depths of sorrow.

Since that week, we have continued to be aware of the effect of the events of September 11, and I am extremely proud of the manner in which the LFA community has responded. Everyone has shown sorrow as well as hope; they have expressed outrage but have maintained a respect for all cultures; and they have offered support to all of those touched by the attack. During the LFA homecoming celebrations, I had the pleasure of meeting with Anna Bowditch, beloved wife of Headmaster Frank Bowditch (1941–51), who four months into their tenure as leaders of the school had to call the entire LFA community together to speak of the horrors of the attack on Pearl Harbor. It was an honor for me to talk about this with Anna and to report to her that LFA had met a modern crisis with similar clarity and sensitivity. At the homecoming dinner, I quoted a LFA report from 1878 that stated, "The most gratifying result of an LFA education is the growth of character among the students." I was certainly proud of the character shown by them on 9/11/2001.

John Strudwick is currently the head of school at Lake Forest Academy. Before Lake Forest, he worked at Phillips Academy as a coach, teacher, counselor, dean, and administrator.

September 11, 2001

Alex Thorn '04
Phillips Academy

As were many American students, I was attending classes the morning of September 11, 2001. Because it was the first day of school for the 2001–2002 school year, we had a hectic schedule during which all classes met, each for thirty minutes. I had just finished my first thirty-minute class, English, and before my second class I was on my way to grab a bite to eat at the Riley Room, a small refreshment/food court type deal with fried food and drinks. In a new addition to the Riley Room, the school had also added a huge white screen with a television projector so that students could have the privilege of watching whatever they wanted in enormous proportions.

As I was making my way across campus to the Riley Room, some friends of mine stopped me and frantically explained what they had just seen on the TV in Riley. It seemed impossible. I broke into a run, and as I neared the Riley Room, I noticed students running from other parts of campus.

The Riley Room was packed, but because of the television screen, everyone could see the chilling video feed that came in minutes after the incident. I can still remember the scene as if it were yesterday. There had to be between two and three hundred students there, all silently staring up in awe.

As the days passed and opinions flared and people pointed fingers, I felt the growing need to honor those who had fought to save lives and those whose lives were lost. While talking with an old friend of mine on the Internet, I became aware of an Internet chain letter. The chain letter called out to all Americans to stand outside on September 14 and hold a lit candle to the sky for those who lost their lives. Receiving this e-mail and subsequently sending it out to everyone on my e-mail address book gave me a sense of pride in my country. Realizing that not everyone at my school would know about the proposed event, I forwarded the e-mail to the student activities director, Kevin Driscoll, and pleaded with him to allow the student body to participate in the memorial candle lighting.

Later that evening, Mr. Driscoll returned my e-mail with a few remarks of his own. He agreed that the idea in the chain e-mail was an excellent one, but he reminded me of school policy on fire and candles. While I did and do understand this policy, I couldn't believe that he wouldn't allow the student body to bend this rule under the given circumstances. However, only a few hours later, I received a second e-mail from Mr. Driscoll, in which he assured me he had not forgotten my plea and had come up with an alternatively good plan, as he agreed that we needed some kind of schoolwide ceremony. In those few hours, he had contacted our school's reverend, Michael Ebner, and between the two of them, they began to organize a schoolwide, supervised candle-lighting and memorial ceremony.

Planning continued. In addition to the students giving Jewish prayers, Muslim songs and Christian prayers, the reverend asked me to deliver a speech during the ceremony. I did not decline his request, and so I spent the next two nights before the memorial service, scheduled for Friday, September 14, writing and editing a speech that expressed sorrow, empathy, and pride for my country.

Classes after September 11 turned into open forums and therapy sessions, with teachers attempting but always failing to offer some sort of reasoning for the events of 9/11. Some students were quiet, seemingly absorbed in their own thoughts; others were outspoken nationalists and called for violent retaliation. People were constantly forming groups around campus—faculty, students, staff—in all kinds of combinations, but there did not seem any way to share what you were feeling that made sense. Students and faculty were angry, confused, and generally frightened. It turned out that the memorial service scheduled for that Friday was just the thing we needed.

The afternoon of Friday, September 14, I spent agonizing in stressful fits of doubt, hoping to God that my speech would run smoothly and I wouldn't make a fool out of myself. I was not worried so much about speaking, for I am usually an easygoing public speaker; rather, it was the thought of reading something I had written and, for a split second, instead of seeing hundreds of students with candles in their hands, seeing the images on the Riley Room television.

It was time. I made my way down to the steps of the Addison Art Gallery, the chosen location for the service, and met with Rev. Ebner. He handed me the speech I had written and said something I will never forget. He said, "Alex, this is a good speech."

More and more students, faculty, and staff poured into the area and soon it was time to start. Rev. Ebner opened the service with some remarks and a prayer and then solemnly passed the microphone to two Indian students who sang a Muslim song of peace. It was beautiful. During the song, candles were passed out to each person in the audience. As I held my candle, it felt like I had a death grip on it, squeezing the frail handle flat. But I didn't. As the song came to an end, a group of students with lit candles passed the flame around the audience, creating a warm glow over the field.

Then it was my turn. I stepped up to the podium, put my speech down, and said the first line without looking up. My heart was racing; I shifted from foot to foot. I had never been so scared in my entire life. I paused and noticed that it was completely silent except for the faint echo of my own voice through the loudspeakers. I raised my head for the first time and gazed across the audience. My heart slowed, and I stopped moving. Suddenly everything I was worried about, everything that scared me was gone. In front of me I saw almost a thousand candles and the same number of barely illuminated faces surrounded by pitch black. Each face was different, but each person's candle was the same. It was the most beautiful thing I had ever seen. The entire school had come together and forgotten their differences and any preconceived notions and it was silent.

And so I delivered my speech, rejoined the crowd, and held my candle in the air.

Alex Thorn '04 listens to all kinds of modern music, is the general manager of the school's radio station board, co-editor-in-chief of the school's general interest magazine, program director of the Andover Barbecue Society, and plays interscholastic football. Away from school he lifeguards and teaches swimming at the YMCA, is a counselor at a summer camp in New Hampshire, writes and produces rap music, and runs his own website.

SOME WAYS TO KEEP IN TOUCH

Your perspective on the world gets clouded the less in touch you are with the communities that you belong to. It's really easy to get so wrapped up in yourself at boarding school that you forget about what's happening elsewhere. More than once or twice, students at boarding schools have been blissfully unaware of major events happening in the world around them. "Oh, so there was a major earthquake in Alaska? Gee, I wonder how come I never knew?" Here are a bunch of ways to keep in touch. Circle the ones that keep you in touch at school, underline the ones that keep you in touch with your home, and put a check next to the ones that keep you in touch with the world. Are there any that cover all three?

_____ find someone who shares a common hobby

_____ read the school newspaper

_____ attend school athletic events

_____ attend school plays or concerts

_____ get a mail subscription to the hometown newspaper

_____ attend school social activities

_____ watch the news on TV when you can (even Headline News will keep you up to date)

_____ join a club or other activity

_____ attend local cultural events

_____ try something you've never done before (ride a kayak, climb a mountain)

_____ write home frequently (if you write, Mom or Dad will write back)

_____ keep an eye on the weather at home from the news

_____ if your town has an Internet presence, check it out regularly

_____ plan a regular phone call home time

_____ get a subscription to *Time, Newsweek,* or *U.S. News and World Report*

_____ start a pickup game of football

_____ get an e-mail address and use it

_____ get your computer on-line in your dorm room

_____ talk to your adviser/teachers

_____ subscribe to *Rolling Stone*

_____ subscribe to *Sports Illustrated*

_____ use the Internet to keep up to date on issues (try *http://www.cnn.com*)

Residence Life at the School of Public Service

Mark Dolhouse
St. Albans

It was the winter of 1960. Ike was in his last year in the White House and a young, Roman Catholic senator from Massachusetts named John F. Kennedy had that winter launched what many regarded as a quixotic campaign for president. Change was in the air and that winter three young African-American students at North Carolina A&T University compared notes in their residence hall one February night. They discussed the treatment that they had experienced in the segregated public transportation system. A few short days later, they "sat in" at the segregated lunch counter at a Greensboro Woolworth's store. They had, that night in their residence hall, conceived of a form of social change that would become known as a "sit-in." The students, in Senator John Kennedy's memorable phrase, had "sat down in order to stand up for human rights." The movement spread like wildfire, and a crucial element of the saga that was the 1960s was launched from a residence hall on a college campus. Four summers later, in the residence halls of Western College in Oxford, Ohio, students from all around the United States sat up late at night discussing what they had learned during the day from the instructors from SNCC (Student Non-Violent Coordinating Committee) as they prepared for their journey into the deep South to register African Americans as voters. One of the veterans of "Freedom Summer" 1964, a young Yale student newspaper editor named Joe Lieberman, would later write of the influence that summer exercised on his conscience and commitment to public service.

The students who gathered in the residence halls of St. Albans School for the inaugural School of Public Service in the summer of 2002 are not unlike those students of an earlier era. Journeying to Washington, D.C., at a time when tension still hung heavy in the air from the previous fall's terrorist attacks upon the World Trade Center and the Pentagon, these students from all around the United States came together to build a community that defined the mission of the School of Public Service and set the standard for future SPS students. These twenty-nine students were the first students to emerge into the post–September 11 world having had their junior year and perhaps their entire youth punctuated by the tragedy of that September morning, not unlike an earlier generation who learned during their lunch period on a Friday that the president of the United States had been murdered in Dallas. It is poignant now to recall that these SPS students received their first packets of information about the St. Albans School of Public Service in the days immediately following that defining national moment in September 2001.

The residential program for the St. Albans School of Public Service demonstrated again the critical role that a residence hall can play as an incubator of intellectual and social development for students. I remember well the night we met the first SPS student to arrive at National Airport late on a Saturday night. Having flown all day from Alaska, Ethan McWilliams had every reason to be groggy and tired. Instead, as we traveled across the Memorial Bridge with the Lincoln Memorial bathed in light, Ethan could barely contain himself. "I can't believe I'm here" was a refrain we heard countless times on the way back to St. Albans. Harnessing the energy behind that awe-struck comment became our goal as a residential staff at St. Albans School as we worked to channel that idealism into the development of future public servants.

As these students arrived at the St. Albans residence hall last summer, the residential staff that greeted them brought individual strengths that collectively made this one of the strongest staffs I have worked with in a ten-year career in student affairs and residence life. Representing talent and experience from the Cate School in California to Washington and Lee University and UNC, the four RAs served as role models and inspiration for the students who arrived at St. Albans that June weekend. There was Katie, who quickly emerged as the "mom" of the students, taking charge by making sure everyone had something to do on Friday nights and offering a listening ear and advice ranging from dating to state dinner etiquette. Mike, newly graduated from college and now in law school, took students on early morning runs through Georgetown and became famous for his "breakfast briefings" on the contents of the morning papers. Rob, fresh from a year as a UNC RA, brimmed with enthusiasm and was full of ideas for programming, and Stacy with her quiet passion for service learning helped remind us that public service is primarily about giving oneself away to others in causes larger than any one individual. The RAs were an indispensable part of the program and their contributions to the success of this first program cannot be overestimated. The RAs coordinated the numerous field trips (from the floor of the U.S. Senate to the west wing of the White House) and they served as a sympathetic and empathetic ear to the students who lived with us last summer.

The RAs lived with the SPS students, ate meals with them, and monitored their studies but, most important, they were there late at night when discussions of that day's activities began and when talk turned to the meaning of life, of politics, and of how one individual can make a difference. Sometimes the most important learning will occur outside of the classroom, and our RAs proved to be superb educators.

The heartbeat of any residential community is, of course, its residents. Community implies a coming together, a convergence of diverse personalities, interests, and beliefs—a challenging balance to achieve on the best of days. Heightening the challenge was that fact that until Sunday, June 24, we knew our students only as snapshot photos attached to an application form. Moreover, many of these students had never lived with roommates and perhaps never for a month away from home. We needn't have worried. No matter what growing pains we experienced as a new program, the one constant was the unity and friendship (and sometimes romance) that blossomed among the students. The memories come flooding back: SPS students eating ice-cream cones together on the steps of the Lincoln Memorial at sunset, the usually noisy refectory strangely quiet each morning as students ate breakfast while devouring their individual copies of the *Washington Post*, the laughter and camaraderie on a Saturday morning when the students helped renovate a house for low-income families, and the intense debates going on late at night as a bleary-eyed resident director secured the doors and turned on the alarm.

Surveying the bright and talented group who lived with us this summer, it is difficult to say which one will be first to create a national nonprofit organization or inspire a new wave of volunteerism among students. What is certain is that this inaugural class proved once again that a residence hall is much more than a place to sleep and do laundry. It is a place, rather, where friendships that may well influence the life of a nation are formed, a place where worldviews may be stretched and challenged, a place where a brief conversation or an overheard comment might inspire a student to gather her or his friends and go start a "sit-in," or register people of color to vote, or go out on a Saturday morning to clean out a basement where one day children who have lived in a shelter might have their own place to play.

Mark Dolhouse is the director of residential life at St. Albans Academy.

In and Around the Classroom

Though the residential life of boarding schools certainly accounts for many of the differences between the schools represented in *Second Home* and public schools, the quality of your academic education at a boarding school is often a major attraction as many student writers here attest. Boarding school teachers *live* on campus. They are your advisers, your counselors, and your coaches. You might meet your Spanish teacher at the dining hall, on the soccer field, or in the dormitory. Furthermore, boarding schools are part of a larger group of schools called *independent* because they develop their educational mission in response to the needs of their students. The teacher-student ratio hovers around 1:10 to 1:15 at most schools. A teacher's course load rarely exceeds four courses, and frequently the teacher has only two preparations (two sections apiece of two courses, for instance). The emphasis, in short, is on teaching students.

Independent, furthermore, refers to another important aspect of a boarding school education. You will find in these essays by students and teachers that the focus is on *learning* more than on *what* is learned. So over and over again, you are invited in these essays to take charge of your own education. Teachers talk about their roles as collaborators in your education, not the sole authorities. Students talk about how teachers have given them the opportunity to create their own challenges. Teachers and students both talk about the importance of hearing more than one perspective on a subject, of asking and answering your own questions, of the primary importance of taking chances over playing it safe. You will find, furthermore, that the academic environment at these schools rewards initiative and inventiveness. There is no limit to what you can learn in the academic environment at a boarding school, both from the adults and the peers in your life.

In fact, support from your peers and adults in the academic community defines many students' most memorable moments, whether they were immersed in very intellectual discussions about Greek philosophy or getting basic help with a test that did not go very well. As several students point out, your peers at boarding school are more likely to support and even celebrate your interest in classes. Both the students and the teachers at a boarding school are distinguished by their dedication to matters academic. Scholars and practitioners in their disciplines, the faculty of many boarding schools are basically college-caliber professors who prefer to work alongside high-school-aged students. They are excited to be in the classroom because you are. Listen to what kids say, here. You will find in every piece that moment when student and teacher connect as colleagues, as two excited people discovering a problem or a solution, together.

There are four subsections in this section: "Class," "Knowing Faculty," "Curricular Matters," and "Reflecting and Moving On." The first two focus on the classroom and the teachers. The third offers four general comments on a school's overall academic philosophy, and the fourth presents two reflections on the close relationship between class lessons and life lessons, concluding with a third piece that invites you to think about how you might decide on your destination after boarding school.

THE CLASSROOM

The Rewards of Taking Academic Chances

Amanda Rubizhevsky '03
The Peddie School

The juggle between choosing classes at school sometimes seems like a simple task that your guidance counselor could handle, but is that really the case? Not exactly. With an abundance of choices— Which science will benefit me most? Should I jump from a "normal" section of a class to an honors section?—every decision can have a profound impact on your school career. These types of decisions strike students year-round at school but this same decision is much harder when you are living away from home and your parents at a boarding school. Yes, you have a faculty adviser who acts as a second parent, advising you on anything you come to them with, but just that extra little push from a parent on whether or not to take the harder course is often needed when selecting courses for your schedule.

Being a risk taker most of my life, and choosing to take the harder, more challenging classes has never been much of a problem for me. But after choosing to take the harder classes I inevitably ponder my decisions. After considering my future work load, I can become skeptical, and the inclination to back out and take the easier route is always lingering in the back of my head. But despite these thoughts I usually end up taking the "academic challenge" and pushing myself to my fullest potential. This is something I have always done and I figure if I am being given the chance to challenge myself in such a way, why not take the challenge. It's a great opportunity to learn. While it might seem I like school, that is not totally the case. I just don't like to be bored. Sure, it would be nice to breeze through the school year and even my entire high school career taking easier courses, but the rewards are not as great in the long run.

For instance, in my sophomore year at my present boarding school I was placed in all classes of the "normal" level—a step up from the public school education that I was used to, but inevitably at prep school my schedule was deemed fairly easy. Having much success that year, I was given the option to challenge myself in honors classes where much of the material learned is self-taught, and therefore the student must take the initiative. It was not such a hard decision to take these challenges because I would now be in the honors courses and thought of as a "smart girl" and people would say, "Oooh, she's in honors." What a privilege, huh? Well, not exactly. I soon found out that these courses required a lot of effort and extra hard work. After much hard work, I ended the year successfully and found myself again in the same position as the year before, choosing classes for the following year. With more options and advanced placement classes open for me to take, this decision was a hard one. Of course, I jumped right into the harder schedule. Fellow class-mates and older students told me that I was going to be in for a real challenge.

After a fairly easy sophomore year I decided that I would take the chance and move into some honors courses. For example, my math class was now honors as well as my Spanish class. In math class we were exposed to many more real-life examples, includ-ing how to get the best car payment and loans from a bank. Much of the basic math from the text was learned through routine homework assignments and then reviewed briefly in class. This was a big change from the regular course where the material was taught in class and practiced for homework and we were only oc-casionally exposed to real-life examples. This made me appreci-ate the subject more and I really wanted to learn so I could use these techniques outside of the classroom. In my Spanish class English was the foreign language, not Spanish. If we spoke in En-glish our teacher would look at us strangely and not acknowl-edge us. This was an extreme help in learning the language and my Spanish truly improved. The rewards are obvious and teach-ers really appreciate students who are willing to learn. Taking these risks my junior year helped improve many skills needed for my personal success in the future.

I thought about my previous year and work load and in-evitably my next question to myself was, "Was it worth it?" Was it really worth all that extra work and struggle just to get a B in honors instead of the somewhat easy earned As in my other classes? Of course it was worth it. Taking the academic risk is al-ways worth it because you get so much out of the experience. A risk-taking student exposes themself to many different perspec-tives on each subject and learns more through the experience. A self-motivated risk taker is looked up to by others and realizes that taking the academic challenge is totally worth it. The educa-tion that I am receiving at prep school is truly superior to what I was receiving at public school. In addition to great study skills, I have learned how to take on challenges not only in the classroom but also on the sports fields, and in the dorm.

Amanda Rubizhevsky is in the class of 2003 at The Peddie School, in Hightstown, NJ. She plays on the varsity golf team, is an active member of several clubs, as well as a photographer for the yearbook. This year she will be busy with several honors and advanced placement courses in addition to applying to college.

The Peloponnesian War and Related Matters

Suzanne Hopcroft '03
Deerfield Academy

I will never forget the moment at which I discovered the truly remarkable nature of the academic experience at Deerfield Academy. It was the first history class of the semester, and bright afternoon sunlight spilled into the classroom unhampered by window shades. We might have thought to adjust a shade or two, but it would have been a shame to shut out the beauty of the scene just outside, where the first leaves were already beginning to exchange their summer green for a breathtaking russet. Besides, we were much too entrenched in our first discussion of the school year to think of the bright sunshine or anything else. Fifteen of us sat around a wooden table, debating the virtues and responsibilities inherent in a life of freedom. With our teacher present to moderate the discussion and the *History of the Peloponnesian War* to guide us, we melded our knowledge of history with our own experiences in the modern world. The focus of the conversation darted from one point to another as we each clamored for the floor and then settled down to reflect on opinions that differed from our own. We all had startlingly different perspectives on the issue, based on our unique knowledge and experiences, but we spoke our minds with intensity and passion and were eager to learn from one another's insights. By the time we reached a cohesive conclusion on the issue, I realized that I was learning more than I could have imagined. It was a truly extraordinary discussion, all the more extraordinary for the fact that such an experience is commonplace at a school like Deerfield.

When I transferred to Deerfield Academy after three years at a public high school, I embarked on a quest for a different academic environment. Tired of classes in which the teacher seemed as unenthusiastic as the students and learning was seen as a punishment rather than an opportunity, I sought a place where I could satisfy my passion for knowledge. From an early age, I had recognized that my understanding of the world and the people in it would be enhanced as I developed my comprehension of academic subjects. Every book and every discussion seemed an opportunity for freedom and empowerment through learning. Unfortunately, although I sought out the most excellent professors at my high school and often had fulfilling learning experiences in their classrooms, I found only a few teachers and students who genuinely shared my philosophy. Too often, teachers talked down to students, as if their seniority entitled them to treat us with contempt. Many students exacerbated the situation through their own disrespect, often treating the school day as a pointless and unwelcome interruption of their social lives, rather than an opportunity to learn, grow, and mature. By the end of my junior year in public school, I was impatient to find a place more suited to my own philosophy.

Needless to say, I soon discovered that the academic experience at a place like Deerfield offers opportunities for learning that I might never have found elsewhere. Naturally, the faculty is one of the most essential elements of such a strong academic program. During the year, I encountered professors so knowledgeable and so eager to share their visions of life that they made learning a pleasure. Although my teachers often have strong opinions of their own, they are careful to expose students to a wide variety of perspectives on every issue. Because they respect us as individuals, they encourage us to reach our own conclusions, even if those conclusions are contrary to their own beliefs. Always dedicated to furthering our understanding of the world, professors are as approachable and helpful outside of the classroom as they are during academic discussions. Indeed, almost every faculty member with whom I interact seems eager to make my learning experience as enlightening as it can possibly be.

Equally important to a truly satisfying experience in the classroom is the student body. In this respect, I found yet again that this new learning experience met, and even exceeded, my expectations. Naturally, in a place where teachers are so quick to encourage and excite their students with the power that knowledge brings, there is little apathy among students in the classroom.

As passionate as our professors and keen on becoming equally knowledgeable, we have strong beliefs and are eager to share them. Many of us come from strikingly different backgrounds, and we often have equally different perspectives on a plethora of issues. Whether we are discussing the relative virtues and drawbacks of the American representative democracy or attempting to explain the equation of a vertical asymptote, we tend to tackle every problem from diverse angles. Luckily, we are also unafraid of confrontation—rather, most of us welcome differences of opinion and the possibilities for growth that those differences can present to us. This dynamic makes for heated, invigorating discussions that are more conducive to learning than any lecture.

The learning environment at a school like Deerfield provides students with an unparalleled academic experience. Indeed, my perspective on the topic of that first history discussion led to a powerful observation about the learning environment here: Students willing to take responsibility for their experience in the classroom will find themselves with all the freedom and empowerment that education can afford them. Those who truly want to excel in this stimulating and challenging environment may work the hardest they ever have. Still, I will be the first to assure them that the knowledge they will gain, and the experience they will have in the process, are wholly worth the effort.

Currently a senior at Deerfield Academy, **Suzanne Hopcroft** transferred from her local high school at the start of her junior year. An avid student of the arts and humanities, she plans to expand her knowledge of music and writing as she continues her education in the years to come.

How I Learned to Like Math

Betsy Pantazelos '02
Holderness School

I glance toward my watch and sigh in disgust; only a minute has gone by since I last looked. The teacher drones on about numbers and variables. I could not be less interested. I am not disappointed, though, because this is how I endure math. As I have experienced, it is boring. It is a concept that I began to grasp long before the complexities of algebra; after all, I am in school to learn, not to have fun.

This scenario represents a typical day in my hometown public school. I spend more time wondering when class will end than understanding the subject at hand. While I was able to gain a valuable fundamental education in that school system, I never acquired an appreciation for learning.

My first year at Holderness put my reality in upheaval. My negative feelings toward math were soon replaced by positive ones. I quickly learned that there was more to education than what was in my textbooks. The primary difference is the faculty. The excitement to teach that they bring to class each day instills an equivalent desire to learn in the entire class. The teachers love what they do, but they are more than just teachers. They also play the roles of coaches, mentors, family, and friends. I could turn to the faculty at any time of day to get answers; the opportunity to have quandaries solved whenever I needed allowed me to progress further academically because I would not remain stuck on a topic until the next class.

While math class does involve using textbooks, calculators, graph paper, and pencils, these elements aren't the only tools used. Rather than hacking through mind-numbing, repetitive problems in a book each night, homework came in various forms. Some of my favorite assignments involved week-long exploration to develop my own understanding. This could require measuring the average distance between lampposts on the path or finding the most efficient way to plant a garden. Since different students were trying to effectively problem solve, we were able to see many different correct answers. This aided us because we viewed a problem from several perspectives. This was not only an important mathematical skill for me, but a crucial life lesson, too.

My freshman and sophomore years, I was blessed with the same great math teacher. She also happened to be my lacrosse coach for three years. Even on the field she was available to answer questions about that day's test or assignment. In her class, I remember taking surveys and making board games. The monotony that I had expected from math was now gone.

My junior year I had a new teacher that knew she had to teach and motivate to the standards of her talented, more experienced colleagues. I would stumble into her morning class and look around at my also sleepy classmates. It would be pointless for her to use the chalkboard now. We were teenagers and we believed that eight in the morning was not only an unhealthy hour to be awake but an unacceptable one, too. Instead of lecture we would do "math aerobics" to get ourselves moving and thinking. She would yell out a function and we would have to mangle our bodies to represent the graphs of them. $Y = x^2$ was simple. Both arms were raised above your head in a parabolic shape. Sinusoidal functions were more challenging and quite entertaining. Sine or cosine would result in a room full of students squirming on the floor like drowning earthworms. After our fits of laughter, we were awake enough for some more traditional learning.

My senior year I took advanced placement calculus. Before I started, I was nervous that I might be in a class that I wasn't ready to undertake. Somehow I was convinced to take on the challenge. It was one of the best decisions I have made. The teacher was determined to have the entire class understand the difficult concepts. We never digressed in class. The teacher remained on task and covered all of the material he set out to teach. Sometimes we would finish prior to our allotted forty-five minutes. At this point, he would set us free early to allow us to think about the quantity of material we had covered that day. While it was a bit overwhelming at times, I often found myself wondering how a class period with nothing but educational material could go by so quickly. I spent less time analyzing the scratches on my watch face and more time engrossed in work.

Homework for this class was different from the assignments from other classes. Rather than settling down on my bed with my notebook spread across my lap and only my own thoughts to attack the assignment, I often worked with other students. We would exchange ideas, suggestions, and possible strategies. We also shared vegetable lo mein, boneless spareribs, and General Gao's chicken. Nothing makes the collective mind process calculus better than take-out Chinese. As a group we not only enjoyed our study sessions, but our work thrived because of them. We worked with each other, we worked with the teacher, and through our combined efforts we were all prepared for the AP exam. Looking back, I cannot imagine having missed this opportunity for group struggle and then success. This class went beyond simply learning. It was an opportunity for discovery and it was a chance to take risks and benefit from them. It was truly rewarding.

Now as I get ready to go to college, my outlook on learning is very different. In the math program alone I experienced phenomenal faculty, I worked with motivated students, and I was granted countless opportunities to push myself harder. Herein the difference is found; you learn because you want to, you learn because those around you want to, and you learn because it is downright fun.

Betsy Pantazelos graduated from Holderness School in 2002. There she enjoyed photography, lacrosse, and was captain of the alpine ski team. She now attends Boston University.

To Be a Teacher or Not to Be: Teaching Becomes a Life

W. Hill Brown '85
Carolina Day School

A teaching career was far from my mind when I graduated from Woodberry Forest School in the spring of 1985. In fact, had someone asked me which fields I planned to pursue after college, I probably would have mentioned architecture or law. Nevertheless, after my freshman year at Davidson College, I received an offer to return to Woodberry as an intern in the summer program. I decided to accept the challenge.

It turned out that I was assigned to work with Mr. Blain, one of my former English teachers, and it was really that summer that unlocked my interest in teaching. Mr. O'Hara, my former adviser and Spanish teacher, was also there that summer, serving as the head of the summer program. Both he and Mr. Blain had been two of my favorite instructors. Now they were colleagues, and I must admit that my new status was hard to get used to at first. Mr. Blain was a dedicated teacher, and I picked up many tricks of the trade from him. I also learned a lot from Mr. O'Hara, and I returned the following summer to teach again.

Although Woodberry had a tremendous impact on me as a student, I began to see things in an entirely different light once I became interested in teaching. Those teachers who had been favorites now also became examples for me as I considered seriously joining their profession. I still can recall striving to do my best to measure up to Mr. Blain's challenges in English class. I remember laughing so hard in Mr. O'Hara's class that I was almost unaware of how much I was learning at the same time. I also fondly remember Mr. Willey, who not only was my teacher, but eventually became my college guidance counselor. He used to share wonderful anecdotes about the St. Louis Cardinals as he prepared to teach us about world history. There was never a doubt that the teachers I had at Woodberry were committed to teaching the material, but the really good ones found connections and common interests with their students, and as trite as it sounds, they made learning fun. They were preparing us for some of the top colleges and universities in the country, but they knew that in order to be effective, they needed to do more than just impart knowledge.

Now, in my eleventh year as an English and history teacher at Carolina Day School, I still find myself thinking back on the many teachers who influenced me along the way. There is absolutely no question that so much of who I am as a teacher comes from those I have witnessed over the years. When you stop to think about it, teaching is really the only profession in which one is in training from the moment he or she enters elementary school. I was extremely lucky to have so many positive role models in the classroom. There have been numerous times when I wish I could somehow thank each one of them for helping to shape my own philosophy as a teacher.

When I first began teaching, I didn't know if this would be something I would do for a few years or if it would be my lifelong career. Yet, as each year passes, I feel more and more as if this is what I am supposed to be doing. The students energize me, and they challenge me each and every day in ways that help me grow. In the teaching of American history, writing, and class novels, I search for meaningful connections for my students. I especially

enjoy sharing my love of the Civil War with my students. I still remember trekking around the countryside with Mr. Epes, Mr.
Rowe, and the Civil War club while at Woodberry Forest. Sometimes I wish I could transport my classroom to that same Virginia
countryside so that my students could experience the things I
did. My challenge then becomes to take them to these places
through my teaching.

Like many of my favorite teachers, I constantly seek to identify
common interests with my students. All the while, I try to pass on
the importance of being good people with character—just like the
teachers did at Woodberry. I then have the privilege of seeing
many of my students move into and through the high school.
With every graduating class, I become more and more aware of
the attachment I have to my students and of the difference they
have made in my life. Recently, I watched our varsity boys' basketball team here at Carolina Day School win its third state championship. I had taught and coached a number of the players when
they were in middle school, and I was so proud of the way they
handled themselves in victory. There were times during the game
when I felt as if they were still playing for me, and that I would be
seeing them in class on Monday. They will always be my students.

So would Mr. Blain, Mr. O'Hara, and Mr. Willey be pleased to
step into my classroom? I hope so. I try to create an environment
that is welcoming and nonthreatening, just as they did, where
students can learn to love learning. I seek to challenge them both
with the material I teach and with the ideas I propose. I constantly incorporate humor in my classes as I have come to realize
that it is a powerful tool. With each day that passes, my students
help me to learn more and more about myself. I can only hope
that I have been able to have a similar impact upon them, and
that they will remember some of what I have tried to teach them.
And who knows? Maybe some of them will become teachers
some day. Nothing would make me happier.

W. Hill Brown is currently an instructor in English at Carolina Day
School, but will join the faculty of Woodberry Forest effective September
1, 2003.

More Than Just a Teacher

Ed Testerman, '02
Woodberry Forest School

As my family and I pulled up to the gates of Woodberry for the first day of my freshman year, I actually felt nervous about school for the first time in my life. Besides the fact that I knew almost no one, boarding school was a big step for a small-town kid from Staunton, Virginia. Yet, by the end of that day, I was ready for my parents to leave and let me get settled. I knew that this was the place I wanted to be.

That morning, walking up the front steps of the Walker Building, I was approached by Mr. Coleman and Mr. O'Shea, who stretched out their hands to me with smiles on their faces. Soon afterward, I was walking down the hall of my dorm, Turner Hall, when Mr. Hudgins, the ninth-grade adviser, began his first of four years of trash talking about Carolina basketball. My first impression of these faculty members was that they really cared about me as a person, not only as a student or athlete. In my four years here, I have found that these impressions couldn't be more true, which has allowed me to develop connections with these faculty members not only as teachers but as confidants.

Looking back on my sophomore year, I can vividly remember my Latin teacher, Mr. Brewster, saying to our class, "Don't come to Woodberry if you only want to get into a certain college." At the time, I didn't wholly understand the extent of what he was saying. However, after spending four years here, the benefits of our faculty have become evident. Not only do most teachers always have an open-door policy for help, but they are enthusiastic about giving one-on-one attention when it is needed. Even if that attention isn't concerning school work, I have found many teachers, such as Mr. Blain, who are happy just to sit down and have a random conversation. When you don't always have parents or other adult friends to sit down and talk to, this quality of our faculty has been incredible.

Several weeks ago, as I was riding back to Woodberry on a Sunday, my mom asked me what I would miss the most about

Woodberry. It didn't take long for me to reply, "My friends and my teachers."

The funny thing is that the more I think about it, I can say that a good number of these people are both.

Ed Testerman graduated from Woodberry Forest in 2002, where among other things he played varsity basketball. He currently attends the University of Virginia.

Potential Energy

Ann Marie Calhoun
Woodberry Forest School

A responsive silence greets me when I enter through the polished wooden doors of the Walker Fine Arts Center. The door handle clicks like a snaredrum, and my rubber-soled shoes whisper and squeak against the black marbled floor as I turn the corner to my office. I have come in early to get some work done, and I gather my thoughts for a moment as I unpack my things in the Red Room. Surveying the space, my eyes adjust to the unexpected red wall and linger on the grand piano that reflects the morning light. I snap my violin case open, anxious to tune my instrument and fill the room with the drone of open strings. As I tune the violin with closed eyes, I feel the beat frequencies of the perfect fifth interval tickle my neck and I know it's in tune. I continue playing on open strings, warming up my arms and feeling the bow grip the string. The sound is elegant and twangy at the same time, and I wonder if I will play a concerto or a fiddle tune. Before I do either, I take out my other instrument of choice, the banjo. I put on metal finger picks and roll across the strings as I tune them to an open G-chord. With only a few minutes left before the first bell, I place my banjo back in its case and look over my lesson plans. I make marks in my chemistry book, and reread the laboratory procedure. When everything is in place, I walk across the parking lot to the Gray Math and Science Building. A typical day is ready to begin.

I am a chemistry teacher, a strings director, a violin teacher, a viola teacher, and a banjo teacher. It is an unusual and interesting combination, but my musical gifts and my love for science make sense together here. I enjoy working for two entirely different departments, and after two trimesters of teaching, I have found a working balance between teaching the performing arts and science. At Woodberry, it is not out of place to have a chemistry teacher who gives music lessons. With a school that embraces the arts, many students have elected to take advantage of the impressive art facilities and students have the ability to make a serious commitment to the arts. Many have incorporated the arts into their academic schedules, and I am not the only one who treks between the art center and the academic buildings.

Sixth former Jessica Broaddus, daughter of faculty member Rich Broaddus, is a violin student of mine, and she has found an interesting way to balance her interest in physics with her talent for the violin. At her last lesson, she asked extensive questions about the harmonic divisions of the violin string. It turns out that she is performing "experiments" on her violin for a physics project. She has brilliantly found a way to turn the orchestra room into a physics laboratory, exemplifying unity between the arts and sciences. One of my fourth-form banjo students, Arthur Hancock, has also found a balance between his academics and an interest in bluegrass music. While he has a normal academic schedule, a banjo lesson is scheduled during his free periods of the academic day. Although he has only been taking lessons for a year, he has made extraordinary technical progress. His musical development has also been supplemented with incredible support at home, and he has taken advantage of unique opportunities to record original lines on his father's CD with renowned bluegrass musicians. Even more extraordinary is Woodberry's ability to recognize the importance of cultivating Arthur's unique talent. In addition to making banjo lessons available to him during the school year, the school granted special permission to attend the "Down from the Mountain" concert in Kentucky. In allowing Arthur to miss one day of class, the school demonstrated academic flexibility and struck a balance between his musical education and traditional academic curriculum.

While my students are finding ways to knit their academic interests with their musical ones, I am also finding that teaching music and science are closely threaded as well. Charlie Nix, one of my beginning violin students this year, helped me realize the connection between teaching violin lessons and introductory chemistry after the first few weeks of school. I remember telling him after our second lesson how amazing it was to see him holding a violin with perfect posture and playing a scale perfectly in tune. Just two weeks before, he had never touched a violin, and there was something thrilling and fresh in hearing him play an ascending scale. At the Parents' Weekend conference that night, I expressed the joys of teaching chemistry to introductory students. Just two weeks ago, my students were beginning to learn what an atom was, and now they were performing unit conversions with balanced chemical equations. The subject may be entirely different, but the rewards of teaching are still the same. While chemistry and music may seem entirely unrelated at times, I have also found that the language of music and the terms of chemistry are both fleshed out through the use of metaphor. In describing how to phrase a passage of sixteenth notes in a Vivaldi violin concerto I may ask a student to picture the confident flow of a waterfall. In defining potential energy for my chemistry class, I may also use a waterfall metaphor, demonstrating how gravity converts the potential energy of an object at the top of the falls into kinetic energy as it rushes downward.

Our chemistry text defines potential energy as "the energy an object has because of position," and it does not escape me that Woodberry is a place of potential energy. In just a few minutes, my moment of reflection in my chemistry classroom will be broken by the hum of conversation and the slap of textbooks opening. My students will learn the foundations of chemistry, and then accompany me on my walk between the science building and the arts center. Every step brings them closer to realizing their potential energy, and it is my job to guide them as a scientist and a musician.

Ann Marie Calhoun teaches Chemistry and Music at Woodberry Forest.

Efficiency

Meghan Cummings '96
Northfield-Mt. Hermon School

When I first came to boarding school, I was completely unpre-
pared for the work load. When my eighth-grade teachers were
helping me choose a high school, they warned me about the
amount of work I would get if I chose to attend a prep school, but
I was sure I could easily handle it. Until I started at Northfield-
Mt. Hermon, I was used to spending no more than two hours a
night on homework. About one month into my freshman year, I
realized I was spending at least twice as much time on homework
than I ever had before. Instead of an easy two hours a night, I was
now faced with between four and five hours of hard work every
day. I was forced to change my study habits and become more efficient at getting my work done well.

One of the most important aspects of homework is finding the
right environment to work in. I found that different types of work
can be done best in certain settings. Obviously if you are writing
a paper, you are probably going to be sitting in front of a computer screen or a typewriter. But, while the best place for me to do
math is sitting at a desk, I find it easiest to do a large reading assignment while I am sitting on my bed or on the floor. I cannot
concentrate on reading if I am sitting at an uncomfortable desk.
Of course, other people might work best in totally different situations. A good place for me to work may be a terrible place for
someone else to work. It is important that you find a place where
you feel you are most productive.

Unfortunately, many people attending boarding school cannot
choose where they work, especially in their first or second years
at the school. Most boarding schools have some sort of a study
hall policy for all students. However, freshman and new sopho-
mores at NMH and probably at many other schools are also required to attend structured study hall for a given number of
hours every night. Structured study hall is a time when students
are required to be in their dorm rooms or in a study room where
they are silently working. Older students also need to be working
during study hall, but they can go to the library or a computer

center, and work with each other on a project. Structured study hall has both its good points and its bad points. It gives students a block of time when they need to be working, and it forces students to use their time a bit more efficiently. However, it can be difficult to get work done in that situation, especially if there are about fifteen other students in a room. Study hall is good in that it makes students get accustomed to always saving a certain amount of time to do work. When we go away to college, we will not have structured time when we are required to do work. It is good for us to get used to saving time for homework.

No one will go through a boarding school experience without entering his or her school library. Some people make use of the library much more than others. I have learned to depend on it as a place where I can really get work done; the dorm is not always a dependable place, especially if it is not study hall time. I personally cannot spend a very long time in a library. I usually stay about an hour, and then I need to take a break and return later. When you are looking at boarding schools, be sure you check out the library. If it is a comfortable spot to do work you will always be guaranteed a place that is quiet and will allow you to concentrate.

Although you can usually get a lot of work done during study hall, it is not a good idea to leave all of your homework for that time. At NMH study hall is two hours long. Teachers are supposed to assign forty-five minutes of homework each night, but they usually give more. Study hall is not meant to be enough time to get all of your work done. You will be expected to find additional time during the day to do some of your work.

I have found that it is often necessary to stop what I am doing in one subject, and move on to the next. If I spend too much time puzzling over one math problem, or trying to write one paragraph, I lose my focus and I have to stop what I am doing and try a different subject. This is sometimes a very frustrating thing to do, but if you have tried as hard as you can to do one subject, you will probably only be wasting time to continue working on it for that particular moment. Often the difficult subject will seem easier if you return to it later.

One of the best things you can do for yourself when you begin at a boarding school is to find people (teachers and other students) who can help you with your work. Most faculty members and teachers are willing to help a student who is having difficulty with his or her work. (They would probably not be teaching at a boarding school if they were not willing to help students.) When I find myself having difficulty in a class, the best thing I can do is go to the teacher for help. Sometimes I schedule private help sessions outside of class, or sometimes teachers will offer to have a study session with a group of students. It is important that you feel comfortable asking your teachers for help; otherwise you will have a hard time understanding a difficult subject, and you will be spending all of your homework time on that one topic.

Homework is not the most enjoyable part of the boarding school experience, but it is unavoidable. All students need to develop their study habits in a way that allows them to be productive without spending all of their time on homework. It is important that you plan your time well, and that you learn to concentrate in an environment that can, at times, be quite stressful.

Some Helpful Ways to Get Homework Done

1. Make a list of places that are quiet and accessible to you during study times.

   _____

   _____

   _____

   _____

2. Buy a three-ring notebook, not a spiral notebook, because the former enables you to include tests, quizzes, and readings simply by punching holes in them. Furthermore, you can move materials around more readily in a three-ring notebook. Teachers hate getting papers with all that frilly stuff from spiral notebooks.

3. Ask yourself these three questions before you sit down to do your homework:

- What is due tomorrow and therefore must be done tonight?
- What preparatory materials should I review before I do the homework (lecture notes, theorems, reading questions)?
- What am I supposed to learn from these homework assignments?

4. For detailed suggestions as to how you can do homework effectively, check one of these references:
   - Landmark College. *Teaching a Study Skills System that Works* (book and video). Putney, VT: Landmark College, 1983.
   - McWhorter, Kathleen T. *College Reading and Study Skills* (fifth edition). New York: Harper Collins Publishers, 1992.
   - Pauk, Walter. *How to Study in College* (fifth edition). Boston: Houghton Mifflin Company, 1993.

   Do not let the titles scare you off! These texts are useful for high school students as well as college students.

5. Set down a regular routine for doing homework so that your roommate, dormmates, and friends know what to expect from you and when.

6. If possible, make a weekly and/or daily schedule that keeps you from falling behind or forgetting dates for tests and papers. A regular calendar will work, though most students get something like an appointment book. Develop your own system of keeping track of your academic responsibilities in this calendar, and then stick to it.

7. Try using a column method when reading school texts. For instance, put the major ideas and key words in the right-hand column and the details about those ideas and words in the left-hand column: any kind of note-taking that forces you to think about the relationships between ideas is more effective than, regardless of the discipline, simply writing down everything that jumps out at you.

8. With respect to note taking, a useful exercise can be the note swap. If you know someone in the dorm who is taking the same course and class, swap the notes you take one night on the reading with those that she takes. Can you follow hers? Can she follow yours? If she can't, there is a good chance that you won't be able to follow your own notes several weeks down the road when it comes time to review for the midterm or final exam.

9. Every week or so, see if you can come up with the week's major themes in each course. This is not an idle exercise. Rather, you are effectively reviewing the material and perhaps even anticipating what the teacher will expect you to know for the final exam.

10. Track down the following places:
   • any and all study halls or tutorial centers in the disciplines you're studying
   • the academic dean's office
   • your teachers' offices (and their office hours)

The most important exercise? Practice coming up with at least one question about the homework each night. You don't have to ask it, but coming up with questions is a great way to start thinking about answers and if you can't think of any answers the questions are a great way to engage your teacher. Talking about a subject is a great way to learn it.

Meghan Cummings graduated from Northfield-Mt. Hermon in 1996. While there she was a member of the Association in the Interest of a Multicultural School.

Wooley has Entered the Building: Passion in the Classroom

William Derringer '02
Phillips Exeter Academy

Dr. Allan Wooley had a habit of coming in late, and at least a few times I knew he was sitting next door in the classics department faculty room. Most of the time, though, he had an excuse, which usually involved some injustice on the part of the school administration. That was the case today.

"Sorry I'm late," Mr. Wooley (he never went by "Doctor") drawled slowly. "They don't give us faculty members anywhere to park," he continued, looking at me quickly as he said "park." His eyes pushed forward as he spoke, not what I would call "bulging," but enough to be noticeable.

Mr. Wooley's appearance is partly comic and partly frightening. He is almost completely bald. He has large, bright eyes and a large mouth, which he can contort to great humorous or horrific effect, a skill he usually reserves for the moments in class when a student clearly does not know the answer to a question he has put forward. He is an older man, but was formerly a diver in college and still maintains some of his former athletic vigor. He wears only turtlenecks and stands not an inch above five-foot-four.

When he walked in I had already been seated for ten minutes. In Latin 520, I was the only student in the class and so I sat in a position I rarely ever sat in otherwise—right next to the teacher. Normally I preferred to sit across the Harkness Table from the teacher, in a position Mr. Wooley himself had termed "the power seat" because it set you in direct opposition to the teacher. The seats right next to the teacher, on the other hand, were the least "powerful" seats. They were for the students trying to avoid the eye of the teacher, trying to be so close so as not to arouse any suspicion or indignation. In any normal, more welcoming class at Phillips Exeter Academy, such strategic considerations were unnecessary, but in Wooley's they were paramount. Many teachers actually moved around the table, varying their seats every day as the students generally did. Not Wooley. He probably had not sat in a different seat since he arrived at Exeter in 1969.

After Mr. Wooley entered the room, he briefly looked at something on his computer in the corner of the room, and then strode past me to his seat at the end of the table. He has an old, green vinyl chair that pivots and rocks. Whether he has a chair like this for comfort or entertainment I do not know. He picked up the daily schedule that sat in front of him, squinted at it, checked the clock, and proceeded to say:

"Well, I guess we'll have to go overtime so you can get your money's worth."

After speaking he looked at me, and when I looked back blankly he laughed.

"Okay, then. Let's begin," he said. "And I see you have your little report typed up. Do you know the word?"

"Providence," I said confidently.

Mr. Wooley lifted his hands above his head triumphantly.

"Providence, that's right," he said emphatically, but with a slight sense of mocking in his tone, forcing a very wide and animated grin.

Several days before we had come to a passage in the first book of Lucretius' *De Rerum Natura* which had alluded to the necessary separation that Lucretius believed the gods felt from humans (*diuum natura . . . semota ab nostris rebus seiunctaque longe*). This separation forms the core of Lucretius's ethical philosophy, and so understanding it was no small matter. Mr. Wooley stopped us at this passage.

"So, what would you call the belief . . . which Lucretius rejects . . . that the gods . . ." (at this point Mr. Wooley paused, looked toward me, smiled, and opened his arms as if feigning an embrace) ". . . *care* about their people . . . that they are interested in what's going on?"

As I had become quite accustomed to doing, I looked back, tried to smile, and shook my head.

"I'm not sure," I said softly.

". . . The idea that the divine powers are looking out for us . . ." Mr. Wooley continued, as if I had said nothing.

I continued to shake my head.

"You don't know?"

"Nope."

"Well, go research that and we'll talk about it tomorrow."

This was not a customary response, even for Mr. Wooley. I had resigned myself to momentary failure and expected that Mr. Wooley would offer a slight insult and then tell me the answer. But he didn't. I was shocked. No one had ever done that before, at least to me. I had never before felt so powerless in a classroom. I looked back at him, angered and amazed.

"Okay," I mumbled.

"All right. Let's move on," he said, and looked back at his book. I continued to translate, reading the dactylic hexameter softly and hesitantly.

I returned to my room after class that day, and hurriedly tried to find out what exactly the word was. I brought up the question with some of my friends at lunch, I checked the Internet, and I even called my dad. But no one seemed able to come up with the word. It became a kind of riddle, a riddle that I did not understand, and so could not even begin to solve. I did not understand the question, and I did not really think about it, and so I could not even articulate the question clearly to myself or to anyone else. I came in to class for the next several days without the answer, and repeatedly Mr. Wooley offered in response: "Well, just keep looking." I offered a few futile guesses, "deism," for example, to which Mr. Wooley had simply shook his head. When I had failed enough times, he did not give in, but instead insisted that I not only find out what the word was, but also outline the spectrum of belief concerning this unknown concept, and then place Lucretius properly in this spectrum. By this point I was well beyond frustrated, and moving toward upset, partly insulted, even genuinely angry.

Having exhausted every other possible resource, I decided to spend as much of a Sunday afternoon in the Class of '74 Library as was necessary to solve Wooley's riddle. Sunday afternoons spent in the library, particularly in winter, are lonely and depressing. It was well into my senior year and I had long since decided to avoid that lonely walk from Main Street Hall to the library for the rest of my time at Exeter. And I would have succeeded had it not been for Mr. Wooley. He had offered something that was not merely an assignment, but a frustrating challenge, a duel, a competition that I had already lost but from which I could not step away.

I climbed the sweeping marble staircases of the library and made my way to the research section on the main floor. I cannot say I remember exactly where I began. I leafed through reference books—encyclopedias of theology, dictionaries of philosophy, the Oxford Companion to religion. I would start with *deism*, or *theism*, or even *atheism*. I spent probably an hour before I finally found what I was looking for—*providence*. I stood up quickly from my chair, and looked around to see if there might be someone I knew who could share my moment of success. But when I realized that "providence" was all that I needed, that this was what I had been looking for and worrying about for all this time, I was startled. It was a word that I had heard so many times, but which I admit I had never really thought about, never explored. I had missed something so obvious, so easy, and I could not help but feel that Wooley had still won.

"Providence, that's right," he said emphatically, but with a slight sense of mocking in his tone, forcing a very wide and animated grin. "And let's take a look at your spectrum," he continued, and took the single sheet of paper from me. "Pantheism . . . ooo, simple foreknowledge . . . Molinism . . . ooo, yes, yes, yes! Great stuff!" he went on, with the same grin and stifled enthusiasm.

With the paper in his hand he stood up from his chair and snatched a dry-erase marker from the tray behind him. He took the cap off, and as he walked to the board on the wall opposite me, he began to wave his right hand in the air, as if trying to write something before he even reached the board. When he reached the board, he drew the red marker across the board, making several parallel, horizontal lines. The last time I had seen him do this was when he was trying to explain his personal interpretation of Book IV of Virgil's *Aeneid* and its connection to Plato.

"So, you see, you have these different criteria by which we understand religion," he began, writing on the board in two columns. "Providence is one of them . . . whether you believe the divine is provident or not."

He continued to explain his different criteria, outlining on the board and waving his pen when he could not think of the word he wanted to write but was too excited to stand still. As he spoke, he looked directly at me, but his face was sincere—no forced grin, no bulging eyes, no laughter or mocking. I pushed my seat back from the table and set my book down on the table.

It was maybe ten minutes before Mr. Wooley was completely finished, before he had filled the board with confused red diagrams and had explained his theological rubric. It did not match the fifty minutes I had once seen him devote to an impromptu explanation of Greek drama, but this was more genuine.

"I'm interested that you choose to put pantheism at that end of the spectrum," he commented after he had finished.

"Well, I thought that since it is the belief that the divine was in everything . . ." I began to respond.

"Yes, but maybe that means that the divine has the most control. . . . Do you see what I mean?" he said. "I don't know, maybe it doesn't fall anywhere on the spectrum."

There was an intimacy in this question that I had not seen all term, or in the four other terms I had been in class with Mr. Wooley. It was the first time that I actually felt him speaking with me, and not just to me.

I had always known that Mr. Wooley was fascinated by the questions of philosophy, but I had not realized until then how deeply he wanted his students to be as fascinated as he was. With his frustrating questions and his vague red lines, he was trying to inspire in me the same appreciation, the same engagement with these questions—of Lucretius, of *providence*, of philosophy in general—that he felt.

Sitting in the library, having just discovered that *providence* was what I had been looking for, I had felt as though I had lost. All that time I had felt as though I was in some kind of competition, that it was a test of will or character. That was not the case at all. Mr. Wooley had asked me to find *providence* for myself, because he knew that was the only way that I would consider it as deeply as he did, the only way that it could captivate me as it captivated him. The whole time that I thought that Wooley had won, I had been right, but not because he had beaten me. Mr. Wooley had won because he had inspired me. He had used a strange combination of mockery, of competition, of intimidation, and of frustration, but he had succeeded.

Phillips Exeter Academy offered me a unique community and an opportunity for intellectual collaboration unlike any I have experienced. It also challenged me as an individual, requiring and testing my intellectual and academic independence. But what Exeter offered most intensely, most powerfully, and most memorably were the connections that I made with other individuals, like Mr. Wooley. The greatest challenge for a student is to relate intellectually to one other person, whether a friend, a classmate, or a teacher. There is something awkward, scary, and uninviting about talking to a friend about an interpretation of a novel or speaking candidly with a teacher about an idea or a difficulty. To speak at a table of twelve people, or to think deeply sitting alone in a dorm room, never proved as frustrating, as intimidating, or as rewarding as that moment when Mr. Wooley stood drawing vaguely on his white board and discussing *providence*. There is a hazy condition that must exist for two people to actually relate on an intellectual level, a condition that is part commitment, part respect, part care. It is a condition that is built into the walls of schools like Phillips Exeter, and which I uncovered in Mr. Wooley's room 24.

William Deringer, from Fly Creek, New York, graduated with a classical diploma from Phillips Exeter Academy in 2002. At Exeter he was a dormitory proctor, a member of the stage band, and an active member of the Exeter Student Service Organization. He currently attends Harvard University. His interests include horseracing and the Boston Red Sox.

KNOWING FACULTY

The Real Resource

David Lombino '96
The Taft School

My friends and I often refer back to our first day at school. Over four years, that day has become a symbol for the fresh start we received when deciding to attend boarding school. It was the day when our parents reluctantly left us, and we enthusiastically departed on a new challenge, leaving everything we had known. It was a total risk, and the best part about it was that our future was entirely up to us; very few times do you encounter a situation when nothing in your past holds you back. That first day the feeling of freedom was overwhelming.

Sometime after your parents leave, and orientation dies down, there will be a lull, somewhat of a letdown. You will find yourself alone for the first time, and doubt and regret might pass through your mind. This will be especially prominent in your first days of classes. Your teachers will seem distant, advanced, and untouchable. You will begin to feel your freedom in a different way. At boarding school, there is no parent to help you, no brother or sister to proofread your paper, and no chance to play sick and stay home from school when you didn't do your homework. There is, however, a community of faculty, rich with knowledge, and dedicated to helping and teaching its students. After your original fascination with the physical plant of your boarding school, you will notice the real resource, the people. For a successful transition academically, you must involve yourself with the faculty who have dedicated their lives, twenty-four hours a day, to enhance your education and your life. These stockpiles of knowledge are dying to share some of it with you. All you have to do is show some interest and they will open up their treasure.

It took me a while to realize exactly how to utilize the teachers because I was rather intimidated by them at the beginning. I had an image of boarding school teachers as strict disciplinarians who cared little for their students. They were an obstacle between me and good grades, rather than a bridge between the two. Soon, I saw that these people were indeed quite human, and also extremely friendly. Teaching is the most noble profession; teachers are real, respectable and approachable, careful and wise leaders of the community. One cannot, however, expect teachers to come seek students out and start relationships. The students must take charge in this matter, and actively pursue friendships with the faculty. I have never heard of a teacher not responding enthusiastically when asked for a personal engagement. In my four years I have established numerous close relationships with faculty. Besides my friends, these are the relationships I will miss most when I leave for college.

I couldn't believe the sight of my first class at boarding school. When I finally found the hidden basement classroom, twenty minutes late, I instantly thought I had been misplaced. There were only four people in the class, and three of them were seniors. At the front of the room was a Latin teacher of forty-one years and his dog Duff. Now, I have had bad allergies all of my life, and I couldn't help but shiver at the thought of spending the entire year trapped in this room, sneezing my brains out, with this old master of a teacher whom I couldn't relate to. Well, as it turns out, Mr. Oscarson was not the stereotypical Latin professor; his methods and attitude were different from any teacher I had ever had—my Latin class was actually funny. I eventually became friendly with the seniors in the class, and Duff . . . well, he came to class every day, and I sneezed my brains out . . . every day.

I can still clearly remember my first grade on a paper my freshman year. I had a bit of an academic ego when I started here, and when I received my first "C" ever in the second week of school, all of my hopes of academic stardom died. On the top of the rushed, flowery paper was the dreaded middle school phrase "See me." I made an appointment with the teacher, and we met that night in his apartment, which happened to be in my dorm.

After I met his wife, he offered me something to eat, and I quickly declined. My stomach was not ready for something like that, as the letter "C" still resonated throughout my body. My teacher did not scold me, or tell me that I would have to take a remedial writing course, but instead offered specific criticisms of my work. He said that I was a promising writer, and he challenged me to take the step up from 8th-English, and push myself in his class. We then moved on to talk about the upcoming NFL season, and my predictions. I ended up accepting the food, and we made it a routine that I would meet with him the rest of the year before my papers, instead of after them. The relaxation I felt talking to him helped me in the classroom as well. While I never brought up the Patriots during English, I felt more comfortable expressing my ideas. It seemed as if the class size got smaller, and we were actually in his living room. This is common at boarding school, as relationships outside of the classroom enhance the comfort within them. As a general trend, you will find that you will do better academically in the classes in which you are friendly with the teacher.

As I now wrap up my four years at boarding school, I am struck with the number and quality of the relationships that I have maintained with the faculty here. At boarding school you will experience a transition of the role of teachers in your life from fear to friendship. There are now plenty of teachers I feel comfortable talking with, even about things other than academics. Teachers have lives outside the classroom, so try to tap into their extracurricular interests. I have gone fishing with my history teacher, and although we didn't have much luck, it was still fun to cast for trout with the man who gives me homework every night. There are no limits to the type of relationship you can have: I talk politics with Mr. Drake; I gossip with Mrs. Everett; I talk about the Yankees with Mr. Piacenza; and I seek out Mr. Shepard for the serious stuff.

The key to a successful academic transition at boarding school is getting to know the teachers. The focus is shifted from academic pressure and stress to interaction and friendship. These people will be there when you need them, and you might even be called upon to help one of them out from time to time. There will be an adjustment period for everyone, some longer than others, but once you pass that there is a whole world waiting for you to give to it and draw from it. That first day we were all so clueless of the experience we were about to receive. It all seems so clear to us now that the risks we took paid off in spades. My advice is simple: Make the effort to become friends with the faculty, and the rest will fall into place.

A 1996 Morehead Scholarship nominee from The Taft School, **David Lombino** served as a school monitor, was a member of the Cum Laude Society, and was editor-in-chief of the school newspaper.

Happy Marriage

John C. Lin
The Thacher School

When I got married in 1989, quite a few people came to our wedding from faraway places, but for me, my former students who attended had made the longest journey. In my mind, they had come from being ninth and tenth graders in my dorm, in my classes, and on my teams to being adults with lives very much like my own and very much apart from my recollection of them as boys and girls. Some were happily embarking on teaching careers themselves. That they came to witness my wedding after almost a decade of lapsed time moved me to consider the profound effect we had on each other—they helped a young, new teacher learn about life in a boarding school, and I hope they learned from me a little more about who they were and who they wanted to be.

How many of you haven't wondered why you were born to such unreasonable and restrictive parents when the rest of the world has such permissive and understanding folks? How many times have you resisted the counsel of these sometimes embarrassing people who drive you around only to nod appreciatively when the same advice comes out of someone else's mouth—a coach, an uncle or aunt, a teacher, or even someone on TV you don't know. Boarding schools are filled with these "other" adults who will do just about everything a parent might do for you— from driving you to a doctor's appointment to watching you play in a soccer game, from helping you with homework to helping you with boyfriend/girlfriend troubles—all without the complicating factor of being related to you. To have at your disposal a faculty full of potential adult friends and mentors is one way to view what a boarding school is all about. The stuff you can do outside of the classroom and off the playing fields is essentially what will distinguish your boarding experience from that of students in day or public schools. There are few situations that I can think of that will allow you to learn and grow in the company of caring adults, other than your parents, in the way that boarding schools can.

The relationships between young and old at boarding schools, in and especially out of the classroom, are based on conditions which we all agree to before starting this great adventure. These conditions, our social contract, ensure a certain amount of clarity in defining the boundaries of our relationships, and this clarity is sometimes impossible when the genetic imperative is present. In other words, we don't have to love you like relatives, and because you know that, you might be less likely to take advantage of us and that unconditional love parents have for you. We can, after all, ask you to leave the school; you will always have a bed at home. Mutual responsibility for making this relationship work can be so strongly felt at boarding schools that only in a few cases does this experiment in community fail. At Thacher, our sense of community is so strong because there is a well-articulated and well-respected honor code which binds our community together, and our kids come to know what we expect of them from the very start. Though this might seem restrictive, I have found that students actually find the clarity of our rules and expectations to be liberating, freeing them to think about things other than how to behave.

When you come to a boarding school, you will be joining a community which will learn about you while teaching you, care about you while pushing and stretching you. As teachers, we will be young, sometimes younger than older siblings of yours, and old, even older than your grandparents. We will bring to you our experience of working with thousands of teenagers over many years, and unlike your parents, who may have learned a lot about that strange beast called a teenager by surviving your older brother or sister, we have many more case studies under our belts. You might not get away with as much at boarding school (if you get away with anything at home), but then you might figure out that you don't need to. When you make a commitment to us, we make a commitment to you—and that's for the long haul. Believe it or not, many schools count among their most loyal alumni those students who were asked to leave for one reason or another, and many faculty members keep as good, lifelong friends these same students. There is no escaping the care that a boarding school can extend to you—whether you're on the honor roll and class president, or the one who keeps missing breakfast check ins and is struggling to get Cs. We will not be better parents for you than your parents, don't get me wrong, because we aren't actually in the parenting or the childnapping business. We are educators, and if you are open to it, many adults at boarding school will be your eager guides through an important phase of your life without the confusion of blood ties and judgment which can sometimes muddle the relationship between you and your parents.

Though all boarding school faculty might appear to be hyperbusy, they do, in fact like to spend time with you, formally for extra help and planned meetings, or informally for a hot chocolate and a chat. Don't be shy about asking a teacher, a coach, or a club adviser to have lunch with you in the dining hall or to join you and your friends for a snack at the student union or to see your dorm room after you get it decorated. If you are too shy to think about doing this, then do it with a friend; maybe a couple of you from the same dorm or class can muster the courage to ask your teacher to talk to you outside of class. You will find for your efforts, I am sure, the human element which, though sometimes invisible, binds every community together. It will bind you and your teacher together. Teachers can be shy too, so take a deep breath and go for it. Some teachers and their families do need more space, and you will figure that out as you go. It's probably a good idea to avoid dropping in on families during dinner or putting-the-children-to-bed time, and some may even find Sundays sacred in more ways than one. Again, don't be afraid to be direct and ask for guidelines which, you will discover, probably differ only a little from those you have grown to expect at home.

Extra help can be one of those awkward things for some students. "If I ask for help, will Mr. Chang think I'm dumb?" "I know I should go see Ms. Robertson, but she lives so far from my dorm, and it's so cold outside." "I don't want to appear to be a grade-grubber, so I'd better keep a low profile in and out of class." What students don't realize is that going for extra help, if done in earnest (and by that I mean not doing it just to do it) is a win-win situation. You *will* learn something. Even if you only learn that your teacher is a real human being with friends outside the school, a family, a pet, or the same computer or stereo system that you have, this is valuable and good stuff. By crossing the threshold into a teacher's more private space, whether an office or home, you will discover a piece of the human element if only you keep a lookout for it. Don't be afraid to share this side of you with them as well. When a student I don't know comes up to me and says that he has a dog like mine at home, that is the start of something—that student will no longer be a stranger to me, and Cody will have gotten a few more pats on the head and the hope of someone else to play ball with. Who loses? Remember: Seeking teachers for help and friendship is a win-win situation.

At boarding school you will make some of the best friends you will ever have. The great thing about this is that many of them will be your teachers. When you go away to school, plan to work hard and plan to work at making and maintaining the friendships you will need to sustain you through school and life beyond. Just as good grades will not just come to you on their own, friendships, especially those with the faculty who are there to test you, advise you, tell your parents about you and on you, will not be waiting for you on your doorstep either. But let me say that I have yet to know a faculty member who will turn down the offer of friendship from a student. Though you might have slightly to extremely different views of what friendship means, and you know there are good and bad friends, you may even find something like friendship possible with the person whose job it seems is to get you into trouble, the dean of students. In fact, who knows, if you and the dean hit it off, you might even get a wedding invitation out of it somewhere down the line.

At the time of this original piece, **Jon Lin** had taught at Taft and Andover, and was the dean of students at the Thacher School where he taught English, coached tennis and baseball, and rode horses. He now is head of the Upper School at Fessenden, and writes elsewhere in this book in that capacity.

How Do I Make Connections with Faculty?

Goga Vukmirovic '95
Choate Rosemary Hall

Fifteen minutes of silence didn't help us. There we were, eleven seniors, sitting in our English class, completely unable to answer the seemingly simple question posed by our teacher: "Are there any heroes left in the modern world?" "Yes," was the obvious answer, but we were hard-pressed to find living proof. After reading stories of the ancient Greek civilization, myths of the godlike powers bestowed upon the chosen men, our minds wandered off the realm of fiction; we searched for celebrities and world leaders who could fit the description of Odysseus or Hercules. Just as we were ready to declare unanimously that the world had lost all of its heroes, my teacher, Ms. Hand, said, "Nelson Mandela" and left us to ponder her suggestion. That was not the only time I had found myself in a class stunned by a teacher's question. There was always the ever-present threat of an unpredictable challenge that would tie the domain of fiction we studied to the domain of reality we lived in. It was the challenge of learning that the teachers presented to us.

Early in the fall trimester, I found myself a part of a slumber party of nine, where we watched Mel Gibson's *Hamlet* and toasted marshmallows in the fireplace until dawn. This concept might not sound unusual, except for the fact that we were high school seniors, sleeping in the house of our English teacher, discussing the themes of the story we were studying as much as the choice of actors and music in the movie. It was a setting with no formalities of a classroom, no limits of time or syllabus, and no pressure of finding the correct answers. At some crazy hour of the morning, the only people left awake were Ms. Hand and I. *Hamlet* long ceased to be the topic of discussion. We talked about Choate, about home (in my case, Bosnia), and about returning to places one feels she belongs to. The world literature class I was taking was the only class Ms. Hand taught. Through the papers we wrote, she had come to know each and every one of the students to a much greater extent than I realized. She understood the perspectives and beliefs that I relied on in my discussions and interpretations of the literature we read. Talking with her that night made me feel as if I were talking with someone who knew me well. It did not take long for me to grow to trust and admire Ms. Hand: the integrity, the strength, and the courage she projected. I have learned a great deal from her. By bringing together her knowledge of literature and psychology, coupled with her complete devotion to teaching, Ms. Hand helped her students grow through the changes the high school age brings. She helped us understand the subtle nuances of literature, and their connection with the world we live in. She made the English class a challenge of ideas, bringing it away from the realm of fiction into the realm of everyday life.

During the summer after my junior year, just as I was getting ready to go up to Maine, Mr. Faulkner, an art teacher at Choate, offered to give me a lift to Portland, Maine. Little did I know how serious he was. Only a few summers earlier, Mr. Faulkner had built an experimental aircraft: a two-seat airplane that could easily be lifted off the ground by one person. It looked like a large scale model of a high-tech toy one could buy in FAO Schwarz stores. How could I have possibly refused such an opportunity? After all, the five-hour drive was to be only a one-hour flight. As I climbed aboard, I could not help but wonder how it must have felt to take the very first flight in that plane: even if all the engines worked on the ground, no one was to say that the wings and the propulsion system would successfully lift the plane off the ground, keep it steady in the air, and ensure a safe landing. There were no highly paid test pilots around. It was Mr. Faulkner, his machine, and the moment of truth.

At first I thought that he must have been either very drunk or indeed insane to embark on such a mission as flying a plane that had never flown before. Right before we took off, as he was checking the engine and fuel/oil levels, I realized what gave him the strength to pursue this goal. The sense of accomplishment a successful flight would offer, coupled with an adventurous spirit and a brave heart, were the perfect incentives to turn the keys, start the engine, and fly. He built the machine from scratch. He knew where every single piece was, how every wheel turned, how the whole mechanism functioned. He had confidence in what he created. Although realistically there was the remote possibility of an unsuccessful flight, failure was truly not an option. As we were safely cruising at 3,000 feet, I came to admire Mr. Faulkner. Art was his life. Through photography and ceramics he was able to express himself beautifully. Yet, he never let his love for machines die away. The aircraft itself was an art piece. Its futuristic design, coupled with a detailed knowledge of aerodynamics and mechanical engineering required to build an airplane, reflected the possibility of merging such different passions in one's life into achieving one's dreams. Mr. Faulkner made me realize that one never has to make an either/or choice: the possibilities in combining one's interests in life are limitless. In his case, not even the sky was a limit.

I developed very close relationships with my dean and my adviser, the two people who created the network of support that enabled me to live away from home. Their role was much beyond ensuring I had enough credits to graduate from Choate—they were the ones I sought advice from, or who I called when I needed someone to talk to. Mrs. Abbe, my dean, and Ms. Perkins, my adviser, are probably the main reason why college seems so different from Choate. Their genuine concern for the well-being of students and their unconditional support of the student's endeavors made the school feel like a much closer community. At each game my water polo or basketball team played at home, I was sure that Mrs. Abbe or Ms. Perkins would be sitting among the students in the audience. At each presentation I made, or each speech I gave, I knew they would be there. Their presence made the extracurricular activities matter even more. I had spent countless hours in Mrs. Abbe's office. She always took time out of her busy schedule to meet with me. I shared my thoughts, my ideas, even my fears with her. Somehow, she always knew when to say exactly the right thing. She encouraged me to try out new classes and new activities. She assumed the role of a parent when I needed one the most.

I have been out of Choate for almost a year now, and I have kept in touch with both Mrs. Abbe and Ms. Perkins. I never fail to ask them for advice about college, or the major I am thinking of pursuing, or the little things in life that have nothing to do with school at all. They are much more than simply teachers at a boarding school I attended. They are my friends, with whom I am certain I will stay in touch for many years to come. Kahlil Gibran in his book *The Prophet* said that "yesterday is but today's memory, tomorrow is but today's dream . . . When you part from your friend, you grieve not;/ For that which you love most in him may be clearer in his absence,/ As the mountain to the climber is clearer from the plain." Mrs. Abbe and Ms. Perkins are a part of my memories and my dreams, for they helped shape both, and helped define the person I have become. In the time I have been away from Choate, I have come to truly appreciate their friendship and all they have done for me.

In many ways, Choate was a home for me. Since I was unable to go back to Sarajevo, Bosnia, where I come from, for three years Choate offered me a refuge: a perfect world of ideas nurtured by incredible teachers who were ready to sacrifice all the rest of their free time to help their students grow to understand the subjects they [the teachers] devoted their lives to. Bosnia lay beyond the impenetrable wall that separated me from the reality and the insanity of war. Choate was, at the same time, both a shelter from reality and an alternate reality in itself.

Talking with Ms. Hand that night helped me understand the transformations people go through at each stage of their life, and how the whole meaning of home and going home changes with these transformations. She shared her invaluable experience of watching generations of students grow through their changes. I finally understood why Nelson Mandela was the perfect example of a modern-day hero. It was not only because he fought for a just cause, and sacrificed twenty years of his life in a struggle almost single-handedly to achieve the end of an unjust political system, apartheid. It also was because Mandela made a conscious choice, each day he was imprisoned, not to give up and just walk away, leaving this struggle to someone else. As he refused to conform to the wishes of his captors, each morning he had to make a decision to spend another day in prison. That choice, the choice that kept him locked away from home and from his family for over two decades, is the strength of a hero. And that existentialist choice is the same choice, often with lesser consequences, that we all make each day.

Ms. Hand made me aware of the individual responsibilities and common destinies. She made me aware that the struggles of modern-day heroes are not very different from the struggles of mythological characters. No fiction can be as impressive as the stories of real-life achievements. Such is Mr. Faulkner's story, a story that stands as a testament of endurance and passion that makes achieving one's dreams a reality. As we landed at the Portland airport, I walked away from the plane with a renewed sense of optimism and satisfaction. By setting an example with his own actions and adventures, Mr. Faulkner touches the lives of all the students who come in contact with him. He certainly has touched and changed mine.

For those three years, Choate was about belonging and becoming. The awesome classes I took, the coaches I played for, and the best friends I made ensured that Choate Rosemary Hall became and stayed my second home; a place where I can always return to, no matter where I have been, or where I am coming from. In my three years there, I became a part of the Choate world, and I never tried to escape. Now, having graduated with the class of 1996, I have come to appreciate even more what Choate has done for me. It has given me a focus in my studies. It has helped me discover and define new passions that now govern my life. Moreover, it has opened many doors to experiences and challenges I previously could not even imagine. Interactions between teachers and students (such as that slumber party) are the best opportunities a boarding school has to offer. The beauty and the biggest advantage of Choate is that it attracts people who are committed to working with their students well beyond class time and are genuinely interested in helping them learn and discover. These four teachers have changed me in more ways than I could possibly describe to you. I have taken a piece of each of their lives with me. The high school years are the years of growth and transformations. I could not possibly have chosen a better school or better group of teachers to give me the tools and set me on my quest to build a monument that will stand as a testimony to a life happily lived. I am in debt to them for making my three years at Choate as incredible and as invaluable as they were.

Goga Vukmirovic graduated from Choate in 1996.

Where You Go for Practical Help

Hugh Silbaugh
The Putney School

There's a whole list of people at your school who can help you with roommate problems, keys that don't work, schedule and class changes, psychological counseling, broken windows, and plain old homesickness. The official list, usually printed in the student handbook, is *somewhat* useful. There are also a lot of helpful people who aren't listed in the index or the troubleshooting section of the handbook. And you'll need help. Boarding schools are a strange landscape, and you should expect to need help finding your way around in them. Teachers will reach out to you, but not always at the exact right moment. They get busy, the schedule is full and relentless, people get caught up in their own lives, and sometimes *you* have to take charge and do the hard thing by asking someone to give you what you need. Having to take charge of your own needs is scary but it's part of thriving at boarding school. So the trick is learning which people are really helpful and which ones only say they are. That'll differ from school to school and from student to student, but I have a few general pointers that may prove useful.

Begin by reading the student handbook. Really. You should read the handbook and do it carefully. Pay special attention to the sections on schedules, grades, calendars, residential life, and helpful adults. Study the map of campus. Find out who wrote the handbook (at my school, it's the dean of students); that person is your best resource for figuring out what assistance the school offers in an official way.

In any event, the dean of students will be important in your life at school. You should try to establish a cordial relationship with her early in your school career—it'll come in handy later, whether you end up in the good citizen corner or its opposite. She's the person who will call your parents if you land in trouble. She also controls the student activities budget. The dean is usually a person of uncommon patience and humor, someone with real affection for teenagers, a good sounding board in your sometimes lonely new life away from home. If only to improve your chances of earning a prized single room next year in the dorm of your choice, know the dean.

Your house counselor (dorm parent, residential adviser, or whatever he's called) and his family may be the closest thing you'll have to family while you're at boarding school. His house is the closest thing you'll have to home. Visit his apartment, be nice to his kids and wife, walk his dog or feed his cat. Offer to baby-sit. The dorm is your house, and the house counselor's apartment is the homiest corner of the building. Don't worry about imposing on the family—they'll nudge you out if you overstay your welcome or come at a bad time (when Junior is making a splatter painting with his Spaghetti-O's, for example). From a faculty perspective, living in the dorm is not living next to kids, it's living *with* kids. House counselors expect you to make yourself welcome in their homes. From your perspective, house counselors and their families offer a taste of normalcy, people living their lives and raising their families, a break from the dorm, a welcome dose of real life.

Pump your faculty adviser for information about The Way Things Work, even if you've been assigned to wizened Mr. Sneezleblitzen, who wears bow ties and is totally uncool, or imposing Ms. Sternfleece, whose name is nicer than her glare. Even if she's some hopeless rookie teacher or intern, go to your adviser early and often. If she doesn't know the answer to your question, at least she will be able to point you in the right direction. At the very least, by reaching out to your adviser instead of waiting for her to advise you, you'll have built a connection with an adult that will prove valuable when you get into trouble later for sleeping through algebra again, or for indulging in wayward after-hours behavior.

Then there are older students, ones who have been at your school a while and know the ropes. They can tell you what and who have worked for them in the past, and they can help you navigate the bureaucracy of your school. School leaders, either designated by the faculty or elected by the student body, are usually the best sources of sane advice. The campus con artists are probably not your best resource; look for students who seem happy at school, who have good relationships with the faculty and with other students. Any advice that tells you to avoid adults is probably going to lead you into conflict with the faculty at your school. Listen to other students and pick thoughtfully the ones whose advice you follow.

Getting to know the head of maintenance, or if your school is too big, a few of the maintenance staff, will make your life measurably easier and happier. Learn their names. Ask them how they're doing and then really listen to their answers. Be more than polite—be interested. The maintenance crew always knows everything about how the school really works (and about who really works). Certainly it's useful to have a friendly relationship with a person before asking him to help you retrieve your nose ring from the toilet (and what was your nose doing there, anyway?). And you'll need assistance with sticky windows in winter, lights that burn out, and showers that sputter when you want them to gush. More important, you'll need someone to unlock your room when you lock yourself out and give you a new key without a big lecture about not losing it in the first place.

The registrar and the academic dean could become important allies, if you seek them out *before* you're failing English. Even after you've fallen so far behind in Spanish that your teacher seems to have given up on you, these two may be able to coach you through hard academic times. The registrar controls the schedule, which controls daily life at school. The academic dean can help you prevent, or at least survive, the personality conflicts with teachers that might arise, and can help you make sense of your grades and comments. Try not to be intimidated by the title or the office, or by the sign-up list for appointments that's posted on the door. The first step over the threshold into the office is scarier for most students than the perfectly normal conversations that happen between students and deans at my school.

There's no stigma attached to being seen with an administrator. OK, so that isn't quite true, but most of us try to make it true. And it isn't a *huge* stigma. Barge in and ask your question. Sidle in and ask advice. Consider taking it, even if it's hard or points you toward the learning center or a psychological counselor. Administrators love nothing better than to drop the reports they're proofreading, ignore the stack of telephone messages on their desks, and talk to students. It's flattering to them that you want their help, and useful to you to get it.

Finally, try to enjoy the adults around you. Relax and get to know them as people. Stay after class and talk about today's assembly with your Latin teacher. Tease your math teacher about his shoes. Sit down with an adult in the dining hall. Ask your dorm parent for a cup of tea. Tell the head of your school (or her secretary) that you want to get to know her. Presume upon the kindness of strangers. It's irresistible—it's disarming and charming to a teacher or administrator caught up in a busy day to have someone like you ask for help. Start with the small stuff—reading your schedule, keeping track of assignments, finding the photo lab or the supply closet in the basement of the dining hall—and see who listens to you and answers your questions. Figure out who's really helpful. Then tackle the larger challenges—teachers you have trouble with, habits you're afraid of, roommates you're occasionally homicidal about, the blues of mid-February. Chances are good that whoever you pick can help, but you have to pick. If your choice of people isn't perfect, listen to the advice about whom you should talk to next and then do it. Even someone you've written off as out of touch, uncool, or even devious, like Mr. Sneezleblitzen, will surprise you. Ms. Sternfleece has an astonishing and dry sense of humor that you never noticed before. Teachers teach because they like students. Even you. Give them a chance to show it.

Need help? Ask for it.

When he wrote this piece for the original edition of *Second Home,* **Hugh Silbaugh** was the assistant director of the Putney School and had worked for Phillips Academy and Choate Rosemary Hall. He taught English at Putney. He is now the principal of the Upper School at Milton Academy, a school represented elsewhere in the book.

CURRICULAR MATTERS

Among the Bright

Sandy Stott
Concord Academy

"My transition to CA was probably different from that of most. I've been in private school since the age of four and so therefore I have always been surrounded by people who are stereotypically 'smart.' Growing up in that kind of environment taught me both to expect a high level of intelligence from my peers, but also to never really expect to be the best. At my former school, however, where the majority of the student body was white, upper-middle class, and frankly pretty ignorant of the world around them, I found that I was unhappy because I felt that most of my peers were book-smart but not really smart about life and anything deeper than the typical teenage existence. That is what struck me about CA. I suddenly found myself among people who thought about learning as more important than just something that was necessary to be successful and make a lot of money. I found myself talking about classes outside of the classroom (something unheard of at my former school) and feeling engaged by what I was learning, and most important for me, finding that my peers felt the same way. I think CA is unique because the people who find their way to CA are interesting and really do believe in learning for learning's sake. This creates an environment where real learning, not just dry, textbook learning, can occur."

L. CA '03

The twelve students in my creative nonfiction class have a problem. Charged with developing a detailed critique of H's profile draft, they've come up against the clarity and beauty of her prose. "What's not to like?" says J, thumbing slowly through the lightly marked, ten-page piece in his hands. "It's beautifully written; the only flaws I find are a few typos."

"J's right," I think as I nudge class conversation toward a discussion of where H might expand her essay, how she might build upon its evident strengths. And even as I hope that we can help H find greater depth in her profile, I hope also that her prose won't discourage others in the class. Here in this province of student writing we've entered a sensitive land. Few pieces of work bear the personal stamp of one's mind like writing, and in this class where we rely on each student's world as source material, the exposure is greater than in other English classes. Given the comparative gymnastics of most adolescents, I'm wise to worry.

Still, there's also the combination of joy and example to be found in H's superb work and in that of this school's many able students. H has both raised the bar (daunting challenge) and opened the window (new view) for her peers. Perhaps at this point in their lives few can match her eloquence, but it is also evident that H's life, and by extension their lives, are the stuff of real stories, the clay of real literature.

Other teachers at Concord and its peer schools offer testimony about gifted students in many academic realms. But before we leave H, let me reflect on an attribute that marks her (and many at our school) and her work finally as encouragement and inspiration for her confreres. H sees her expressive ability as both gift and aid. In her hands what could be a caustic weapon wielded to assert superiority is instead an offering of story about an eternal literary subject: parental relations. "This," I think as the class warms to its work, "is a point of joy in working with able kids who mix kindness and a touch of humility with their ability."

It may seem a lengthy trail back from a classroom to a school's mission statement, but during my twenty years at Concord I've found it a short hop. A particular phrase resonates year after year in class after class; it even survives the sometimes disillusioning "college process," where ideals at times meet the hard news of comparative statistics and seemingly capricious, opaque decision making. Concord aspires to be a school "animated by love of learning," and its decision to forgo honor rolls, awards, and class rankings helps center its work in this love. Such a philosophy also places great responsibility on Concord's students, who are expected to be the animators of said love.

As T, a junior, put it while reflecting on her freshman year, "I found it incredible that from reading a few lines of *The Odyssey*, we could get so much meaning and link it to other parts of the story. It was exciting to be around people with so many ideas." At the same time for this student and for others, the flocks of ideas found routinely in Concord classrooms kept her quiet. Her previous school (in Hong Kong) hadn't encouraged divergent ideas or their expression, and her natural reticence added another bar. Learning to speak her mind became a necessary burden, one she began to shoulder during the spring semester when another teacher replaced me in the class. Her new teacher's style and confidence in T put her "more at ease, and I spoke much more often. She also helped make my transition less stressful by being patient."

T continued her thoughts: "History, biology, and French were somewhat different. There were some very smart kids in my classes. It was intimidating and at times I couldn't help but feel left out. Some of them already knew each other, and, even if they hadn't gone to the same schools, they seemed to have had pretty much the same material. I came from a different style of learning; I was used to having the teacher tell us the answers. Now I had to find them myself." Finally, T noted, "The experience has made me much more independent." In this realization lies the hope of a school like Concord. Independence of mind and spirit, along with sound grounding in academic disciplines, should serve students well in college and beyond.

After teaching in other places, Concord faculty often comment on the curiosity and expressive capabilities of the students they meet. A, an English teacher, spoke of some of the tutoring she had done before moving into the Concord classroom: "Hired to tutor students in English, presumably because of their language difficulties, I 'helped' a native Thai speaker, who was comfortable reading articles that had been assigned to me as a graduate student in English Lit.—she only needed help because she had never been taught to write a précis. Another tutee, from a U.S. inner city, mastered five-paragraph essay organization in one tutorial session—something most University of Wisconsin remedial English students got in about three weeks, at best. In five years of tutoring English here, I never did get over my feeling that I actually was working with undergraduates who happened to be a little young for the courses they'd enrolled in." I highlight a tutor's observations because this small group of teachers works with the school's strugglers, those who don't glide across course material, often because their preparation has been different or inadequate. Tutees suffer the burdens of incomplete academic backgrounds and ramped-up expectations; they sit next to kids for whom Concord is a happy extension of prior excellent schooling. That they too find eventual traction in their work is testament to their grit and ability. The few who do fail often do so because they've not yet reached the point where they can motivate themselves to keep struggling until difficulty eases.

Surviving the comparative jostling of entering a school peopled by many bright students and teachers can be unsettling, but (as noted above) in the long run (over three or four years), few students are unhorsed by it. Many more are lifted by the ability and work of their peers, and, finally, by learning as an expression of love.

This fall I've again been granted the gift of teaching twelve students as we snoop and snuffle into the world of creative nonfiction. Today, we talked about conducting interviews and the need to wait for stories to emerge in conversation as my twelve prepared to gather material for their first long essay (a profile of someone at work). M asked a question about dealing with the simultaneity of what she thought she'd experience while watching the head of Boston's MBTA work. And as other students leaned forward to offer ideas for sorting and recording experiences and ideas, I thought about the deep pleasure of setting a problem for bright kids and then watching them teach themselves.

Sandy Stott teaches English and serves as dean of faculty at Concord Academy. In addition, he is the former editor of the conservation journal *Appalachia*, and, until lured to the dean's chair, a longtime soccer coach.

Editor's note: The following piece appeared in *Far and Wide: Diversity in the American Boarding School* (Avocus, 1997). Though it was written by a faculty member of the Choate community for faculty, it offers prospective students and their families important insights into what many boarding schools consider the residential curriculum. We therefore include it here.

What Is a Residential Curriculum—
An Outreach Program?

Mary F. Pashley
Choate Rosemary Hall

As I popped the tape into the VCR, I had hoped that the cookies and hot chocolate would have a relaxing effect on the eight students in the living room of my dorm apartment. Although I knew what they were about to see, and they knew of the topic we were to discuss, I had no idea how they would react to what was on the screen. Teenagers—in their seafoam Henleys, weathered college mascot baseball hats, and faces that depicted life from every corner of the globe just like the latest J. Crew catalog—giving very real testimony to the temptations, joys, and dangers that come with drinking or drug use.

The images on the screen seemed more real than any other speaker, or pamphlet, or conversation with a parent had been to them. The students were still, almost frozen. Each watched, and I watched each of them. We all heard the adolescent voice on the tape talk about the thrills of being high, and how being "cool" was all that mattered:

> . . . some of my friends were doing it, and nothing ever happened to them, it seemed cool to do it with them. We had a lot of laughs, being high was awesome, and there wasn't any hangover to deal with. . . .

The voice turned to justification,

> . . . it seemed pretty safe, I never thought anything would happen to anyone, and certainly not to me. Besides, I really liked getting high, it made me deal with everything so much easier. . . .

Then the voice turned to regret,

> . . . my expulsion was really hard on my parents and my friends, but I think it was the hardest for me. I just didn't think. I just didn't think it would be me who got caught. I wish I never got involved with all of this mess. My life will never be the same again.

I sipped my hot chocolate and realized it couldn't remove the chill in the air at that moment. The tape continued with six more vignettes about adolescent experimentation use and abuse of controlled substances.

The buzz of the VCR filled the room as the tape rewound. The eight students shifted, stretched, coughed, ate Keebler cookies, and fidgeted with backpacks. The hard part was about to begin; the dreaded "follow-up discussion" with an adult. Gosh, kids would have to talk openly and frankly with each other and with an adult about this important issue. It scared the heck out of them and little did they know, it scared me, too!

I wondered, how could I seriously engage in a dialogue with teenagers about such an issue? Then I thought again, how could I not?

In Loco Parentis

As adults who serve "in loco parentis," a term I use often as I explain to my mother why I don't have children of my own, we owe it to our students to prepare them for the "real world" as much as and as well as we prepare them for college. Boarding schools typically do not do a great job at the former.

Enter the buzzwords of the '90s—"cocurriculum," "residential curriculum," "second curriculum"—call it what you want, it has become our call to duty. We have to go beyond the classrooms, the athletic fields, go past the playfulness of the common rooms and food runs; we have to get down and dirty and have serious dialogues among adolescents and adults covering a variety of topics. Harvard professor Robert Coles suggests that the best learning takes place within the context of a relationship, and I have adopted this as a personal and professional belief. Students in boarding schools hopefully connect with at least one adult within the community. This social agenda, then, if done right, creates room for social dialogue. It naturally draws on the experience, wisdom, and knowledge from adults and is nicely accented by the diversity, innocence, and pure adolescence of our students.

Cocurriculum topics are not merely "taboo social topics" as one might guess. Although I have chosen to recall the advisee meeting where we discussed drugs and alcohol, I realize that that specific subject still surfaces as the number one concern of prospective families touring campuses and remains top among discipline cases in most schools. However, it is safe to say that the majority of students are not engaged in such behaviors. Students should still be educated about such issues, not just for themselves, but in an effort to understand and help friends who struggle with difficult decisions. In talking with a diverse group of students, it is not uncommon to learn that in certain countries, drinking is "not really an issue" and that a conversation with an adult about drinking may never take place. Such comments can be quite valuable to the group, and can lead to interesting comments. Let us also talk about some positive social trends and enjoyable topics, too.

We have discussed some of the following topics in the past two years:

- Celebrating multiculturism
- Religions across our campus (38 of them!)
- Performing random acts of kindness
- AIDS awareness
- Effects of tobacco and smoking
- Teaching tolerance
- Volunteering: What is a community? Our call to service

These topics have been covered within small advisee groups. Ideally, content and dialogue will be age and gender appropriate. What is said to our freshman females can be (and is) drastically different from our message to senior males.

The Entire School Reaches Out

Annually, we devote an academic day in the fall to community service and a day in the spring to diversity. On Community Day, over 1,200 people can be spotted in town raking leaves of needy senior citizens or working in one of the seven town parks. Elderly men and women wave gratefully as our students and faculty return to campus. With leaves in their hair and tiny blisters on their palms, students always prefer a day of raking to a day in the classrooms. This altruistic activity is a long-standing tradition at Choate Rosemary Hall, dating back to World War II.

Our current community outreach program places students in local service agencies such as the YMCA, Big Brothers & Big Sisters, the American Red Cross, the Boys & Girls Club, Habitat for Humanity, Brookhollow Health Care Center, the Wallingford Day-care Center, and the Masonic Home for the elderly. The demonstration of complete compassion in our students is utterly amazing to witness. The skeptical student frightened by the antiseptic smell of the convalescent home is seen by term's end comfortably pushing the wheelchairs of local residents along whitewashed corridors while sharing favorite knock-knock jokes. Surprisingly, by the time students reach graduation, they have spent a significant amount of time volunteering, and that is an encouraging statistic. The hope is that this experience will be the start of a lifelong commitment to service.

In the spring, Diversity Day is designed to showcase our personal experiences, our cultures, our travels, our religions, our sexual orientations, and our traditions. Through storytellers, panel discussions, video presentations, student performances, dances, songs, workshops, demonstrations, and even through the menu items served in the dining halls, we celebrate our diversity.

What is learned by walking barefoot in a palm-tree–lined theater room while tying a Samoan lava-lava (sarong wrap which is worn by both males and females) and speaking such words as *fafetai* (thank-you), *malo* (hello), *umu* (oven), and *Salapuala* (the local village) cannot be extracted from any textbook. Neither can the level of awareness be measured as students and adults hear candid words from their "favorite teachers" and colleagues in a discussion titled "Growing Up Gay: Our Stories."

And the list goes on . . .

Good Advice, Talk Among Yourselves . . .

When engaged in a productive dialogue, all of the voices are speaking, and heard, appreciated, and encouraged. At any given advisee meeting, I can count on input from a wealthy, eccentric Jewish student, an African American from the Bronx, an Indian (I am being politically correct: he is from India, not America) a day student from Wallingford, a Southern-raised conservative, and a student whose mother is African and whose father is Caucasian. Clearly, it is our students who represent a harmonious international existence (well, most of the time!) on our campuses and we as adults can learn much from that ability.

In an increasingly busy world seduced by the age of technology, we have to actually work at finding the time to simply TALK. Without distractions. So, turn off those computers, don't worry about voice-mail, gather your advisees together, bake some cookies, make some hot chocolate, pick a topic, and then SAY SOMETHING. Don't forget to listen, too.

Mary Pashley is the director of community service at Choate, where she is also a member of the history, philosophy, religion, and social sciences department.

Models for a Modern Age

Craig Thorn
Phillips Academy

Most likely, you will have more freedom to design your course load later in your career at boarding school than you will in your first few years. However, boarding schools tend to have a broader, more flexible curriculum than the typical high school offers, even in the ninth and tenth grades. Because boarding schools encourage students to think for themselves and also pride themselves on their attention to the individual student's needs, you will enjoy both the freedom and responsibility that comes with lots of choices in your academic career that reflect both your needs and interests. The school will insist that you focus on needs early on so that you are well prepared to pursue your interests later on. However, it will be up to you to keep sight of your academic goals as you work through the four-year curriculum.

To start, you probably would share a similar looking class day with most of your fellow freshman. A typical ninth-grade year might look like this:

	Monday	Tuesday	Wednesday	Thursday	Friday
1	Math	Math	Math	Math	Math
2	English	English		English	English
3					
4	Spanish	Spanish	Spanish	Spanish	Spanish

5	History	History	History	History
6	Biology	Biology	Biology		Biology
7			Biology (lab)		
8					
9					

Schools vary in their schedules. Some use Saturdays, for instance. Some stagger the classes so that your biology would meet in a different period each day. Some operate on semester calendars, some on trimester calendars. Some even have special terms of two to three weeks during which you engage in a project in the community or even in another country. Some schools have forty-five-minute periods; others have sixty-minute periods. Some expect you to take a half course in art or music in your ninth-grade year. Some specialize in certain disciplines. You could be taking several hours of Latin and studying the classics all day, but devoting only a few terms to history. Some schools offer classes after afternoon sports; others try to finish academics up before a late lunch. Some require a minimum of four courses per term; others will on occasion expect that you take six. Some schools use a block schedule: for example, you may take some courses intensively one term, and the others during a second term. Do not be alarmed by the seeming complexity of your school's academic schedule. You will be amazed at how quickly you pick up on the most obscure idiosyncrasies of your school's Byzantine schedule.

In the tenth-grade year, you may have some choice as to when you take some single-term required courses or in what combination you take courses. You may be able to defer a second year of science in order to take two languages. Or you may settle on a yearlong music course that means you have to postpone fulfilling some other requirement in religion or math. At this early stage in your academic career, you and your adviser have probably figured out some of your strengths and weaknesses as a student, so that assessment might influence how you balance your course load. You probably have to take several required yearlong courses. However, you and your adviser should be thinking about possible scenarios for your junior and senior years. Do not worry about having more than one plan. Chances are your plans will change. Making them with your adviser, however, helps you because if forces you to think beyond the next assignment in history. It puts you in charge of your education.

For most schools, the junior year is very important academically. At this point, you have developed some basic skills in several disciplines. Your teachers are now expecting that you will begin to sound like young scientists, historians, and writers. At least in one discipline, you are literally learning how to speak the language, be it Spanish, French, Japanese, or German. Junior year is also the year when many students develop a feeling about what interests them and what doesn't. Now your schedule is very, very important because junior year is also the time when you are most involved in sports, extracurricular activities, and a social life. Though we have presented here the most basic daily schedule, imagine that you are unlikely to be taking courses every period of the day. If you have not done so already, now is the time to learn how to use the "dead" time in your academic daily schedule. Recommendations I have heard from students in my twenty years of teaching include:

- Getting your mail.
- Doing the most basic homework you have for that night.
- Taking at least ten minutes to write down the bare bones of what you have to do for homework and for errands.
- Checking your courses' syllabi (term-long assignments) to anticipate weeks when you have more than one assignment due.
- Eating healthy snacks. Unhealthy snacks taste better in the dorm at night.
- Reviewing notes you took in class. At this level, teachers expect you to master both ideas and details. Anyone will tell you that a day after having taken notes, you will have no idea what they mean unless you have tidied them up shortly after the class.
- Making appointments to see teachers and/or tutors to resolve questions quickly before they lead to more problems.
- Catching up with friends during free periods so as to avoid doing so at night when there is no bell-ringing to make stopping a rambling conversation easier.

All these suggestions may seem like a lot, but they reveal just how efficient you want to be when you have a demanding course load, while protecting some of your time for activities other than schoolwork.

The better prepared you are for your senior year, the more fun you will have when you get there. Again, schools vary remarkably in their approaches to senior year. More and more schools are requiring a senior project, often interdisciplinary in nature (involving more than one academic discipline as it is applied to a particular subject). Some schools insist that seniors try something new, anything from community service for course credit to a performance of a major project in one of your courses.

Here is a possible senior year schedule:

	Monday	Tuesday	Wednesday	Thursday	Friday
1	Biochem		Biochem		
2	Biochem	Math adv.	Biochem	Math adv.	Math adv.
3		Math adv.			
4	Sr. Eng.	Sr. Eng.	Sr. Eng.		Sr. Eng.
5	Sr. Span.	Sr. Span.	Sr. Span.	Sr. Span.	
6					
7					
8	Religion	Religion			Religion
9					Religion

A senior schedule might consist of five courses, but several of them may be very small because of the advanced nature of the material. They may be taught as seminars, too. In other words, the classes might not meet as often, and for a much longer time when they do. Furthermore, students might collaborate with the teacher on the content of the course and the method in which it is learned: student presentations, guest lectures, round table discussions, and groups projects could all be part of the course. Or you might have the opportunity to do an independent project that counts as two or three courses. Notice that the amount of freedom you have in your senior year is in part related to the amount of responsibility you showed in your first three years. The more requirements you have fulfilled in the beginning, the more opportunity you will have to experiment in the end.

Most schools will require yearlong ninth-grade courses in math, English, science, history, and a language, and something similar in the subsequent two years, though you will probably be expected to take courses in the arts, religion and philosophy, physical education, and life issues as well. While schools also vary on diploma requirements, most expect 4 years of English, 2 years of language and 2 years of science, 3 years of history, 1½ years in the arts, and about 3 years of math. Depending on your ideas about college, you may end up taking more science, more math, or more courses in the arts. Furthermore, even these basic requirements vary and often within a single school. In fact, many schools try to be somewhat flexible in the way you honor the school's requirements so as to accommodate special circumstances. For instance, you may be proficient in math, fulfilling the course requirement quickly. Or you may be exempted from one requirement because of a proven facility with language or music or physics. Though all your classmates may take math and language in your freshman year, you may take different courses in those disciplines' sequences depending on your ability and prior education. Most schools have diploma requirements (number of course credits) that allow you to take nonrequired courses during your senior year and even during your junior year. In other words, the average student will earn more course credits than she needs if she simply passes all her courses. So, many departments offer electives, courses that can be chosen by the students. Furthermore, most schools invite students to apply to do independent projects in collaboration with a favorite teacher, to double up in a discipline they particularly enjoy, or to consider academic programs off campus.

Every school has some kind of "course of study" guide, a list of courses with descriptions, usually by department. Often in this same guide, you can find all the rules about how to transfer from one course to the next, drop a course, petition the school to have a requirement waived or to take an extra course, evaluate your performance based on the school's grading system, and determine what courses require prerequisites (courses that you need to take in preparation for another course). In addition, you can learn a lot about what each department's expectations are for a student over the course of four years. You can improve your chances for success *if you know what each department's ideas are about successful student work.* Some departments will explain their expectations for each level of their curriculum. Most departments will offer departmental, multisection courses that may share the same syllabus and surely will reflect a similar approach to the material from section to section. Still, knowing who is teaching what and when are important factors in how your academic workload evolves. Some course of study guides will tell you who is teaching what. However, sometimes you have to rely on the scheduling officer and/or wait until the master schedule comes out.

For better or for worse, colleges can influence what you choose to do with your academic career as well. For instance, the NCAA has its own stipulations as to what you should have done in the course of four years of high school. Ivy League schools tend to favor the student who has excelled in all his/her courses, but sometimes they'll take a student who has gone very, very far in one discipline, her success or lack thereof in all her courses notwithstanding. Generally, the better schools will rely on your test scores heavily, but not exclusively. A good grade point average (GPA) goes a long way. However, colleges will be aware of the fact that you are going to a very good, very demanding school, and in fact many, many boarding schools refuse to rank their students by GPA. Furthermore, many boarding schools count their mainstream curricular track as an advanced placement (AP) track. In other words, the better colleges probably take your school's demanding academic reputation into consideration when perusing your transcript. Do not be alarmed, therefore, if you discover that you are not at the very top of your class in boarding school, even if you were at your old school.

The bottom line is this: You have heard over and over again from students and teachers in this section that what lasts is not what you learned but how you learned it. If you have taken your courses seriously, then you will thrive in college no matter what college you attend. Brilliant kids go to colleges you have not yet heard of, and they go on to great things. The idea that there are eight colleges worth going to is an illusion. There are brilliant professors and brilliant courses waiting for you everywhere. Learn how to learn, and how to take charge of your own learning. That's the real education at a good boarding school. The curriculum is just a means to that end.

Craig Thorn is an instructor in English at Phillips Academy, where he has been a house counselor, adviser, administrator, and coach for twenty-one years. In addition to writing and editing books about education, he writes essays about literature and reviews of alternative rock music.

Academic Mission

Hugh Jebson
Lake Forest Academy

At the heart of the boarding school experience is the academic program and, most important, the student-teacher interaction that takes place primarily in the classroom. At Lake Forest Academy, we design course work to provide students with the skills to work independently as well as part of a team, and to provide confidence so the student can tackle greater challenges.

One of the greatest things about this is the faculty who are dedicated to working with each and every student in a variety of settings. The same adult, for example, who teaches science during the academic day will also coach sports in the afternoon and then work equally hard to support and mentor students in the dorm during the evening. What this means for the student is that he or she will enjoy frequent opportunities throughout the day to learn valuable academic or personal lessons from teachers who are interested in the development of the "whole" child. Furthermore, by truly getting to know each other in different settings, the teacher and student(s) develop a stronger and deeper bond, leading to better classroom instruction and enhanced student performance.

Perhaps the greatest single benefit of boarding school is that a majority of teachers actually live on campus, either in a dormitory in a self-contained apartment, or in separate on-campus housing. This gives students wide-ranging access to their teachers and allows for interaction long after the formal academic day has ended. This can make a world of difference to a boarding student who might be struggling with a particular academic topic or piece of work because his or her teacher(s) can be available to help and support at times simply not possible in a day-school setting.

Another common feature of boarding school academic life is

the faculty adviser. Typically, each student is matched with a particular teacher when the student joins the school. In fact, a great deal of preliminary research goes into the process of matching the adviser and advisee even before the student arrives on campus. Every attempt is made to match the pairing based on mutual interest and student need; this is, arguably, the most important single relationship the student will have during his or her time at boarding school and much depends on a successful adviser-advisee relationship.

The adviser/advisee partnership can, and does, develop into a very meaningful relationship that is remembered and valued by the student long after he or she leaves the school; it is not unheard of for the two to keep in touch long after the graduation year. At Lake Forest Academy each advisory group gathers every day to hear school news and to share personal stories. The faculty adviser is primarily responsible for supervising and mentoring six to seven students and guiding them through school. He or she will monitor and report student progress, share information, and act in conjunction with the parent or guardian to address any problem or concern. Furthermore, the adviser will be on the phone or send an e-mail to share good news with advisee parents, whether it comes from the classroom, the sports field, or the school play. Open, ongoing, and "two-way" communication between the faculty adviser and the home serves to support and benefit the student a great deal. Of course, particular importance is given to curriculum planning; adviser and student will meet repeatedly throughout the school year to discuss student performance and progress, and to determine the most appropriate curriculum for the individual.

Boarding school academics place great emphasis on student responsibility. The role of the classroom teacher is to guide the student through learning by encouraging him or her to take responsibility for his or her education. Classes are, without exception, challenging and hard work is an essential ingredient for success. Students are expected to play a proactive role in their own education. Teachers utilize a variety of teaching styles and approaches in the classroom such as lecture, discussion, debates, and role-playing in order to encourage maximum student participation in the learning process. That is not to say, however, that continuous support is not available—quite the opposite, as teachers will frequently make time to meet students in order to help them. At Lake Forest Academy class sizes are typically small with a teacher to student ratio of 1:12. This allows for a high level of personal attention before, during, and after scheduled class. Basically, boarding school teachers share a belief and expectation that each student actively wants to be in the classroom, wants to learn and, most important, is prepared to work hard. So, in order to get the most out of the academic experience, students need to come to class prepared; they need to have done the assigned reading or readings before meeting and should be ready to participate during class meetings. Indeed, the most meaningful class meeting is one during which the teacher and students engage in lively discussion or debate about a particular topic.

At Lake Forest Academy, the faculty emphasizes the development of particular academic and intellectual core skills within each discipline. Academic departments continuously evaluate what they are teaching and how they teach it in order to make sure the curriculum is designed to provide students not only with a deep understanding of the subject matter, but with the ability to think critically and creatively. Once identified and defined in the course description, these goals guide classroom instruction. In other words, students need to master certain core skills during the freshman year, for example, in order to move on to the sophomore year where previously learned skills are further developed but also supplemented by new ones. And so on. As students continue to develop these skills, those who excel and/or discover a deeper interest in a particular discipline have ample opportunity to pursue a passion through Independent Study (IS). This is an excellent way for a student to work closely with a faculty member who might have expertise in a specific area. IS meetings tend to be less formal and frequent than regular classes, and involve only the student and the sponsor teacher and center on research work done by the student on a topic or area of his or her choosing. The freedom provided by the opportunity to work independently allows students to delve more deeply into areas of academic life not usually permitted in a typical high school curriculum. It is not surprising, then, that much of the best student work I have seen has been the product of independent study.

The Lake Forest Academy history curriculum is an excellent example of the approach to skills-based education. History courses here are designed to provide students with much more than a narrative survey of the period studied. At the end of a course, history instructors expect students to demonstrate an understanding of the historical themes, topics, and periods studied. The instructors, moreover, teach students to assess the significance of individuals, ideas, and events in their historical context. Additionally, instructors require students to demonstrate that they can conduct investigations of historical questions, problems, or issues in order to analyze, use, and interpret historical sources in their historical context, and therefore draw on historical evidence, accounts, and arguments to explain, analyze, and make judgments. History instructors nurture the development of these skills in the content of the introductory survey course World History I and continue to do so throughout the department curriculum with elective courses such as "Twentieth-Century China," "War and Peace in the Middle East," and "The Rise and Fall of Adolf Hitler." In effect, teachers teach history to students in a way that encourages students to think for themselves as historians.

So, in closing, it is important to remember that academic life at a boarding school is rigorous, lively, and challenging. For the student who is prepared to work hard, to take responsibility for his or her education, and to seek out the type of teacher support that is found only in a boarding school environment, the potential reward is an academic and intellectual experience that better prepares the individual for the college experience and beyond.

Hugh Jebson attended the University of Iowa and graduated with a B.A. history and political science. He completed his graduate work at St. Andrews University in Scotland and earned a master of philosophy. A twelve-year veteran of secondary education, Mr. Jebson is currently the academic dean at Lake Forest Academy where he teaches a course entitled "The Rise and Fall of Adolph Hitler." A 2000 Mandel Teacher Fellow of the United States Holocaust Memorial Museum, Mr. Jebson has given numerous presentations and workshops on Holocaust education. He is currently writing an "Essential Word Dictionary" for high school historians that will be published in England in 2003.

REFLECTING AND MOVING ON

In Whose Faces Do I Find Friendship Now?

Diana Lopez '97
Phillips Academy

Friendships are what I remember most about my years as a student at Phillips Academy, the ones I made when I came and the ones I learned to keep when I left home. When I compare my friendships at a prestigious boarding school in a wealthy all-white suburb to my friendships in an urban city, I discover that they are actually not completely different.

I grew up in East Los Angeles, a place where a friend is a lot more than someone you call to get the homework assignment. Faced with the challenges of inner-city life, I learned to turn to my friends for support and help. Because I was always trying to be a good student, I wasn't always considered a cool person. Many students in my school did not care about grades, and many hardly came to school. However, one of my closest friends, Irazema, supported my work even though she wasn't always interested herself. I first met her when we were working on a history project about the colonists. We were supposed to combine English, history, and science, but I was the only one doing any work. When I told Irazema and the other two girls that they had to help me, one of the girls said to me, "Why are you having a cow about this assignment?" and the other told me that she wasn't going to do anything. But Irazema didn't say anything, she just started to help me. I could tell that she thought a lot about how important the assignment was to me. I knew that she didn't care about the assignment, but she cared about me. When she started to help me, the other two girls started also. Irazema brought them over to my side.

Another friend taught me how to be strong despite the trouble all around East LA and in her family. Her dad is a Vietnam War veteran who is hooked on drugs. He doesn't get any benefits and spends most of his time in and out of gangs. Her brother is the same way. Her mother works all the time as a nurse but her paycheck goes to lawyers to keep them out of jail. They lost their house and had to move to East LA, a block away from where I live. Because her life is always hard, she has learned how to fight. Though she is skinny, I've seen her beat up people much bigger than she is to protect her honor. She can fight because she has a rage in her. So now she has graduated from high school and is going to Cal State even though she is pregnant. I have no doubt that she is going to survive. Knowing her, I know I can make it through any trouble.

Sharing the same Mexican traditions and celebrations added an extra bond among us. After being part of their quinceañeras (debutante balls) and having them help me organize a Cinco de Mayo (a Mexican holiday) celebration, these friends are no less than a family to me. I organized the celebration because I really wanted to have something special for Mexican students in the school. I got all my Mexican friends to help me. We had to get families in the community and the whole school involved in order for the daylong celebration to work. We made posters that told of the history of Cinco de Mayo. And when the day came, we actually had a folklorico dance team. A folklorico is a special style of dancing that celebrates Mexican traditions. The girls wear really bright skirts that they can wave around. The men are much more conservative. They wear tight black pants and black jackets and white shirts. The costumes are very important because the attention is focused on the girls. We got food donated from families in the neighborhood. The celebration took on a life of its own. In fact, some parents were so excited that they found a mariachi band that day which they brought to play at the end of the day. Everybody was dancing—parents, students, and faculty. I was proud to have returned this tradition to my school and to see so many generations of people having fun.

To be part of a friend's quinceañera was a great honor. The quinceañera is like a religious ceremony that celebrates the coming of age (the fifteenth birthday) of a young woman. So to be invited to do the waltz, a special dance during the ceremony, is a high honor. For months and months you go to the quinceañera's house and you practice and practice to get the waltz perfect because it is carefully choreographed. It is much harder for the quinceañera, however, because she has to organize the event, which can involve from 200 to 2000 people. The quinceañera is a great way to meet everyone in the community because you are part of a profound event that welcomes a young woman to her adulthood. You make new friends of her family because you spend so much time rehearsing. All the women dress in the exact same clothes, usually made by an aunt, in a design chosen by the girl who is being honored. The other girls, mostly family such as cousins and sisters, dance around her to show her off. To be invited to be part of this formal dance when you are not part of the family is like being adopted into a new family.

When I was fifteen, I took the red-eye from Los Angeles to Phillips Academy in Andover, Massachusetts, after saying goodbye to all my family and friends. I was greeted by a bunch of screaming teenagers who wanted me to fall backward off a stump into their arms (a trust fall), which I refused to do. The TV show *Turning Point* was doing a special on me. The whole time I was preparing to leave, the camera crew was in my face telling me to turn this way and step over here. And then when I arrived, all I wanted to do was to blend in and I had to deal with this camera crew that was hanging microphones on me and hovering around me. How different it was when I graduated and the pictures of me were with my friends Nashira, Vanessa, Juan, and Lindsey. When I came, I was the object of a television camera, sort of like a weird human interest story. When I left I was part of a graduation picture with my friends, just one of the gang that stuck together for three years.

"Class of 97: It's All About The Friends We've Made," was my message in my senior page in the yearbook. When I first came to Phillips Academy, as a new lower, I never thought I'd be one to make such a statement. But the three years I've spent here and all the experiences that my friends and I have helped each other through have allowed me to grow, redefining myself and my friendships. Being so far away from home and old friends raised my understanding of the responsibility of being a friend to a higher level. It meant helping someone with their homework instead of just giving them the assignment, running an errand for a friend who was ill, or even writing a friendly note for a person who was really homesick.

The daily support and encouragement that I used to get from my family I learned to receive from my peers and friends on campus. One of my friends, Nashira, always lifted my spirits when I would get a bad grade. Most students here set such high expectations for themselves that when they aren't met, there is a feeling of disappointment. Nashira, in her own creative way, managed to cheer me up and encouraged me to do better the next time. So I was never surprised when she would perform an improvised ballet for me after hearing the bad news of a test grade.

On a campus as friendly as P.A. it was very common to receive encouragement and support while walking down the path or having a meal in the Commons. Juan, another friend, went above the call of duty last November. While working on my history research paper, I had an accident in which I misplaced many of my notes. So I was put in the position where I had to pull a much dreaded all-nighter. I was terrified because I didn't think I'd be able to stay awake the whole night, as tired as I was. When I told Juan my problem he not only gave me the courage to meet the night head on, but also called me every hour and a half to make sure I was still awake. It was thanks to him that I got a 4 (or B) on my research paper.

Stress is definitely a component of everyone's life at Phillips Academy. I came very close to being overcome by the stress and giving in to the demanding schedule that is routine for all students. Lindsay and Vanessa always made sure that I scheduled in some fun and hang-out time. In many cases Lindsay spontaneously showed up in my room throwing clothes and makeup on me so we could rush off to a dorm party or some other school activity. Despite my resistance, she always convinced me with her "anything-is-better-than-staying-in-your-room" saying. Vanessa, who was a day student, helped me realize that there is a life off campus. She randomly picked me up to wash her mom's car, have dinner with her family, or shoot some pool. Besides leaving all the stress of school behind on campus, I was able to enjoy and be a part of her regular life.

And regular life included some of the same crises and celebrations of regular life back home: broken families, battles with addictions, betrayals, loneliness; but also romances, dreams and hopes, reunions with family members, personal success stories in sports and school and you name it, and lots of friends.

The day I graduated from Phillips there were thousands of people on the great lawn and so many of them were people I had to say good-bye to. We marched around the inside of the stone wall led by a Scottish bagpipe band. We marched up through the corridor made by parents and friends toward the steps leading to Samuel Phil. I heard my English teacher shout "Diana, you go, girl!" After the speeches, we made a circle on the great lawn and passed around our diplomas until every student got her own with her name on it. I remember hugging friends from my dorm, my classes. I remember hugging teachers and parents of close friends. Everywhere there were women in white dresses and men in blazers. There was a long white buffet table with sandwiches and drinks and melting ice sculptures. And there were little circles of chairs where families waited for their children to finish saying good-bye.

Although it was hard sometimes to live and grow with my friends, I feel that we've all learned a new meaning of caring and supporting. I can appreciate the fact that I can count on these people as if they were my family, because in a way, they have been for three years. I'm sad that we will be separating after graduation, each of us headed in our own direction. With Nashira at U. Penn., Juan at U. Miami, Lindsay at U. Mass., Vanessa at Columbia U., and me at UCLA, keeping up with everyone's daily life will be impossible. But I don't think it will be necessary because I feel that our friendship is at a deeper level that surpasses the need of common daily events to survive. That's what I learned about friendship in East Los Angeles and I learned the same lesson at Phillips.

Diana Lopez graduated from Phillips Academy and returned to LA where she currently attends college and now works, while keeping close ties with her family.

What Did I Learn About Other People? Myself?

Louise af Petersons '96
St. Andrews-Sewanee

The clay room at St. Andrew's-Sewanee School is a quiet place. No matter how upset or troubled I am, I can retreat there, take on some huge project and relax. I take a lump of clay and step by step go through the process of shaping the unformed mass into something different and useful. The same thing happens to each of us in our lives and happened to me as I experienced an American boarding school.

All of us are molded by our place of origin. When I lived in Sweden I went to a small rural school. The importance of school was not emphasized very much because we did not get grades until we were in eighth grade, so I basically did not care. In the back of my mind, though, I did have some vague idea of what I wanted to do with my life. After all, when you get toward the end of your ninth-grade year you have to decide what you want to do in the future in order to go on to the gymnasium [high school]. All in all, I was still an unshaped lump of clay.

My transformation from one form to another happened in stages, just like a piece of pottery grows on a wheel. I did not come directly from another country. I lived in the States for a while and I became accustomed to the American ways. First, my family moved to Florida from Sweden. This was a huge transition for me and I had to adapt to it. When I first came over to the States I had to change my ways of living, but I still had ways of looking at things that were part of my old culture. In Sweden people tend to be open and honest. If you ask a Swede how they are doing, you know that they will give you an honest answer. I continued to answer honestly, even when I began to learn that Americans would say "I'm okay," or "I'm doing great!" even if it was the worst day of their lives. Finally, I began to change as I realized that a sense of distance was as much a part of American culture as intimacy was a part of Sweden's. Going to school was even more different.

When I was in tenth grade my parents decided to send me to boarding school. One day my parents mentioned to me that we were going to go visit a boarding school in Tennessee. Tennessee!?! I thought. What will become of me and my "Swedishness"? I identify with everything that has to do with Sweden. In Florida I could still feel some sort of identification with Sweden because my parents were there and we spoke Swedish all the time. Even on Christmas, we held on to our traditional Swedish celebration—December 24th instead of 25th, and ham and meatballs instead of turkey. Going to boarding school would pull me further from the culture I identified with, further from my values and morals and the land that shaped me as a child. I was afraid.

When I arrived at boarding school my way of living and looking at things changed again, and once again my form was altered. It was like coming from another country all over again. Not only do you leave the comforts of home and your parents but you also learn how to live and take care of yourself with total strangers from other cultures and backgrounds. In order to live at boarding school, you must grow into the culture. I slid further and further away from my Swedish culture because at boarding school, and St. Andrews-Sewanee in particular, I was brought together with people from other cultures and given a certain framework to live in. I saw that what I had expected to be a narrow environment was wider than I thought, and that the school community was a mixture of cultural forces. Because I am receptive and flexible it was very easy for me to live within this framework. Through the years, though, I have encountered people that were not as receptive as I am.

One year there was a girl at St. Andrew's-Sewanee from Germany. She told me several times she was very excited to be in the States, but somehow this did not quite reflect her behavior. She constantly remarked about how everything back home was better. She argued with her chemistry teacher about simple equations, and I tried to tell her about my experiences of coming here and how you have to accept new and different things and be willing to adapt, but she simply did not listen. I don't think her experience here was positive because she did not have an open mind about the situation. You must have an open mind about something in order to accept and learn from it. Still my experience of coming to boarding school has been extraordinary, and it has given me new insight to myself and other people.

The school itself—its culture, morals, and values—has shaped who I am today. One place where I learned these new qualities is my clay work. Working with clay and making pottery is the best thing that has ever happened to me. I found something that I love to do and can use to express my feelings. I was never exposed to clay before because not every school has this opportunity and it was only fate that I ended up where I did. Like my clay work, school has shaped me in terms of how I identify myself and with other people. Last year I decided I would apply to be a proctor. A proctor acts as an assistant to the teachers and helps out with a lot of things in the school community. I did not think I would be appointed proctor. I didn't think my grades were good enough, and I knew I was quiet. But what did I have to lose? It was worth trying. To my surprise, I was appointed. I suddenly realized that my perception of myself and what other people thought of me were two different things. I didn't think I would be a good leader, but found that I could be quiet and still lead. I matured because I understood that my position of leadership brought with it a responsibility to others. I learned to accept the rejection I sometimes received for doing what I thought was right. Still, my time as a proctor taught me that even though I came from a different culture, I could be accepted as a person of importance and responsibility. They still may make fun of my accent, but they don't make fun of me.

Despite all of the good I have gained at boarding school, I will take some sadness with me as well. All of these changes have made me feel distant from my native country. I would not say that I am Swedish anymore even though I've been in this country for only six years. Most of this change from a Swedish person to an American has happened in my time at boarding school. Even though I am very receptive to new ideas, this change was really hard for me. It is still difficult for me because when I go home for vacation I bring with me the ideas from school and they clash with my parents' ideas and way of living. I am forgetting my native language and my parents insist I speak it, but I feel more comfortable speaking English, because it is what I do almost every day at boarding school. When I talk to my parents, I don't feel like I belong at home because I know what they are saying, but the language that I used to speak now sounds foreign to me. I feel adrift between two cultures, one foreign but familiar, and another new and comfortable. I need somewhere to belong—one culture, not two. It can be very confusing at times.

I will take from this school a sense of place to identify with, as I before had done with everything Swedish. Here, I found something new to identify with, this place, Sewanee, and different cultures. There is something about boarding school, and this place in particular that stays with you, no matter where you go or how bad things are going for you. You can always feel like yourself and feel a sense of place. William Wordsworth wrote a wonderful poem on this particular subject called "Lines." In it Wordsworth describes the beauty of Tintern Abbey and how that beauty has stayed with him even though he has been away from the place for five years. I know that the same thing will happen with me. I will always remember this place because it is the place where I came to know who I am, and where my character grew to fullness, just like the sculptures I create with clay. Unlike those sculptures, though, while my shape may remain the same, the way I perceive different surroundings will change as my experiences grow.

Louise af Petersons completed her career at St. Andrews-Sewanee in 1997. After she graduated from St. Andrews-Sewanee, Louise went on to attend the University of Miami, in Miami, Florida. In December of 2001 she received her bachelor of arts in sociology with a minor in art. Louise is currently studying for a master's degree in science of elementary education. She will graduate with her master's in the summer of 2002, at which point she hopes to start teaching at a local elementary school.

Matchmaker, Matchmaker Make Me a Match

Kimi Abernathy
The Webb School

I love the city. I love the energy, the people, the activity. I love the markets with their vibrant displays of fruits and vegetables and buckets of fresh flowers. Going to plays and museums, sitting in a diner, walking down the crowded streets—all of this recharges and invigorates me. However, I do not want to live in the city. I am a country girl at heart. I do my best work in a place where I hear crickets at night and see the stars in a sky unaffected by light pollution. I want to walk to the creek and ride bikes on dirt roads. Both environments –city and country—have wonderful characteristics to recommend them. I have chosen to live and work in the environment that best matches my needs and lifestyle.

When you choose a college, you will be asked to think about

much more than the brand name of a school, though that often seems to be among the primary criteria. You will walk through a process of self-discovery and evaluation in order to arrive at a group of schools that best match your needs not just academically but also socially, extracurricularly, and emotionally.

Why is a good match so important? Each student has a different set of needs and issues. Every school has a specific culture and a variation on ways to meet students' needs. What works for you may not work for me. The criteria by which you choose a college are most likely different from those used by your parents, your best friend, Aunt Sally, or Great-Uncle Joe. The criteria must be your own, discovered through thoughtful reflection and careful evaluation of all of your options. Your best friend must find his/her own place, and one presumes Aunt Sally and Great-Uncle Joe have had their shot at college. You will ask their advice and help, but ultimately this is your search, and the reward, a wonderful college experience, is yours as well.

You are already farther along in this process than your peers in day schools. You understand finding a good match. When you looked at boarding schools, you and your parents worked from a set of criteria to find the school that met as many of your needs as possible. You visited campuses, read curriculum guides, checked out sports teams, talked to students and faculty, asked about college placement, inspected dorms, and tried to get a feel for the culture of the school. All of this was to see if the school would provide you with an environment optimal for your success.

I once worked with a young woman who had everything a highly selective college or university would want. Sarah had an impressive academic profile: a 4.0 in all honors and advanced placement courses, 1590 on the SAT I, and above 750 on her SAT IIs. She was president of the honor council, on a nationally ranked Quiz Bowl team, was a committed volunteer at the hospital, had the lead in several school plays, played varsity tennis, and tutored underprivileged children. Sarah was an aggressive student with much natural ability and an impressive work ethic. Everyone thought she should shoot for the stars, or the Ivies, as the case may be. Sarah felt great pressure to go with a school that matched her profile in terms of admissions selectivity, to choose a name brand school and to matriculate to the "best" school to which she was admitted. Sarah, however, was a small-town girl and did not really want to leave the region. While she was completely confident and accomplished and would do well academically at any school, she chose to stay closer to home. In the end, the criteria that were most significant to Sarah were not the criteria that you or I may have used. They were, however, the things that made a difference to her and to her success in college.

Finding a good match academically may actually be the easiest part. Schools publish their curriculum, mid-50 percentile for test scores, and average GPAs. However, the intangibles often make the good fit. A good college placement program will ask you to take a hard look at yourself. It will require you to explore the kinds of environments you need to work best. Do you need the energy of an urban environment? Do you want a large campus with tens of thousands of people, or do you prefer a small college where you will have close faculty interaction? Are you looking for a campus that is heavily Greek (fraternities and sororities) or one that does not have a Greek system, or do you even care? Is distance from home a factor for you? Are you a warm-weather person, one who loves the cold, or one who needs seasons? Is a strong advising system important? Would you consider a college abroad? Do you need academic support services? Are scholarships and/or financial aid a factor? Are specific activities important to you? Do you want a diverse student body and faculty? Are you more traditional or more nonconformist? What does your gut tell you when you visit a school?

One day a young man came to my office to tell me he had found the perfect school. He outlined his criteria—no core curriculum, highly selective, strong math program, opportunities to work closely with professors, looking for male students, offered National Merit money, was in or close to an urban environment, and was not Greek oriented. Seth wanted to apply early decision. I would not sign off until he visited the school. When he did visit this perfect school, Seth was stunned to see that everyone looked as if they stepped out of a 1950s beatnik poetry reading—wearing black, smoking, and in deeply earnest conversation. Few looked as if they were enjoying themselves. Seth would have been miserable in that environment, yet on the surface, on paper, the school met all of his criteria.

There will most likely be more than one or two or even ten schools that meet your criteria. There will always be a number of schools where you will find a good fit. Be open to schools about which you may initially know very little. Look beyond the glossy brochures and Fifth Avenue marketing for the essence of a school. Read the various guide books with a jaundiced eye, taking the hard data but treating the rankings as relatively irrelevant and self-serving. Be flexible. Be open-minded. Be proactive.

And finally, as I tell all of my students, use your time in high school to the best of your abilities. You are in a college preparatory school. Therein lies the magic. You have been given an opportunity to prepare for college in a way most young people can only dream about. Dorm life will be old hat for you. Negotiating with a roommate will be within your comfort zone. You will already know how to prioritize your time and study. Laundry is no problem, and you have learned how to augment school food with specific items (read contraband) in your dorm room. You are already so far ahead in the game. Now you must leverage that edge by making the best grades you can and being actively involved in the life of your school. Finding activities or concerns about which you are passionate and pursuing them with vigor as an underclassman, looking hard and realistically at yourself and your needs as a junior and senior, and making a thoughtful college search will assure you of plenty of schools with which you are a perfect match.

Kimi Abernathy is the director of college counseling at The Webb School in Bell Buckle, Tennessee. Founded in 1870, The Webb School is a coeducational college preparatory school for boarding and day students in grades 7–12. Ms. Abernathy has been at The Webb School for ten years serving as director of admissions prior to assuming duties in college counseling.

Ending with You and Your Family

Adults—teachers, administrators, and parents—write most but not all of the essays in this closing section. In fact, several of the essays are deliberately written as much for your parents as they are for you, and a few are excerpts of essays written by educators for other educators. So why is this section in a book for young people thinking of going to boarding school and not in a book for your parents and educators? As future members of the boarding school community, you ought to know what adults think about when they think about how boarding schools should work and how they should work with your parents to give you every opportunity to shine.

These essays address practical subjects (financing a child's education, following rules) and philosophical subjects (developing a curricular mission, defining role models, addressing issues of diversity). It also offers some very personal stories told by parents who have had children at boarding school, teachers who have devoted their lives to boarding school education, and in closing one student who reimagines her four years at boarding school.

In between a few introductory and concluding essays, there are four major sub-sections: "Diversity," "Community Values," "Contact," and "Curricular Philosophies." You are at a distinct advantage over most students coming to boarding schools. You have the opportunity to know what people who work hard to make the boarding school experience rewarding are thinking. Certainly it helps to have had all these students and teachers talk to you over the course of this book and to have had the opportunity to add your own two cents in various exercises. Now you get to eavesdrop on the adults as they talk among themselves, something you have never, ever done before, right?

At the very least, you'll see how boarding schools constantly challenge themselves to educate the whole student. If there is a coherent theme in this provocative closing section it is that the academic experience is only a small part of what makes you who you are and what schools want to give you. Schools want to support the development of your religious beliefs, your creativity, your cultural identity, your particular talents and interests, your family, your emotional and physical well-being, your ethical sense, and your understanding of and appreciation for what it means to be a responsible, happy individual in a thriving, complex community. It is a tall order that preoccupies us daily. Wish us luck.

INTRODUCING YOU TO YOUR FUTURE

What Kind of an Education Should Colleges Expect the Twenty-first Century Student to Have?

John R. Eidam
Wyoming Seminary

Twice we packed the car to deliver our son and daughter for day one of their respective college careers. Twice Dr. Ed interrupted his evening stroll to impart the same advice, "Don't let your studies get in the way of your education." We chuckled—some of us through tears—and Dr. Ed ambled on his way.

Good ol' Dr. Ed was singing my song. Thirty years of boarding school living demonstrates that students learn some of the most important lessons outside the classroom.

When Alida, a sixteen-year-old East German, came to our boarding school in Pennsylvania, it was not long until her dormmates realized that, indeed, Alida had lived under Communism and had witnessed, firsthand, the collapse of the Berlin Wall. They listened as she spoke of walking with her grandmother from East to West. At ten years old, she saw for the first time in her life fresh bananas and grapefruit. Lighted brightly and with shelves stacked full, the stores of West Berlin contrasted sharply with all she had known. Faces of window-shoppers sported smiles, not the gloom and despair with which she had grown accustomed. The well-dressed mannequins seemed like an illusion. She had neither seen nor known of this other world.

Where were you when Desert Storm erupted? Our family sat at dinner among students who lived in Saudi Arabia, and our daughter wept with friends from Dhahran. Their families were in the direct line of scud missile fire. Our news vigil was packed with emotion. The fear of aggression was real; the tragedy of war was personally and emotionally felt.

When Zagreb, Croatia, came under seige, Jelena's parents and grandmother were in the midst of it all. Suddenly, the conflict in Bosnia-Herzegovina became less distant. Jelena was a friend with feelings and opinions, which brought this critical world situation poignantly into our hearts and minds. We read the news and listened to the telecasts, trying to sort out the issues.

Most Americans can conjure up images of the Berlin Wall collapsing, but few comprehend the ramifications of that great event. To reside in a dormitory with Alida of Germany, Nora of Hungary, Jana of Slovakia, or Nicoll of the Belarus is to learn how myopic and arrogant the American perspective can be. We assume that democracy and a free-market economy are right for the rest of the world, but we are blind to the possibility that any other political and economic system might have merit. Listening to their Eastern European dormmates, students temper their arrogance and broaden their perspective. The American way is not the only way. The boarding school experience opens minds.

When I was a youngster, my brother brought an African-American friend home for a visit to our provincial little Pennsylvania town. That we had a black man in our home was an extraordinary event among my parents' generation. That my brother and he shared a Coke from the same bottle was astonishing. For years this story was retold. One generation later our son met for the first time his college freshman roommate, an African American. They were unaware of the difference time and circumstance can make. Both had lived in diverse boarding school communities. From their perspective this introduction had no meaning beyond the fact that they, like thousands of other roommate combinations, would live together for at least one year. I doubt that the issue of race crossed either of their minds.

When our son and daughter faced the freedom and independence of college life, they benefited from one other boarding school gift. They lived a routine that balanced academic priorities with personal and community responsibilities. Day after day they lived that routine—classes-activities-dinner (with teachers and peers)-evening study, classes-activities-dinner-evening study, classes-activities-dinner-evening study. To those in the real world this routine seems akin to Pavlov's experiment. When the 6:15 P.M. Nelson Tower Bell rings for dinner, we begin to salivate. The same sound at 7:30 and 9:50 begins and ends the evening study. Almost on signal books open and close.

The routine became a lifestyle. Sans the Tower Bell it was the modus operandus of their college years. Newfound independence and freedom from parental oversight led many of their freshmen peers to disaster; our children's productive lifestyles helped them stay the course.

Activities—strongly encouraged or required in most boarding schools—forced each of them to pursue something that would broaden their development and contribute to the community. Swimming gave our son self-confidence that he may never have found otherwise. "Feeling good" about himself, he developed a personality and a sense of humor that are among his greatest assets. Music, drama, and government allowed our daughter to test her leadership skills. Both became more rounded, developed new interests, and through participation, contributed to the quality of campus life and opportunity.

The boarding routine benefits each person in different ways. International students develop a sense of what it means to be contributing members of a community. Like colleges and universities, boarding schools depend on each member of the community to contribute to the quality of life. Being a good student is not enough. Soaking up experiences for one's self, without giving anything in return, is not enough. The degree to which any community provides vibrancy for all is determined entirely by how much each gives of himself or herself on behalf of the community. Responsibile students leave the school a better place than it was when they arrived.

Were I a college admission officer, I would turn Dr. Ed's advice into a question: What have you learned beyond the classroom from your boarding school? I would hope to find that exposure to different ideologies has reduced parochialism and has opened minds, that friendships among people from diverse cultures has improved tolerance for those who are different, and that a self-disciplined lifestyle has been adopted which balances work with personal growth as well as contributions to the community.

Listen to Dr. Ed: "Don't let your studies get in the way of your education."

John Eidam is presently the dean of admissions at Wyoming Seminary.

Second Home

Lynne Brusco Moore

Several years ago one of my ninth-grade students left Florida to attend a well-known New England boarding school. He is an only child. I was concerned for him until I understood the culture of the school and the legacy of a headmaster about whom books have been written. This student desired a more challenging environment. His belief in teamwork, coupled with a love of athletics, were other factors that pointed toward a kinship with this school. I envisioned him studying in a leather chair, pausing to consider who sat in that chair before him, and keeping a promise to remember the faces in the photographs lining the main hall. True to form, he is resilient, feels connected to his peers, and flourishes scholastically and socially. He is a loving son who wanted his parents, and the faces in the photos, to be proud—as proud as *he* was to have been accepted.

Over the course of a career, the fortunate teacher meets with a handful of students whose presence enriches the classroom and school community. I have been fortunate in my work as a teacher and administrator in independent schools. My students have had a wide range of abilities and interests, and each possessed essential traits that ensured his or her success—the most important being resilience and a sense of connectedness.

A student's greatest strengths can be his/her greatest weaknesses, and understanding this duality is part of the learning process. Motivation may overshadow process. Curiosity may curtail caution. Industry may cloud insight. Resilience, however, is a key attribute in each student's success. Like Horatio Alger, it is the ability to pick oneself up by his/her bootstraps and appreciate something in each challenge, whatever the outcome, and forge ahead. Quiet or outgoing, this student navigates carefully, adjusts to changes and, though perhaps discouraged with his/her own performance or that of others, refuses to be bogged down by the minutia that clouds achievement.

Whether considering independent day or boarding schools, students should have a sense of connectedness to the school. History, mission, and philosophy are the crux of the school's culture—its ethos—and are present in every detail. While students need not be versed in all aspects of the school's background, they should have an appreciation for its traditions and feel a connection to the school community (a class, mentor teacher, peer group, club, team, etc.).

The girls in my classes, and for whom I wrote letters of recommendation to single-sex and coed boarding schools, are determined to find schools that fit their interests. They realize this is the precursor to college and beyond. One has ventured to New Hampshire to pursue dance, another to New York to be closer to journalism internships. Each has supportive parents concerned about distance. Yet, their daughters are passionate in their pursuits. One is quiet, the other gregarious and forthright. Both are fortitudinous. They take advantage of opportunities, hold fast to their goals, and excel.

Each school is different. Each student is different. The final common denominator for all students involves the knowledge that learning is a privilege and that the classroom, the campus, and the world around them is their movable feast.

Lynne Brusco Moore received her B.A. from Purdue University and her M.A. from Columbia University where she participated in the Klingenstein Seminar in Private School Leadership. She has conducted graduate research in writing, discourse, and culture at the Bread Loaf School of English, Middlebury College, and Lincoln College, Oxford University. Mrs. Moore has been honored by a Barnes Foundation Fellowship for her study of the arts in education and was appointed by Florida's secretary of state to serve on the arts in education panel. Mrs. Moore has worked as a middle and high school English teacher and upper school dean of students in South Florida independent schools. She has presented at the National Association of Independent Schools national conference in Washington, D.C., and consulted with corporations and schools in South Florida and New York.

Some Hidden Costs of Independent Schooling

David Arnstein
The Putney School

You're thinking about sending your children to a private boarding school? It's hard to imagine that cost will not be a critical, perhaps overwhelming, consideration. Knowing that you are not alone (only a fraction of one percent of families in the U.S. can easily afford boarding school tuition) is not much solace as you navigate the financing options and make hard decisions about how to create this opportunity for your child. But are there other costs, hidden costs, associated with boarding schools? What is the true cost of sending a student off on this amazing adventure?

I have been teaching in independent schools for almost twenty years, the last fifteen of them at a small boarding school in southern Vermont. It wasn't until my daughter enrolled, however, that I really became acquainted with our school's "bookstore" and I glimpsed the beginning of an understanding of the costs associated with independent boarding schools. I am modestly confidant that books are actually sold at the bookstore. For instance, I can see books stacked floor to ceiling against all the walls when I go there to say hello to Jane (who knows every student on campus in a way that teachers never will). I have to admit that for years I had never actually seen a student buying a book at this store. Clothing, snacks, art supplies, batteries, toiletries, camping gear, maple syrup, wool, wood chisels, office supplies, computers (all from a tiny little space no bigger than my pantry at home . . .) but never a book.

Until the day that I received a statement listing a few books—some which were ones I already owned—that had been charged to my credit card. Since it was the middle of November and far beyond the time when students would have bought books for classes, I was puzzled. Thinking this must be a mistake I called Jane only to find out that my daughter had, indeed, picked up a couple titles for interest and pleasure reading. She had become curious about her peer's classes through various conversations, had browsed books that were lying around, and finally gave in to curiosity and temptation. There are many such temptations and a powerful need for students to feel that they "belong" and are part of the scene. Boarding schools bring together students from all over the world and offer a bewildering variety of activities. The list of new ideas, experiences, and, sometimes, new "things" that students feel compelled to acquire can be long. My daughter's bookstore bill prompted a little conversation about the do's and don'ts of charging items when it is my charge card on file. I recommend this conversation for any parent to have with your child; in this area clarity is like money in the bank. If your children aren't used to budgeting, aren't clear about an "allowance," and will have the ability to charge things to your account while at school, some caution is in order.

I thought everything was cleared up concerning charges at the bookstore until the next month's statement came in: several hundred dollars for horseback riding lessons. How I missed the fact that my daughter was taking riding lessons is still a mystery to me; I mean, I work at the school! But then I imagined what it must be like to ride on the school's trails and through the surrounding forests and fields during the brilliant colors of Vermont's fall foliage season; the school's founder's words about how "A happy childhood is a priceless possession" scrolled across my mind (along with her closely following words ". . . with great privileges come great commitments"). I was also reminded about the kayaking activity I lead at the school: like riding, kayaking the white water rivers in Vermont represents an amazing opportunity, but one that is expensive relative to other activities. While most of our school's afternoon activities involve no additional costs, some involve costly equipment (such as lacrosse or cycling) and others are simply expensive (such as downhill skiing and kayaking). So I paid the bill and tried to stop worrying. But paying the bill was the easier of the two tasks.

The issue—how to account for the different costs of different activities—is one we talk about, and struggle with, in many areas of our school's program. Very often individual families shoulder these costs. While any student can take jewelry as an evening activity at our school with a nominal activity fee ($15), if they choose to use gold, semiprecious, or precious stones, or even gems, than the student (or parent . . .) pays for these materials. Often the line between a "normal" expense for an activity (generally covered by tuition or a lab fee) and an excessive one is unclear. Our school's Project Week presents hundreds of examples of difficult cost assignments as students build telescopes, carve marble, record sound tracks, learn to fly, produce movies, create and print etchings, build musical instruments, choreograph dances, rebuild tractors, and follow their dreams and passions in many different directions. Our five-day Long Spring camping trips, that range from Canada to the Outer Banks, are another example of wildly divergent activities that are paid for through a combination of tuition, a common charge, and individual contributions.

Because of these opportunities, it is probably more difficult to predict expenses associated with our school's program than many other schools. While our parent/student handbook details many anticipated expenses and tries to present an average cost (we publish $1,000–$1,500/year in additional expenses for boarders to cover travel, allowance, books, typical fees, etc.), there is so much variety and opportunity that expenses could be significantly higher (or lower). Good communication and clear boundaries are needed so that your children are aware of financial limits that may apply. For instance, at our school students must purchase a season ticket to participate in the downhill skiing program (several hundred dollars), but cross-country skiing is free (and the school has some equipment to loan as well). Similarly, a five-day Long Spring trip to Montreal will cost much more than five days hiking on Vermont's Long Trail.

Tuition represents an incredible commitment on the part of families. In all boarding schools, tuition includes an outstanding and diverse educational experience. But, amazingly, it doesn't cover everything (and development offices will explain it doesn't even cover the school's annual budget). Our school offers an exchange program with Kazakhstan, and has offered vacationtime trips to rain forests, deserts, high mountains, and the Galapagos Islands. Your child may want to visit close friends at their homes around the United States, Asia, Europe, Africa, the Americas, from any one of dozens of other countries. You may find yourself hosting these students for days or weeks at a time. Trips to major cities and cultural events, local colleges, political rallies, museums, national parks, athletic competitions, etc. are examples of the type of requests that might come up and the requests may be frequent. I know that my daughter's school is a tremendously rich and enriching environment and I am thrilled with her experiences here, but trying to support a teenager as they transition into adulthood is a challenge worthy of Sisyphus. And often not cheap, either. The real hidden cost of an enriched educational environment is the result of an ignited curiosity, a new passion, an expanded worldview and an attendant sense of limitless possibility. This is what you were hoping for, right?

After attending public schools in Westchester County, New York **David Arnstein** went to Princeton to study chemical engineering. After graduation, he taught for three years in an all-girl's day school in Baltimore (the Bryn Mawr School) before joining a large chemical engineering firm for fourteen months. He then came to Putney where he began teaching chemistry and physics while being the network designer and administrator for Putney's computer services. He recently received a master's in education from Antioch University in Keene, New Hampshire. Currently he is dean of students (second year) at Putney and teaches one class in the science department. His wife Allegra (and her brother and three sisters) graduated from Putney and his daughter, Jillian, will graduate this spring. He also has a twelve-year-old son, Jeremy, who plans to attend Putney if the school builds an indoor basketball court.

Thirty Questions

Craig Thorn
Phillips Academy

If you are a new family to boarding school life, the experience can be as much a shock for you, the parents, as it can be for your child. When I first interviewed at Phillips as a prospective teaching fellow, my understanding of high school amounted to the memory of Hudson High, a ¼-mile-long single-story complex that looked more like a coastal defense system outpost than a school. I could not get over the idea that some disciplines had their own buildings, that you actually had to walk outdoors to get from one course to the other. Of course, I was finishing up in college and so I did not make a complete idiot of myself when asking questions. As visiting prospective families, however, you will find that no question is a dumb question. Basically, you have two goals when you visit a boarding school campus: you want to learn about this school's culture; and you want to figure out if this culture is one in which your child can thrive. Let's assume that you and your child are on the same page (I know, but it's okay to dream).

Academic Life

1. Does the school have a curricular philosophy that matches the course offerings as listed in their course of study guide?
2. Does the school have a daily/weekly/yearly calendar that suggests a healthy balance of structured and unstructured time?
3. Does the school have a balance between what is required of the student and what is elective in the curriculum? How far can a superb student in a particular discipline go with the support of the faculty?
4. Does the school have a college counseling office that is actively engaged with the student body early on? Is there a good counselor-to-senior ratio?
5. Does the school have a good academic support system for

students who may struggle with parts of the curriculum? Does the school have the means to address some learning disabilities? Does the school offer English as a second language?

6. Does the school's curriculum cover the range of disciplines that suit your family's interests and needs?
7. Does the school have an evaluation system that you like and that is relatively consistent across disciplines?
8. Does the school clearly state its minimum expectations for graduation? Are there opportunities to make up for insufficient performance? Is there a process of early warnings to give students a chance to avoid failure? Is there more than one "track" to a diploma?
9. Does the school seems to have a strong faculty (check their Web site and on-campus documents for profiles)?
10. Does the school's classroom architecture match what the stated philosophy is? What is the student-faculty ratio?

Behind these questions are some basic expectations:

- The school has a curricular philosophy that does not answer solely to college or parental pressure.
- Families are not sending their children to this school solely to get into a certain college. There is nothing wrong with being that kind of family, but if you are, you had better make sure that the school you're considering is that kind of school; otherwise, you will be sorely disappointed.
- The school does more than "grade" a student—specifically, the school supplements formal evaluation with counselor/adviser letters, instructor reports, and other opportunities for feedback that acknowledge the whole student; skills that are not measured by grades, improvement, motivation, effort, good character, and citizenship.
- The school offers students some independence and active engagement in his/her career as a student. Frankly, if they do not, even if you are looking for a school that specializes in students who have trouble succeeding in academic courses, you may want to reconsider. (This is my personal bias.)

Residential Life

1. Does the school have good coverage? In other words, who is minding your student at any given time of the day or night?
2. Do the dormitories seem adequate for a good living experience? Is there a common room where kids can congregate? Is the faculty apartment accessible? Is there a laundry room?
3. Does the school have a clearly stated, reasonable disciplinary system? Does it seem educative or punitive? Is there a process that invites students to think about what they may have done wrong? Does the process reflect a balance of openness and discretion so as to protect your child's privacy but also promote a sense of consistency and fair play?
4. Do you like the chain of command in residential life? In other words, who speaks for your child? Who is expected to know your child best? A residential counselor, a college counselor, an academic adviser, a coach, a favorite teacher? Is there more than one faculty member who could be a logical candidate for this role?
5. Does the school offer a variety of healthy experiences for kids when they have time on their hands? Is there a social functions director? Are there events offered that are pure fun? Events that represent good fun and enriching experiences, too?
6. Does the school offer access to the local community? Are there field trips, off-campus experiences?
7. Does the school provide Internet and/or phone access from individual rooms? If not, is there easy access to more than one phone in a common area?
8. Does there seem to be a good layout to the campus? In other words, are there natural places to congregate outside and inside for kids? Are the farthest points still manageable in bad weather?
9. Does the school hold regular all-school meetings, meetings by cluster of dorms, dorm meetings (formal or informal)?
10. Does the school have a cocurricular program that addresses appropriate living in a community? Faculty and/or program in place that supports varied religious observances,

cultural diversity, respect for sexual preference? Is there institutional support for varied political points of view?

Behind these questions, there are some basic expectations:

- Families do not expect Club Med. House counselors and faculty are available, but they are not second-class citizens, nor do you want your child to think so. In order to be good to your child, they need to have a personal life of their own. Otherwise, they will be bad role models for a well-balanced full life. In loco parentis does not mean that they will baby-sit your child anymore than you would. If you want someone to watch your child every waking moment, you have forgotten that fostering intelligent independence in your child is part of nearly every boarding school's educational mission.
- Schools are educating latchkey kids. Residential life is more than just providing room and board. You should expect that your child is making contact beyond formal exchanges with at least one adult *every day*. You might even check to see if the school has some kind of formal life-education curriculum: a life-issues course, required sessions that all students must attend about substance abuse, sensitivity to gender and cultural issues, and/or more general issues of responsible adolescence such as conflict resolution and dorm living.
- Schools and families alike understand that education in community living renews itself because the community changes every year as new students arrive and old students leave. So, both schools and families accept that in order for students to learn about living in a diverse community, they must be allowed to make mistakes.
- Families and schools both understand that the wonders of boarding school life rely heavily on mutual trust and respect. The law is doing its level best to divest schools of all possibility of honest accidents. Read Don Grace's article (see page 000) carefully. The end result of most spurious litigation is a lesser school, not a better school: a school without a wrestling team, an Outward Bound experience, a riding range, a diving board, or a community service program. A school with policies in place to minimize accidents and eradicate any possibility of

negligence is one thing. A school without programs that have some risk is quite another.

Athletic and Extracurricular Life

1. Does the school have a broad range of facilities like tennis courts, basketball courts, places to run, fields for a variety of sports? Are they up-to-date? Is there a fitness center that is open to students and faculty not involved in interscholastic sports programs?
2. Does the athletic department have a physical education program that all students participate in at some level?
3. Does the interscholastic program allow for students to participate all four years? Is there a postgraduate program that makes the upper levels too competitive for students coming up through the teams?
4. Does the school have experienced coaches where they need them?
5. Does the program have a good record placing its best athletes in college sports programs?
6. Does the school offer a wide variety of intramural and specialized programs for students who prefer alternatives to the interscholastic programs? Do those programs feel marginalized? Do the intensive interscholastic programs feel marginalized? Is there a good outdoor program for hiking, camping, climbing, canoeing?
7. Does the school offer decent facilities for major student activities like student publications, political and cultural organizations, drama, photography, dance, choral and orchestral groups?
8. Does the school have active faculty advisers in these organizations who teach students, or just monitor them? (This, too reflects a personal bias.)
9. Does the school have ways to honor nonathletic performance (stages, galleries, publications, fairs, assemblies)?
10. Does the school enjoy some conventional success (trophies, championships, community recognition) in any of their athletic or extracurricular activities?

Behind these questions, there are some basic expectations:

- The school includes physical well-being not only in their education mission, but also in their daily program and practice.
- The school has a good medical facility and/or trainer's facility on campus or close by.
- The facilities allow family and friends to visit campus and support the school and their child in athletic contests.
- Where possible, the school will support students with modest regional and/or national involvement in their sport.
- The school has a healthy mix of coaches who specialize in sports and teacher-coaches who are deeply involved in residential and academic life so as to ensure that the athletic department remains vitally connected to the rest of the school's program.
- The student feels that he or she might have an opportunity to start a club that reflects his/her interests with faculty support, if such an organization does not already exist on campus.

Needless to say, there are many more questions that might come up in your visit to the school. Furthermore, after reading through a school's materials or studying its Web site, you may have some very, very specific questions. As you may have noticed, many of these questions do not have a single right answer. Rather, you are looking for your family's right answer. Ultimately, all of these questions are secondary to the most important one. Does your child like the place? There are all kinds of questions that follow from this one, most of them specific to your child and your family. Will he fit in? Will she fit in too well? Will she feel like a stranger in a strange land? Will he feel like it is a second home?

There are some clues, but choosing an appropriate school is not an exact science. Look at the students on campus during your tour. Do you see kids who look like your child or your child's friends at home? Excepting the strangeness of seeing a new place for the first time, do you feel comfortable walking around the campus? Did your son or daughter feel comfortable during the tour just for students? My own experience is not far from the norm, I think. My son is a good student in the conventional sense.

My daughter is a great student in the conventional sense. Yet, I did not hesitate to send my son to Phillips Academy because I knew that the size and scope of the place would not overwhelm him, his success with the rigorous academic program notwithstanding. However, my daughter is another story altogether. She's now in seventh grade. She has great study habits, does well, is engaged in activities. And she is also very sensitive to setbacks, very dependent on a close circle of friends, something of an at-home child. We're not sure this is the best place for her. It might be too big, the emphasis on speaking up (part of the PA culture) too prevalent. Some days, she wants to apply; some days, she doesn't want to apply. We have lived here all our married lives: twenty years. And still we're thinking about it. I should probably ask these questions.

Craig Thorn is an instructor in English at Phillips Academy, where he has been a house counselor, adviser, administrator, and coach for twenty-one years. In addition to writing and editing books about education, he writes essays about literature and reviews of alternative rock music.

DIVERSITY

E Pluribus Unum: Maximizing the Potential of Cultural Diversity on a Boarding School Campus

Charles Cahn III and Amparo Adib-Samii
Suffield Academy

Cultural diversity is a distinctive feature of the boarding school's overall educational mission. Yes, you just read that. Student populations are no longer culturally homogenous. Because a boarding school community tends to be small and intense, schools must address issues of integration and difference. There are 110,000 schools in this country—25,000 schools are private, while 1,500 are independent (unaffiliated with any church or other such entity). It is this independent 1.4 percent of the total pie about which we are writing. There are, for example, 12,000 international students enrolled in independent school, most of whom attend boarding school. Yet the cultural backgrounds in our schools are much broader than our students from overseas alone reflect. In addition to students from abroad, American students come from a wide range of ethnic and religious backgrounds to a school like Suffield, which is home each year to only 390 students. It is fair to say that the old "blue blood prep school" is a thing of the past, a dying myth.

Located in a beautiful, historic New England town populated largely by upper-middle-class white families, our school's enrollment is a microcosm of many boarding schools: 25 percent non-white; 17 percent from overseas; 36 percent receive financial aid. Earlier than many other independent schools, Suffield had a small, but important, international presence on its campus. Beginning in the 1960s, we attracted students from Venezuela, Africa, Iran, and Japan. From the mid-1970s until the mid-1980s, there was a gradual increase in the number of international students at Suffield. In recent years we have leveled off with about 14 percent of our students coming from eighteen different countries. Given this reality, Suffield has asked how to best capitalize on the rich cultural diversity that exists on our campus. Clearly, putting a diverse group of students in the same classroom is not, in and of itself, a celebration of cultural identities. It is but a means to an end, far from an antidote for creating an intellectually charged, exciting classroom. A central philosophical tenet here has been the intentional integration of all students into the structure and culture of the campus. Our goal has been to prepare all students to become comfortable and successful citizens of the Suffield community. What we have found is that an essential component in celebrating the rich cultural diversity on our campus is to emphasize our shared traits and common values and goals. In a sense, the parameters of our approach to maximizing the impact of an array of cultural diversity are similar to what Arthur Powell writes in *Lessons From Privilege: The American Prep School Tradition*: "Economic, racial, gender and other differences (in independent schools) are muted by what everyone has more predominantly in common: high family and school educational expectations and enough student capacity and willingness to do college preparatory academic work. The triumph of the contemporary generic or standard independent school is its capacity to attract enough families recognized as "diverse" who nonetheless share general educational values."[1] As Powell notes, though our students are culturally diverse, their motivation for seeking a private school education is often quite similar.

This fundamental premise—that we will celebrate differing cultural backgrounds while simultaneously emphasizing our commonalities and connections—permeates our approach to capitalizing on the potential for learning that rich cultural diversity presents. At our family-style, community lunch, we remember a Senegalese student standing for an announcement (amidst comments about weekend activity offerings, evening plans, and other business of the school). "What a nice meal this has been," he started. "I have been thinking today about the fact that in my home, meals like this are not the usual—we are lucky, and we should appreciate that we have such plentiful food. Let's give thanks." The dining room was silent. This student, loved by all, had us stop, think, and appreciate our good fortune. There was no assembly or splintered group discussion. His comments came within the context of an all-school, community gathering (lunch). In a sense, this exemplifies how we celebrate cultural diversity at Suffield.

We do not sponsor a series of groups representing specific cultural perspectives—for example there is no Asian students association, or Muslim group meeting. Rather, we have a broader International Students Association, a Multicultural Students Association, and an Interfaith Discussion Group. There are of course exceptions, and specific faith-related celebrations (like a Passover Seder for our Jewish students), but a fundamental part of our plan for best capitalizing on our various cultural backgrounds has been an emphasis on inclusiveness. This, we believe, has served our school and our students quite well. Moreover, the specific clubs and positions we do have serve a tangible purpose. The international student adviser, for example, has responsibility for addressing student visa issues, travel schedules, problem solving, integration into school life, relationships with parents, and points of intersection with the school and staff. There is a clear purpose and mandate.

The case we're making is that while a celebration of our diverse cultural backgrounds in boarding schools is a priority (that inquiries into different ethnicities and backgrounds are an important part of our school culture), it is under the umbrella of fundamental, shared core values relating to how we will live together in a residential school community, and to the importance of intellectual pursuit. The celebration, which is genuine, comes within a larger framework about the nature and values of the school.

We encourage all students to celebrate their cultural identity while at the same time asking them to be members of this family. A symbol of this approach is a dinner we have each spring, featuring food from all of the countries represented at Suffield Academy. It is a highlight of the year at the school. It is a community celebration, and every student takes something important away from the event, especially great food. Parents fly thousands of miles to help their son or daughter prepare an exotic dish. It may seem unimportant, but it's not. What this evening symbolizes is our overarching approach to celebrating cultural diversity: eradicating distinctions in the context of personal relations, and celebrating differences in the context of togetherness. We celebrate cultural backgrounds at Suffield by making it an inclusive community for all, and by celebrating our shared priorities (whether they are good schools or good food).

Charles Cahn III is the associate headmaster of Suffield Academy and **Amparo Adib-Samii** is the coordinator of the international students program at Suffield Academy.

Where Do Role Models Come From? How Do You Support Them? How Do Programs and People Make a Changing Community Thrive?

Charlotte Knowles
St. Timothy's School

How has a small all-girls' boarding school met the needs of an increasingly diverse student body? Where have our students gone to find role models and how have they benefited from the diversity of the ethnic and cultural backgrounds of our faculty and staff? These people have served as role models in very important ways for the many students from other backgrounds. Here are a few of their stories.

Maggie Cho is a first-year biology teacher, dorm parent, and cross-country coach. As an Asian American, Maggie feels an immediate bond with the students whose cultural background mirrors her own. She has been able to help the Asian-American students sort out the conflicting traditional expectations of their Asian parents and the more liberal expectations of American youth. Janet Cho, a senior at St. Tim's, explained that her parents only wanted her to apply to Ivy League colleges. They did not approve of any of her college choices. The most important thing to Janet's parents was her education. They had uprooted their family from Korea solely for the sake of their children's education. Janet felt like only another Asian American would understand this type of parental pressure. Maggie helped Janet to understand her parents' fears and expectations. She even offered to call Janet's parents to help them understand the pressure their daughter felt.

Renee Hawkins is our English-as-a-foreign-language teacher. She has served as a role model for the Asian international students. Although she is not Asian, she lived in Japan for five years. Her experience and knowledge of Asian traditions and expectations enable her to support and comfort these young girls in their first experience in American living. Aileen Suh, one of our international students from Korea, described a cultural miscommunication that Ms. Hawkins helped resolve. Aileen explained that when she first arrived she thought it was rude to refuse someone anything. She was unhappy because people were borrowing her things, but she had told them they could. In her country she would never ask to borrow things from a friend. Ms. Hawkins helped Aileen learn that it was okay to say "no."

Neha Vapiwala teaches science and math and lives in the dorm. Priya Bhandula is a sophomore now living in Turkey, but she is originally from India. There are aspects of American culture that made her uncomfortable. She felt Neha would intuitively understand her feelings. Although from different regions of India, Neha could understand how Priya would feel uncomfortable wearing tank tops and short shorts. Priya does not wear traditional Indian dress, but her cultural customs have instilled in her a more conservative approach to clothes. Wearing tank tops is not a huge issue for Priya, but it's a small thing that she felt only Ms. Vapiwala would understand.

Leroy Levi is a professional tennis player and he coaches our tennis team in the fall. Leroy's passion for tennis and his warm charismatic personality are the main reasons our girls go out for the tennis team. He also knows that his African-American background has helped some of the African-American students realize they can play the sport too. Levi likes seeing the black students learn how to play tennis because "it's an opportunity for networking and socializing. Tennis is a life sport and it puts people from different backgrounds in the same social arena." Nearly half of the African-American students at St. Tim's play on the tennis team. Levi has been an instrumental role model in opening the doors of tennis to our African-American students.

Sometimes the students' desire for leadership helps the school to appreciate the value of role models. Four years ago the African-American students started a Black Awareness Club (BAC). They have talked to the head of school about their desire to have a more diverse faculty, especially an African-American full-time faculty member. They understand she is trying and the task is not so easy. The BAC has worked hard in expanding their membership to all cultures and ethnic groups. They struggle with philosophy behind a club focused solely on issues concerning African Americans. They want to be inclusive of all minorities, yet at the same time the African Americans represent the largest minority group in the school, and they do not want to dilute their focus. The BAC has searched hard for role models too. On Martin Luther King Day, the Black Awareness Club arranged for one of our African-American board members to speak to the student body about stereotypes and diversity. For this event they looked beyond the faculty of the school for their role model.

Some of the Jewish students at St. Tim's have struggled with the Episcopalian school's required attendance at chapel once a week. Every student knows when they enroll that St. Tim's is Episcopalian and chapel is required; however, those students who lived in Jewish neighborhoods and had predominantly Jewish friends did not realize how difficult the twenty-minute requirement would be. They turned to the Jewish teachers for support. The students felt empowered by these adults who listened and understood, and students and teachers worked together to find solutions.

During Passover they organized a chapel service that explained the traditions and meaning of Passover. With the support and advice from her teachers, one student had her rabbi talk to all the students about the history of Judaism and its fundamental principles and philosophy. To complement the activities in chapel, Ellen Glassner, a Jewish teacher who teaches Spanish, had a seder and invited Jewish and non-Jewish students who were interested in participating. During Passover our dining service supplied matzos at every meal. This conflict brought the Jewish teacher/student population closer together and it also enabled non-Jewish people to understand more about Judaism.

These are just a few snapshots of how role modeling has occurred at one boarding school campus. All schools struggle with diversity on their faculty and staff and like many St. Tim's is doing a good job, but has a long way to go. Faculty role models can often help students as they work through difficult moments, and as students work through those moments they themselves often show us how to be better role models.

Charlotte Knowles was a graduate of St. Timothy's '86, a faculty member, and presently serves on the 2002–2003 board of governors as Charlotte Knowles Higgins.

COMMUNITY VALUES

What Is the Culture of a Boarding School?

Ted Lutkus
Westtown School

Most years, the swallows return to Westtown on Shakespeare's birthday in April. Some years they come a few days early, some years they come a few days late. But for the last two hundred years that there has been a big red building on this hilltop in

Pennsylvania, the swallows have come here in the spring, stayed for the summer, and then return to Brazil in the fall. During the day the swallows are out gliding in tight circles, catching insects. I notice them the most after dinner, between 6:30 and 8:00 when there is free time before study hall. Boarding schools are busy places and even though there are meetings of different committees or rehearsals going on, after dinner seems to me a more relaxed time. A time to look up and notice the chimney swallows.

The present building is an eighth of a mile long with one hundred and one chimneys in which the swallows make nests, a kind of swallow development complex. It can be rather daunting to see this old red building which has been here so long. I think it strikes people the most when they see it for the first time. During the summer when I first arrived as a new teacher I felt the history of the place by just entering the door. When the students came for orientation the building seemed to awaken; their faces, and all their stories—these are what makes up a living community. Coming into a community each person brings their ideas, their viewpoint, and their voice. They all comprise the collective vision, a collective culture that is the true essence of community—of boarding schools.

Every school creates its culture. It is one of the beauties of being in an independent school. Faculty and students live and work together in boarding schools and are able to define how they want to live together. What is important? What is not important? What values do we uphold as a community and then how do we govern ourselves to uphold these values? When students and faculty are coming from so many different backgrounds and places the conversation becomes that much more rich.

Some of the school culture is written down in handbooks. Some culture is written in brochures. Pictures and words try to capture important elements of the school. Often an included mission statement speaks to the values of the school. Schedules, courses of study, and school expectations of behavior all strive to reinforce these ideals. Most of the culture of a school, however, constantly defines itself through everyday practice—that part of the education that is hard to capture in admissions brochures. You become part of a community's creation by participating in the daily life of the school, thereby creating a common vision. Students and faculty share a responsibility to that vision and it is a unifying force.

For each school there are certain "nonnegotiables." Strong schools are able to set boundaries which hold true to their mission statements. Many nonnegotiables reflect concern for health and safety. These lines drawn in the sand often carry strong consequences if broken. For instance, at Westtown, if a student lights a flame in a school building he is automatically dismissed. A second drug or alcohol offense results in dismissal. Fighting will most likely lead to dismissal from the school.

When parents and students come to a school they are accepting these non-negotiables. Faculty and students live and work together in boarding schools and are able to define how they want to live together. Boundaries protect the community and uphold core values. To truly be partners with the school, families need to be knowledgeable and supportive of these values before coming to the school.

There is also an incredible opportunity for diversity within the framework of common core values. Ideally no one gives up themselves or their family traditions, but is exposed to other people's outlooks on life. The diversity of religions, ideas, practices, and values gives strength of each and every boarding school. Students and faculty are exposed to difference. It is a little like going to another country, experiencing different things. You see basic assumptions that you make about your life being challenged. When you return home, you reexamine what you have previously taken for granted and develop a new perspective.

Parents sometimes ask me for the best advice they should give their child going off to boarding school. My answer is simple. Try things—reach out. Get to know people. Do something new. If you have never been on stage, try being in a one-act play. If you have never played field hockey, try it. If you have never lived with someone from a different country, do it. New perspectives raise consciousness. Hopefully, they offer a wider view of the world and people. Encouraging your child to broaden his or her experience is what boarding school is all about.

I recently took a group of students to a Thai restaurant on a Friday night. Two girls from Thailand were eager to go so we had a sign-up for anyone who wanted to join us. Twelve students signed up and we piled into a van and went to a local restaurant. On the way over, the discussion turned to languages and different phrases used in languages. It was not until we were in the van for a while that I realized that there was one American student and the rest of the students came from seven different countries. At the restaurant, the Thai students recommended dishes to order. People described different foods that they typically have for dinner in their homes. On the way back we spoke about Westtown's tobacco policy—a four-step series of consequences and education, with the fourth step being dismissal. It was interesting to hear students talk about how cigarette smoking is viewed in their cultures. In some students' homes smoking was a common activity. For others, it tore at their family's values. Pros and cons were weighed. The differences were many. Because of these differences each of the students now view Westtown's tobacco policy from a slightly different angle.

The swallows come as a group from Brazil each year. One Westtown student comes from Brazil, the rest come from other parts of the world. The swallows and the students come to the same place. The swallows bring their songs and their flight, and students bring their culture, heritage, and traditions. They bring these to a place that has its own culture, its own heritage, its own tradition. In this mix of experience is knit together a community called Westtown School.

Ted Lutkus is chair of the science department at Westtown School.

The Religious Boarding School

The Reverend Patrick Gahan
St. Stephen's Episcopal School

I would have scoffed at the suggestion that I was "religious" during my boarding school years. I can only remember effectively praying before basketball games, trigonometry tests, and dateless Saturday nights. But the special grace I received as a four-year boarding student at a religious school was that I was not quarantined from the spiritual world. What's more, I was spared empty notions of a god who was fashioned like a kindly great-uncle, some syrupy sweet Sunday school invention implausible to my questioning adolescent mind.

I remember our daily retreat into that musty, stuccoed chapel whose landscape was dominated by the yellowing, wood-hewed, life-sized crucifix centered on the north wall. Elizabethan English mingled with medieval Latin, incense burned so thick the altar appeared to be floating, and the chilling, crisp ring of the sanctus bells reverberated through our ears disturbing our adolescent resistance. The god inhabiting that chapel bore little resemblance to the one I had encountered in Sunday school. This was a serious God, a Holy God. I learned that He was a "jealous God," a "consuming fire," and that He wanted all or nothing, and that the yellowing tormented Christ was testimony to just how serious God was. This was told to me by men and women who, for no rational reason, taught, pushed, chided, coached, nudged, and urged me and a host of other hapless boys through our secondary education as if we had some intrinsic worth.

Those boarding schools which take their religious foundation and life seriously are places of inexhaustible grace. The students who matriculate in these schools bask in an unconditional love that frees them to be themselves truly, to create, to seek, to delve deeply beneath the surface of human existence. They are places standing in opposition to the sterile materialism of this age, where students and faculty are free to worship and seek those things that far outlast concrete.

The heart of a boarding school serious about religion is the freedom it offers its community to worship and to seek that which is the source of our deepest yearnings. The soul of such schools is the confidence it maintains that all people have great value and much to be discovered and given. At their best, the two boarding schools I have served realize that you are not just a vessel to be filled. They have dared to believe that the inventors, the explorers, the actors, the politicians, the judges, the missionaries are not just people caught between the prefaces and indexes of a book; they are the students they serve. These schools have had the courage to maintain that the culmination of your time with them is more than credits on a transcript, more than numbers on the SAT, more than "4s and 5s" on AP exams, more than the collected letters of acceptance to East Coast colleges.

Certainly these boarding schools appreciate the importance of standardized testing, college acceptance, and career planning, but they recognize that those things represent the surface of life, not its substance. These schools have a wide range of religious expression, but seem uniform in the belief that a life truly lived means more than a ribbon on a diploma, an invitation to attend the most prestigious college, or an offer to join the best firm. These schools maintain that to live truly is to go beneath the surface of things where our most urgent questions rumble. Why are there black holes? What makes a family? Who is my neighbor? Why do we dream? Who made the rainforests? Who made racism? Is there hope for the world? What is faith? Is there anything worth dying for?

While the course descriptions for religion classes at the many boarding schools in this country vary considerably, students at these schools will be pulled beneath the surface of their existence to wrestle these questions and the throng of questions like them. They have the courage to let you grapple well beneath the superficial and seek the most important mystery, "God." This is not some airy movement, some flight of fancy harboring a disregard of the facts. To seek God is to face the hardest facts of this life. These schools aren't trying to convert you, or equate God with a divine menu of morals and values, as if He were some celestial fax machine.

The paths most students in boarding school will forge are exhilarating treks connecting God to flesh and blood. You will follow Abraham on his journey from one end of the Fertile Crescent to another, and follow Mother Teresa along Calcutta's endless streets. You will sit with Paul and Peter in prison, and Buddha under the Bo tree. You will glean the pragmatic leadership argument of the Tao Te Ching and consider the radical contentions of the Beatitudes. And you will see that while the path to God led Joshua to the land of promise, that same path led Dietrich Bonhoeffer to Hitler's gallows. You will discover that to consider Dr. Martin Luther King's painful pilgrimage apart from those hard roads walked by Moses, Gandhi, Amos, and Jesus is empty fantasy. You will travel along the powerfully symbolic road from one garden in Eden to another in Gethsemane. Along the way, you will likely see your own worldview greatly challenged and altered toward the high ground of service to God and humanity.

George Carey, the present archbishop of Canterbury, laments that we in the West have fragmented human life to an "unattractive gray materialism." We have relegated our existence to a colorless, hopeless single dimension. Carey states, "No longer dwarfed by questions about the transcendent, no longer thrilled by the wonder of creation, we have settled for a life that is basically functional and materialistic." The archbishop urges us to look courageously again at the three questions Immanuel Kant put to the eighteenth-century world in his *Critique of Pure Reason:* "What can I know? What ought I do? What may I hope for?" Those are the three questions that are the essential landmarks on the road provided by religious studies departments of many of our boarding schools. It is the high road for those students who take it.

The Reverend Patrick Gahan was the executive director of the Society for the Promotion of Christian Knowledge, an international organization. He also served as senior chaplain at St. Stephen's Episcopal School in Austin, Texas, and as director of development at St. Andrew's-Sewanee School.

CONTACT

Contact from the Mothership

Peter Durnan
Holderness School

"Mr. Durnan, I am so sorry to be bothering you at home. It's Claire Mc-Manus, Molly's mother. We met at the game on Saturday. I apologize, I simply didn't know who to call."

"That's OK. And please, call me Peter. Is everything all right?"

"Well . . . no. In the three weeks that she's been at school Molly has managed to find herself a boyfriend and have a breakup. She's left me a frantic message and now I can't reach her. I . . . really, I wasn't sure who to call."

This is an approximation of the beginning of a conversation I had with a parent last year. The family was new to boarding schools. Dropping off her daughter, Mom had met dorm parents and advisers, but in this moment of panic the only number she could find for the school was the main switchboard, nothing more than a message center after working hours. She remembered my name from a JV girls' soccer game where we had met a couple of days before this trauma and was able to track me down by calling information.

This isn't a particularly unusual situation. Even as the means available to parents to contact their children and the residential schools they attend have proliferated, parents continue to struggle to keep up with the lives of their kids once they've left for school. By all appearances, keeping up should be quite easy: parents return home from orientation flush with assurances, names, and numbers of deans and teachers and counselors. The campus, they have found, is equipped with cutting-edge technology and staffed by thoughtful, personable professionals. Nonetheless, parents often find their first attempts to contact the school frustrating. They play phone tag with dorm parents and leave hopeful but echoing e-mails for teachers.

There are no simple solutions to this problem. It helps to get to know the school's receptionist; invariably this person knows the ins and outs of the school better than the headmaster does. Dealing with faculty and staff, parents need to be flexible and sensitive. Like most teachers, I communicate academic information best through e-mail. The time delay allows me to read and digest at leisure, to compose replies with an eloquence and correctness that escapes me on the phone. I'm not caught off guard on e-mail. Parents, I know, are desperate for news of their child's academic development. But what if they could only see me in my classroom answering their questions, phone cradled under my jaw as I claw vainly for the grade book I realize I've left at home, frantically checking my watch to see how many minutes I have before the team bus is scheduled to leave for Exeter? Is this really the moment they were hoping for when they sought news of their daughter's work in sophomore English? For the love of God, drop me an e-mail, I think, as I peel myself from the phone in such instances. Give me the time to make sense of my grade book and the behavior I've seen from this kid in the past couple of weeks. I promise to be as concrete and specific as I ask her to be on her weekly essays.

Surely there are moments when parents confront situations that are immediate, pressing, and even frightening. Imagine receiving the horrifyingly elliptical messages that high school kids are so adept at leaving on their parents' home phone machines: "Mom and Dad, I got a little concussion in the lacrosse game today, but I made a big hit. And we won. Talk to you Sunday." This is the sort of message that leaves parents reeling, the sort of message that necessitates the immediate contact of a call to the adviser or dorm parent. All parents need a reliable connection with the school, the home number of an adult who knows them and their child and can act quickly. This is the single phone number that should be posted by the phone at each parent's home, and the relationship between parent and dorm parent should be cultivated with respect (a little humor goes a long way, too).

Initially, at least, this can be an awkward connection to make. Often calls to a dorm parent come in the early morning or late night. Parents of my advisees have come to expect the screams and banter of my daughters in the background of our conversations; for less pressing matters they simply ask for a quick call back. At times, though, there is no waiting, and I shush my girls and address things as best as I am able. These are human moments, often painful ones, but they are parents and I am a teacher because we care enough to take these moments with the seriousness they merit. Such was the case when I talked with Molly's mother, a parent I have come to know well and like immensely. And our friendship began with that simple needed call:

"Mrs. McManus, did you try Martha Baker? She's Molly's adviser, she lives right there with her in the Yellow House."

"Of course, that's it. I just couldn't find the right piece of paper. Do you have her number? I'll give her a call right now. I'm so sorry to have bothered you."

"No trouble, really. Actually, I was just heading over that way. I'll drop in on Molly and see how she's doing, and I'll stop by Martha's place, too. She'll call you within the hour. I know she'll want to talk to you about all of this."

"Could you do that? Thanks so much."
"Really, I'm glad to do it. I'm glad you called."

And I was.

Peter Durnan is the English department chairman at Holderness School where he teaches, coaches, and lives with his family in a dorm.

A Chorus of Guiding Voices

Jill Pate
Darlington School

As the director of personal counseling, I represent only a small portion of the services available at Darlington for the support of our students. I share a variety of responsibilities with the dean of college guidance, twelve college advisers, fifty-eight faculty advisers, and six heads of house. Collectively, we hope to inspire our students to take advantage of their God-given gifts and work to nurture them in the six areas of personal growth defined by our mission: intellectual, spiritual, physical, social, moral, and cultural. My principle responsibilities are to be proactive toward this end and to be available to respond to the occasional emotional crisis in an individual or the institution.

Sam Moss, our dean of college guidance, is an icon in the field of college admissions. Sam is well known and respected by his peers in the Southern Association for College Admissions Counseling and the National Association for College Admissions Counseling. Recently, Sam was named the first recipient of SACAC's Larry West Distinguished Service Award. Sam has held offices in both of these distinguished organizations and is currently serving on the National Merit Scholarship Selection Committee. Sam brings a wealth of knowledge, wisdom, and experience to what he does.

Under Sam's expert guidance our twelve college advisers start working with students in the spring of their junior year. Students are allowed to express a preference for which college adviser they wish to work with. During the junior year, college advisers assist their group of advisees in preparing a list of suitable colleges based on interests, ability, and ambition. They help students in their senior year narrow their college choices, complete applications, and are responsible for writing the school recommendations. In a nutshell, our college advisers become the experts on the students while Sam remains the expert on the colleges.

In addition to the twelve faculty members and administrators who serve as college advisers, all of Darlington's faculty serve as faculty advisers to our approximately four hundred and fifty Upper School students. Each faculty member has five to ten students in an advisee group. Advisee groups meet formally on a monthly basis, but also informally for social activities such as eating out or going to a movie. Faculty advisers also meet individually with advisees and are in frequent contact with parents via the student's confidential Web page.

The role of the adviser is to become actively involved in the lives of advisees and monitor each one's growth, development, and well-being while at Darlington. To this end, our students are asked to establish year-long goals for their intellectual, spiritual, moral, physical, cultural, and social growth. These goals are committed to writing in September and serve as a tool for advisers to get to know their advisees and support their success at Darlington. Ideally, the adviser/advisee relationship is one of mutual respect, friendship, and admiration that will last throughout the student's career at Darlington, and in some cases, the years beyond.

Life at Darlington is organized around the English house system, a system that is unique, so far as I know, among American boarding schools. We have six houses, three each for girls and boys, which include both day and resident students. Houses are run by a head of house whose primary responsibility is the welfare of the students in that house. heads of house do not coach or teach; however, they serve in the admissions office and largely control admissions to their respective houses. Each house consists of approximately thirty residential students and forty to forty-five day students ranging from ninth to twelfth grade. Twelve upperclassmen serve as prefect leaders in each of the houses. Prefect positions correspond roughly to the six areas of personal growth already discussed, and prefects are selected after a thorough application and interview process. They manage the life in the houses and also sit with the heads of house on the house Senate where they help to shape the rules by which everyone at Darlington lives. In addition, our entire faculty is assigned to a house, and many faculty live in their respective houses or on campus in one of the faculty homes.

The house system provides a nurturing home-like atmosphere for students. It has changed the face of what I, as the personal counselor, do at Darlington. Because of the close relationships that are developed within each house, many concerns and/or problems are identified and addressed prior to becoming major obstacles for students. Heads of house and advisers are often in daily contact with parents through Darlington's Web page. Advisers and teachers can post daily grades, assignments, deportment reports, and comments on the student's confidential Web page. In turn, parents are able to access their student's Web page at any time and e-mail faculty directly.

As the personal counselor, I am privileged to interact with our students on a variety of different levels. I help to coordinate tutorial services and extended-time testing for students with needs in these areas. I oversee the student support team, a confidential referral and support service for students struggling with alcohol, drug, and/or eating disorder issues. I enjoy working with our parent association and facilitating a parent-to-parent program. Most of all, I am available to students on a daily basis for support through the normal adjustment issues of adolescence. I maintain an open-door policy with students, which I hope makes them feel comfortable and welcome at any time. Students often come by my office just to relax and visit, or at other times to discuss such things as relationships, family, stress, extracurricular activities, and other day-to-day occurrences in their lives. Of course, there are times when we have to deal with more difficult issues such as depression, anxiety, grief, and crisis intervention.

We are a family at Darlington, and we all share some part in counseling our students. Whether it is for college admissions, academics, life away from home, or just life in general, our goal is to nurture and support each student. We want to ensure that every boy and girl who attends Darlington is challenged to live an examined life, conscious of their obligations to themselves and to others. We strive to graduate students who exemplify our School's motto: Wisdom more than Knowledge; Service beyond Self; Honor above Everything.

Jill Pate, director of personal counseling, has worked with adolescents for almost twenty years. She is a graduate of the University of Denver and Presbyterian/St. Luke's Medical Center. She is a certified mental-health nurse with extensive experience in adolescent drug and alcohol rehab, as well as, teenage depression and suicide.

Boundaries

John C. Lin
The Fessenden School

I worked at a school early in my teaching career where there raged a debate as to whether or not faculty should be friends with students. Ridiculous, I thought. Of course we should be friends with our students. Why wouldn't we want to reciprocate the offer of friendship from our students? After all, wouldn't it be better if my students actually knew me and liked me as a person rather than merely someone who taught and graded them? Wouldn't that make teaching them easier and more rewarding? Wouldn't my effectiveness as their mentor be enhanced? Wouldn't I enjoy the experience of teaching, coaching, house parenting, and advising more?

Even the headmaster knew enough about the situation to declare that teenagers craved the attention of adults, despite any sign they might make to the contrary. As a young, naive, single, male English teacher I was all too ready to meet this need head on, to invest myself completely in the business that seemed to be at the heart of boarding schools especially. And as I launched myself blindly into the work, how could I anticipate that some twenty years later, I would be writing this article having come full circle, enlightened enough to know just how young and how naive I actually was then.

This is not to say that in the intervening time I have become aloof and distant from my students or believe now that they should not know me beyond the classroom. On the contrary, in this time, I have refined what I powerfully felt into a more thoughtful, measured, and reasoned approach to student-faculty relationships. To be sure, the years have widened the gap between my students and me, especially now that I have moved to teaching middle schoolers, but what I have learned is how to be an adult, *the* adult, in the lives of young people who might need the boundary setting and structure that only an adult can give. Previously, I had focused on the nurture part of my relationship with students and failed many times to set appropriate boundaries for them, partly because I was still too young and inexperienced to know how to do this for myself. Now, as a parent in his middle years, I have come to know with acute sensitivity just what balance of structure and nurture is needed to be an effective parent. And this learning has made all the difference in my teaching.

When Chris walked into my apartment to check in that Saturday night some twenty years ago, I could tell that he wasn't quite right. When I sidled up to him at the sign-in sheet on my dining room table, I immediately noticed a hint of alcohol on him. Faint, but nonetheless indisputable. I engaged him in some small talk in order to improvise some response. Why didn't I know what to do immediately? Had I not been trained to respond to situations like this? Had I not read the faculty handbook? The student handbook? Had I not recently sat through a new faculty orientation that discussed what to do in just these circumstances? Well, whatever formal training I had, I could not bring it to bear on this case before me. As I chatted with Chris, now eager to go to his room to crash, I became aware that the other students in my apartment, as they made their way to sign in and checkout, had some inkling that something was up. This could have been my first bust as a faculty member. If I had turned Chris in, called another faculty member to corroborate my suspicions, and actually turned him in to the administrator on duty that night, I would have busted my first student and one of my advisees.

The next day, after a fitful night, I went to Chris's room after brunch. He was still in bed. I walked in and sat down at his desk as he awoke. I simply asked him if he knew why I was there. He nodded, and I must have told him never to do that again, or never to put me in that situation again, and with that, I left his room. We never talked about that situation again, and though he never got into any formal trouble in his remaining time at the school, I could never claim that my "intervention" had anything to do with that. For all I know, he never signed in again without brushing his teeth and washing his mouth out with plenty of Scope, or chewing some strongly scented Teaberry gum or chomping on an Atomic fireball or swallowing a dollop of peanut butter. We never became very close, and in fact, he may have switched to another adviser before he graduated.

In retrospect, what I think kept me from doing the right thing in that moment was a fear of alienating Chris, my advisee, and then not having the relationship with him that I thought we should have. In the process, I probably made it into the annals of the school's popular culture for chickening out and being a pushover, for enabling major rule violations and being a hypocrite. How did I know that when I would bust my first victim, this case that I had almost put behind me would be brought back in a powerful outburst that rendered me speechless and defenseless. "How can you bust me when you let Chris go? You're so unfair. You're such a hypocrite!" I think that I had to lie and deny that I knew anything about my advisee being drunk on Saturday night a month ago. After all, who was going to believe a student who was actually caught for drinking over a faculty member of the school?

I had crossed a big boundary and didn't even know it.

Boundaries are crossed for many reasons and many of them can seem like rationalization because they are. Often these boundaries are negotiable because the adults involved have not clearly set their own personal boundaries. Often some aspect of the student-faculty relationship serves only the faculty member, some hidden, blind need that needs to be fulfilled. The most egregious cases have led to firings, arrests, personal and institutional humiliation and embarrassment. Often, not only are individual faculty members at fault, but the school, which usually has known about the situation, is also implicated. How can this happen? Given a strong culture of politeness and an aversion to conflict within our schools, it should not be that surprising that there is a high level of enabling behaviors present in schools. Without formal and meaningful evaluation processes in place and administrators trained to do the hard work of setting boundaries for colleagues, a school is vulnerable to boundary crossings at many levels. Though clearly individuals must regulate themselves in the end, a school must be very direct and act decisively whenever improprieties are uncovered, and, I would say, even sensed.

At a recent faculty meeting, the school's consulting psychiatrist asked the faculty to take a short test, devised by the dean of faculty, to take the group's temperature around issues related to boundaries. Is it okay to take a student out to lunch off campus? How about dinner? How about at your house? If you are single? Married? How about a group of students? Is it okay to hug a student? A student of the opposite gender? An elementary student? A high school student? Is it okay to accept a gift from a student's family? How about if the gift is worth over $100.00? If you are the student's current teacher or coach? Does it depend on what kind of student we're talking about? The faculty pored over several pages of such questions, and in a follow-up session, we had the opportunity to review our collective answers. What emerged, more importantly than a "right" answer to any question, was a sense of the group's norms. If the majority of faculty rated it un acceptable to take a student out to dinner on your own and you rated it okay, then this should serve as a clear indication that your personal boundaries are out of line with that of the school and perhaps you should stop and rethink your position. There may never be an articulation of the rules to cover all possible boundary crossings, but these occasional and salubrious community check-ins could provide much needed feedback to individuals about their behavior set against the norm of the whole group and the school.

Jon Lin has taught at Taft and Andover, and was the dean of students at the Thacher School where he taught English, coached tennis and baseball, and rode horses. He now is head of the Upper School at Fessenden.

Parents, Boarding Schools, and Students:
Time to Lay Down the Law

Don Grace
Chapel Hill-Chauncy Hall

Author's Disclaimers:

I sent my two children to boarding school, and they grew through the challenges of that experience. I have headed independent schools for twenty years, including Chapel Hill-Chauncy Hall School (a boarding/day school in Waltham, Massachusetts) for the last five years. Two of my three brothers are lawyers.

I have tremendous respect for the law as a potential source of good in our society and in the world. At the same time, I worry about how litigious our society has become and how frequently involving lawyers in a dispute results in no clear winners—other than the lawyers.

These experiences and viewpoints have not shaped the following essay in any way, except to provide the whole basis for what I am about to write.

Whitney Tyler, the dean of students for Robertson Academy, was certain of one thing: Mr. Bernie Parent, the father of Angel Parent, would be calling back soon. Whitney had just left a message on Mr. Parent's personal voicemail to indicate that Angel had violated the academy's disciplinary probation by riding off-campus in a car with a few other students and engaging in smoking pot at a favorite student hangout. Angel was already on probation for similar violations of the academy's driving and drug/alcohol regulations, and this latest incident would mean possible expulsion.

Whitney was far less certain about Mr. Parent's response. Two years ago, Mrs. Parent had arrived with Angel for student registration, and they fidgeted through the process together. It was Angel's first time away from home and first time in an independent school, and both parent and child preferred asking questions of school officials to imparting any information about Angel or the family. Unfortunately, Mrs. Parent had a pressing work commitment that prevented her from attending the new-parent orientation that day, and Mr. Parent was away on an important business trip. Mr. Parent called in later that week to introduce himself to Whitney, and they had a lengthy phone conversation, filled with questions like those Mrs. Parent and Angel asked. Apparently, the registration and orientation process had left the parents with some ongoing concerns about how Angel might fit in to this new environment. Whitney ended by reminding Mr. Parent that Angel's adviser, Carol Diligent, was the primary resource for their child's adjustment to the academy.

In the two years since that day, Whitney had had only occasional contact with Angel and with Mr. and Mrs. Parent. Angel had done reasonably well academically, though final grades were not as high as they had been in Angel's public school. Angel's quick wit and fertile imagination had impressed the Academy teachers. At the same time, Angel's writing did not display that spirit and creativity, and some grades reflected the variance. On the social side, Angel struggled to connect with grade-level classmates, in part because of the differences in social experiences, attitudes, and ways of expression and dress (Angel was a bit more sophisticated than classmates in these arenas). Angel connected more readily to students a year older, particularly in activities outside the classroom. By the second year, Angel was firmly embedded in that older group. That led to some problems with the school's rules. At first, the violations were minor enough: lateness and an occasional absence from class, clothes outside the dress code, lights on later at night than the time for lights out in the dorm. By year two, however, those violations had grown to more serious levels: a pattern of class absences, riding off-campus without permission, and finally, a pot smoking incident that left Angel on a probation that did not allow for further violations connected to driving and to drug/alcohol consumption.

Whitney had supervised the discipline committee process that led to putting Angel on probation, and that involved a lot of contact with the Parents. They had mixed emotions about the violations. While they voiced support for the school's rules, they were also critical of how restrictive those rules were generally, and how unreasonable some of the rules were that applied to Angel's violations. Both Mr. and Mrs. Parent called Whitney to voice concerns about the disciplinary process before, during, and after that process. Whitney noticed that questions continued to be the preferred mode of communication for both Parents. After Whitney communicated the final decision to Mr. and Mrs. Parent, they appealed to the head of school, David Solomon, for a different decision. Mr. Solomon, after consulting with Whitney, turned down the Parents' appeal.

With this latest violation, Whitney needed to set up a disciplinary process that might lead to expulsion. Whitney had already met with Angel and Carol Diligent, to confirm the chain of events and to inform Angel that this violation was a serious one. Whitney's phone rang. It was Mr. Parent on the line. . . .

Scenarios involving possible expulsions or major violations occur several times a year in a boarding school. Neither the frequency of violations nor the frequency of school responses seems to have changed much over the twenty years since I first started heading schools. What *has* changed is the nature of parent responses, particularly as connected with the law. In comparison with twenty years ago, parents are more likely to have one or more of the following responses when they contact Dean Tyler:

- "Angel is innocent, and I believe my kid. Angel never lies to us as parents."
- "This is going to eliminate Angel's chances of getting into Price University."
- "Angel was not able to confront student witnesses. You have not proved Angel's guilt beyond a reasonable doubt. We were not allowed to attend the hearing. The process is unfair, and the result must be unfair."
- "We are contacting our lawyer and are demanding transcripts of the student hearing. We are considering suing the academy if there is not a different result."

No wonder deans of students are sometimes reluctant to pick up that phone!

This constellation of responses is connected to some important shifts in parental feelings about disciplinary processes in boarding schools. Here are a few of those shifts:

- Parents are less likely to accept the school's understanding of what happened. They are more likely to accept a child's version of what happened.
- Parents are less likely to accept the school's vision of appropriate consequences for a misdeed. They are more likely to see their job as getting the least possible consequence for their child, in fear of the negative impact on college admissions and the future.
- Parents are less likely to accept the school's disciplinary process. They are more likely to see the process as needing to conform to a court of law.
- Parents are less likely to accept the school's decisions about major disciplinary consequences. They are more likely to threaten the use of a lawyer and to imagine that the weight of the law is in their favor.

With these shifts, parents and school are much more likely to get stuck in an adversarial exchange and legal maneuvers that absorb tremendous time and energy from everyone and rarely serve the needs of the student involved.

How do we begin to escape from this trap? I have some advice.

Parents: Consider the following adjustments in the way you work with the boarding school your child attends:
1. Introduce yourself to your child's adviser and keep relatively frequent, relatively positive contact with that person.
2. Try to attend parent orientations and events designed to help you understand the culture of the school.
3. Read the school's handbook, particularly the language around the process and the consequences in major disciplinary cases.
4. Be careful about making any public pronouncements about your child's version of events in a disciplinary matter. In private, press your child for the whole set of facts in a particular case.
5. Understand that your job as parent is not to remove all chal-

lenges, failures, and consequences from your child's life; in fact, your job is to help them move through the inevitable failures, and consequences of life and to emerge more mature as a result.

6. Independent schools are not obliged to proceed as a court of law or even as a public school would; they simply have to follow the process outlined in their handbook.

7. Avoid threatening use of a lawyer if you are not prepared to use one. Avoid using a lawyer in any but the most extreme cases, given the time, energy, and money involved and given how difficult it will be to meet the needs of your child in the process.

Schools: This problem will not get addressed by parental adjustments alone. Consider the following in the way you work with parents:

1. Spend more time training your advisers, particularly on how to work with parents and students who have difficulty adjusting to the school.

2. Provide parent orientations at convenient times (evenings rather than during parents' workday) and plan for how parents of boarders from far away will get their orientation.

3. Make your handbook more reader-friendly. Insert language about the behaviors you hope to foster in addition to the consequences for misdeeds.

4. Make sure your discipline process is described adequately and that you follow that discipline process consistently.

5. Hire a great school legal counsel who talks you through each potential legal challenge in a dispassionate way.

6. Keep the needs of the child in mind!

Students: You have the ability to affect this dynamic, as well. Consider the following adjustments in the way you work with your school and your parents:

1. Talk to your adviser about your struggles as well as your successes.

2. Read the handbook, especially the sections on what can get you into major difficulty—really!

3. If you get into major disciplinary difficulty, tell your parents

the complete story early. If you cannot manage that, tell them the complete story at least before you go into a disciplinary hearing.

4. You can grow from defeats, failures, and even consequences. That is less likely to happen if you invest a lot of energy questioning the school's authority to give you consequences or if you mislead people about what alleged violations you may have committed.

5. If your parents are threatening legal action, talk with them about how that might impact your life at the school.

6. If you really want to leave a school community, try to let your parents and the school know that in a positive way first, before you get expelled because of a violation.

Boarding school students have a hard enough time growing through their challenges when their parents and their school are not in an adversarial relationship. Those same students will have a much a more difficult time growing through their challenges when parents and school get to hiring lawyers to resolve the issues. In major disciplinary cases, it is time for parents and schools to lay down the law—literally—and focus on the student's needs together.

Don Grace has been an independent school educator for thirty years and has headed schools for twenty of those years. He is currently president of Chapel Hill-Chauncy Hall School, working primarily on raising funds for the school. He has presented to national and regional audiences at conferences and in a variety of publications. He is married to Catherine O'Neill Grace, a free-lance writer and editor, who has authored two recent parenting books with Dr. Michael Thompson and who has written an upcoming book on the history of the White House, for a middle school audience. Catherine and Don live on the campus of Chapel Hill-Chauncy Hall School in Waltham, Massachusetts.

Andover Story

Susan and Chuck Glass
Phillips Academy

In Chuck's town the only kids who went to boarding school were usually wealthy and in trouble—family trouble, academic trouble, police trouble, alcohol/drug trouble. They disappeared in September, returned briefly at Thanksgiving and Christmas and then were away at summer camp or resort compounds and we would occasionally hear of their continued dysfunctional behavior.

Susan had mixed feelings about boarding schools, having attended Miss Porter's School in the early sixties when friendships and education were offset by confinement. It was, therefore, with some degree of skepticism that we approached sending our oldest son to boarding school. Why would parents decide to split up a family? Why should we send a son away before we had to? Why wouldn't our own wise advice and parental role modeling suffice?

There was never a problem at home. But, we knew that our comfortable, homogenous Midwestern suburb had its limits. We lived with landscaped yards, big trees, and good schools, but when our oldest started looking for more excitement, we all started looking at boarding schools.

We did a hurry-up tour in the winter as application deadlines approached. Any notions of delinquent or unhappy students were quickly dispelled. Incredible physical facilities and depth of available teachers and counselors were obvious. The talented diversity of the student body was understood, but less obvious. Our concerns about what might be happening to our family were not addressed.

Charlie chose our least favorite of the schools where he'd been accepted (Phillips Academy, Andover) because he could get to Boston quickly on a bus. We dropped him off that fall and ran the usual errands to help make his room as comfortable as home. We then drove him part way to a rally and let him out on the corner as he walked into his new life. We waited for him to look back over his shoulder to signal that he had some of the uncertainty about this that we did. He never looked back. We headed home.

So the first one left and had a chance to be on the ski team and write for an English teacher who expected more than a simple half-page book report. He found a new challenge in a place where it was cool for a teenager to be smart instead of the other way around. There was independence that was simply not available at home. He found freedom within a structure based on community that gave new meaning to rules and reinforced guidelines we set as parents.

At parents' weekend we discovered incredible teachers and small classes. We got to know the daily life of the school. And though short, parents' weekend was a way to enjoy being together again.

Vacations too were happy and warm family time. For the boys it was a relief and a chance to regroup. In a way, the long separations had made our togetherness more appreciated.

We began to notice that these young, bright, competitive, and popular young men who were our three sons seemed to be developing very healthy friendships with one another. The younger ones, proud of what their older brother was doing, seemed intrigued by his adventures. The older seemed more tolerant and charitable to those he'd left behind.

At the time we sent off "number one" we had little idea of the impact that it would have on "number two." As he approached high school, he too wanted a shot at racing for the Andover ski team and a chance to live apart from hovering parents. When Andover recognized the need for a common family commitment and accepted Carter, that's when the family relationship with the school deepened.

By the time our third son left for what he already considered a second home, it seemed totally natural. Will left eagerly, for four years, taking his drum set along with him. When he got a locker for his drum set in a soundproof practice room where he could play at every opportunity, he was in heaven and we found new reason to justify the tuition.

Because the school accepted the second brother, and later the third brother, too, Andover gave us a family glue. Equal and shared experience among the three brothers has brought us all closer together. Although each boy certainly made his own way, there were variations on an Andover theme that continue to connect and anchor our family. Rarely is a harsh word spoken on vacation. There is a mutual respect among the three brothers which is not commonly found. They enjoy each other's company and now seek each other out for fun and serious advice. Although the boys never lived at school together, the easy familiarity they developed with books and music, history and politics they share readily with each other and their somewhat astounded parents.

Boarding school has been not an early end to our family but an integral, challenging, and cohesive part of it for ten contiguous years. We never sent our boys "away." Rather, we all went "to" a new place.

The Glass Family has graduated three children from Phillips Academy: Charlie, Carter, and Willie.

Students, Parents, and Teachers: The Educational Trinity

Cecil Lyon '68
Suffield Academy

Linda's and my decision to send our daughter away to school was a tough one. We felt a little bit like we were passing the baton in a relay race. Things were going well and we were hopeful that the recipient of our baton would continue to run a good race. The eventual drop-off of our child at Suffield was filled with trepidation. It took a full Suburban, hours of bed making, closet organizing, and some teary eyes.

This contrasted sharply with the manner in which I arrived at Suffield. That leave taking was akin to the 82nd Airborne parachuting in the troops at the start of Operation Overlord.

I was the youngest. By the time I was due to arrive on the second floor of Fuller Hall my parents had already done seventeen drop-offs—eight for my brother, eight for my sister and one for me at pre-prep school. My mother had become world class at sending children off to school. At Suffield, the car barely slowed down. Rugs were kicked out, posters tacked up, bureaus filled, hugs and kisses exchanged, and off they went. My roommate,

Don Cohen, took all this in and then politely asked, "Who were those people?"

That is the way it went. Parents turned their child over to the school, and the kids stayed at school. Parents and teachers did not work together. They exchanged places. Given the technology and highways of the day it couldn't work any other way. It missed taking advantage of the educational trinity. Best results are gained with a prodding parent, a willing student, and a provocative teacher. The parent and teacher need to consistently reinforce each other's message—to encourage and to help.

This wasn't an option for the boarding student of the 1960s. When we were at school, we were socially isolated. In fact, I arrived at Suffield in September and did not leave until Thanksgiving. There wasn't much in the way of communication either. Each dorm had one very public pay phone from which expensive long-distance calls could be made. In our house there was an egg timer next to every phone. Notes were made before the call was placed so you would stay focused. And, finally just before the call was dialed (yes, we dialed), careful planning had to go into whether the call was to be made on a person-to-person or station-to-station basis. Never was a call made just to say "Hi." They were brisk communiqués intended to exchange information. Letter writing was also a bad idea. We were usually too far behind in our homework to even consider getting out the stationery we had been thoughtfully provided. Furthermore, it would only go to show how little we had learned from Mr. Glover, our English teacher.

Then Suffield wired the campus. When first we heard about this, we thought only of the educational benefit—the information exchange and research benefits, a bold attempt at the paperless environment. Never did we perceive the sociological implications. Parents and kids can easily stay in touch. Don't have to schedule a call, just fire off an e-mail, send a picture, or ask if the math teacher accepted her (weak) explanation as to why her workbook was incomplete. Just like day school. We are there and yet we are not there. The campus, the students, the faculty are all more accessible. There is no more social isolation. Many of the differences between a day and a boarding school have disappeared. In fact, we never really passed the baton, but we still show up with a full Suburban.

What is the Right Amount of Participation in Your Daughter's Boarding School Experience?

Linda Lyon
Suffield Academy

On occasion my husband and I compare our experiences at boarding school in the sixties to those of our daughter's thirty-five years later. Our first observation is the difference in parental involvement. His mother dropped him off at Fuller Hall in Suffield, Connecticut, in such a hurry his roommate's mother was speechless. A few months went by and his roommate asked, "Why don't your parents call or come to see you?" My husband responded, "I know they love me; they don't need to be here to show it." My situation was similar due to the distance factor, going to boarding school in Massachusetts from Indiana. Still, in spite of a parental void, we survived. We relied on friends, faculty, coaches, and the school community. This partnership between students and school formed the boarding school community. We learned to make our own decisions and rely less on our parents.

Times have changed the way we communicate at boarding school, but the partnership is still there. Even though our children are away from home, they are more accessible. Thanks to new technology, calling home is much easier and faster. Gone are the days of standing in line for the pay phone. Suffield was the first boarding school to take advantage of recent technology by requiring laptop computers for every student. Access to phones and e-mail makes staying in touch easier. If you are anything like me, then you would like to hear from your daughter every other day. This may be excessive, but it makes me feel connected. Soon enough they get busy and stop calling. Other ways to stay connected are participating in parent events (parent weekends, for instance) and attending programs (speakers series) and sport events.

Suffield Academy is one hour away so I find myself looking for reasons to make the trip. I love visiting. The campus is beautiful and the students are so full of life. My daughter is a senior so she is not necessarily looking for the mom to show up to embarrass her. But I do anyway, to watch games and to take her out for a quick lunch. School is their turf so I try to use good judgment about the right amount of mothering. Emotionally they still need us, but maybe from a distance. Remembering why we sent them to boarding school in the first place is important: to grow and mature with the help of qualified teachers and mentors in a safe, nurturing, and stimulating community. Letting go is difficult, but Suffield is a small, nurturing school that watches over and engages their students.

The boarding school community depends on the involvement of the students; so it is important for the child to join in the fun and become a part of it. From our experience at Suffield, it did not take long for our daughter to become engaged in the school community. She speaks up in class, joins team sports, helps out as a proctor, and gets involved in leadership programs. The headmaster and faculty encourage a loyal school spirit and a partnership that fosters good values and has little tolerance for unacceptable behavior. Teachers at Suffield are accessible and willing to give extra help anytime. My daughter finds relationships with her teachers invaluable.

Sending a child away to boarding school is a hard decision. Watching them grow into a mature, confident adult ready to take flight is the payoff and worth all the worry and time put into being a boarding school parent.

Cecil and Linda Lyon are proud parents of Eliza Lyon, class of 2003 at Suffield Academy.

CURRICULAR PHILOSOPHIES

A College Prep Program

Rufus McClurer
The Bolles School

What constitutes a sound college preparatory program? There are, after all, those who attend college and succeed, sometimes remarkably, without even the traditional high school diploma. The General Educational Diploma (GED) was instituted as a federal program after World War II to enable millions of men and women returning from the military, millions of whom had not completed high school, to enter college immediately and without the traditional high school diploma. These individuals attended hundreds of colleges and went on to remarkable careers in all kinds of businesses and professions, including the teaching profession, the first ever significant influx of males into academia, a truly transformational phenomenon. In fact, this program, which still exists, is arguably the most successful single education initiative ever launched.

Moving backward now from college to high school, one might ask why so many of these individuals were so successful. The answer obviously is an amalgam of experience, curiosity, motivation, and maturation. Therefore, the ideal high school curriculum must provide for a similar pattern of growth and development of the whole person: mind, body, and spirit. This assumption implies that such college preparation must go beyond the confines of the classroom. The Bolles School's all inclusive curriculum does, in fact, provide for this desideratum. In order to optimize the development of the whole person and therefore his/her readiness for college, the classroom must be extended, reconceptualized. In fact, at The Bolles School the entire campus becomes a learning laboratory that extends the classroom where the seed is planted and germinated, but the activities and experiences that occur elsewhere provide the nutrients that continue the process through fruition. This elsewhere includes the dorms, where experiences and activities are designed to expand upon the classroom, the playing fields, and the stage and studio. It might be argued that the ideal boarding school college preparatory program is a twenty-four-hour endeavor that blends all of the basic experiences one encounters in college, including a diverse residential population, which, at The Bolles School, includes approximately 25 percent international students from twenty countries from all over the world, about fifty girls on one campus and about seventy boys on a nearby campus. It should be emphasized, however, The Bolles School is not an isolated, rural community but rather a large school (1,200) that blends boarding students with local students in an urban setting, which is itself a rich learning laboratory with superb cultural and educational opportunities, including two universities. Hence, The Bolles boarding program is a microcosm of the college milieu that the student will transition into upon graduation.

At Bolles, college preparation consists of a large body of collective experiences—some structured, some unstructured—that provide our students the multiple activities and myriad challenges that constitute growth and development in four primary areas: scholarship, physical development, spiritual and/or aesthetic fulfillment, and character and moral education. Therefore, it must be clearly understood that college preparation extends far beyond academics in any narrow sense, nor is such preparation confined to the classroom or the textbook. It must also embrace an awareness of the physical self and the development of the body because we believe that a sound body necessarily promotes psychological fitness, indispensable for both college preparation and preparation for life. Our comprehensive definition must also provide for spiritual and aesthetic development because we believe that each of us is more than mind and body. Man's spiritual dimension, which embodies values and consideration of values, leads us finally to character, upon which all future success and personal fulfillment are predicated. While recognizing that the student is a harmonious entity and not a compartmentalized list of attributes, we believe nevertheless that some useful purpose can be served by viewing separate dimensions independently.

Obviously, our academic curriculum covers the basics, a sound, traditional program that embraces the essentials: English, math, science, history, the arts, and humanities. But we also offer a host of electives, many of which go beyond the traditional and which therefore allow students to explore new interests and expand their educational experiences as far and wide as they can reach, including a comprehensive advanced placement curriculum in all disciplines.

The Bolles academic program is designed to prepare each student not only in the various disciplines, but also for his/her future involvement in a societal world of flux. To achieve this goal, we have built, and continue to sustain, a superior, committed faculty. The school, in turn, is committed to the faculty because we recognize that however good the curriculum, however capable the student body, only a qualified, involved faculty can translate the curriculum into a meaningful, lasting instructional experience. We believe our faculty succeeds in this endeavor because of a developed sense of community manifested in our student-faculty fellowship and camaraderie. In the broadest sense, academic preparation for college presupposes a mastery of the concepts and skills required: to perform successfully at Bolles and later in college itself; to develop the mental skills necessary to think logically in a disciplined manner; to absorb and retain those concepts of primary importance and thereby differentiate between the essential and the trivial; to clarify the student's personal values and goals necessary to enable him/her to perceive the moral issues that circumscribe his/her world; and to understand the ramifications involved in the behavior he/she follows or the stand he/she takes—in other words, academic independence.

Our physical development program is an integral part of every student's educational experience. We recognize that competitive sports are not for everyone. Therefore, our programs are designed to provide instruction in such skills as will permit competition for those who desire it. To this end, we have developed extensive interscholastic competition in a variety of team and individual sports appropriate for our geographical locale including award-winning programs in every sport, from football and lacrosse to Olympic swimming. However, we have developed additional programs that ensure individual physical development for all students that will, therefore, provide them lifetime physical activities.

We recognize that the student's spiritual self is, to some extent, developed and fulfilled through academic and physical endeavors. But we believe that the spiritual and moral dimension is best served through the individualized flexibility of the fine arts/ humanities and student activities experiences. Since man has historically expressed his emotional and spiritual self through philosophy, art, music, literature, religion, drama, and science, we believe that every student should have the opportunity to explore his own spiritual self in terms of the best that our civilization can offer because it is the great creative achievements, both scientific and artistic, that we revere and preserve. Therefore, we have designed and provided comprehensive cocurricular and extracurricular experiences (of which the student activities program is an integral part) which enrich and ennoble students' lives by providing them myriad opportunities to pursue and develop new interests, skills, and friendships. To this end, we have sought to develop programs that awaken and recognize the creative impulse in all fields of human endeavor. We believe that such experiences foster cooperation, leadership-followership traits, independence, creativity and growth in emotional and spiritual areas, although we are fully aware that such intangible aspirations are difficult to implement and even more difficult to measure.

Finally, we believe that all Bolles's programs are and should be formulated and implemented with a view to character building and development. Recognizing that increasing social pressures thrust upon our youth during the coming decade necessitate an active school role, we believe that we must support the home and community in a collective effort to promote moral education and positive character development. We must, therefore, assist students to develop citizenship consistent with democratic principles, leadership-followership potential in the classroom and in campus organizations, responsibility toward the needs of others, and a personality with constructive values. It must follow then that all of the foregoing philosophical tenets and aspirations culminate in this final dimension of college preparation: character— which is the ultimate manifestation of the Bolles experience.

Rufus McClurer writes: I signed my first contract with The Bolles School in 1951, $2,200 plus room and board. I expected to remain for a year or two, save my salary and return to graduate school, but I met a

Jacksonville girl, married her and lived happily ever after. I retired, more or less, after a forty-nine-year career, which concluded in the same workplace where it began. During those forty-nine years, I served in just about every capacity possible except headmaster. From 1963 until 1980, I served as director of studies/academic dean, but my first love was the classroom, where I taught AP English; so I returned to my first love in 1980, and to my former position, chairman of the English department, until I turned sixty-five, when I decided to pass that particular torch to someone else. From June 2000, when I officially retired, until May 2002, I maintained a small office and continued to piddle around the school. In May 2002, the president, Dr. John E. Trainer, approached me and requested that I return to one of my earlier incarnations and resume that former life as interim academic dean. Since I never truly retired in the first place and since I continued to piddle around, I concluded that I might as well get paid for my piddling, so I returned to the payroll on August 1, 2002, interestingly at the highest salary I've ever earned. I still haven't devised a strategy to mix it up with students, a big factor in my decision to return, but I will. However, I have reestablished a collegial relationship with the faculty, another important criterion in my decision to return to the workplace. On September 24, I turned seventy-seven, and I am now well into my fiftieth year at The Bolles School.

What Is a Multicultural Course?
A Multicultural Curriculum?

Craig Thorn
Phillips Academy

As the former chair of the English department at Phillips Academy, I cannot say what I think a multicultural course or curriculum might be without first remembering my own history as a student.

My high school English teacher, Frank Sullivan, turned me on to literature with Charles Dickens's *A Tale of Two Cities,* a romantic tale of brave souls in England and France during the French Revolution. The heroic melodrama of Sydney Carton's life enthralled me. After all, he sacrifices his life to save the woman he loves even though by doing so he reunites her with the man she loves! My history teacher, Dale Nicholson, was marching us through the French Revolution at the same time. I was lucky because these two guys were the best teachers I had at Hudson High School. Were they aware that I was taking what amounted to my very own interdisciplinary course and therefore experiencing the complex dialogue that can take place between history and literature, fact and fiction? I doubt it. Mr. Nicholson was the president of every faculty organization and Mr. Sullivan was the adviser to every student organization. They were certainly too busy. But I wasn't. Literature became real to me when reading Dickens and studying the chaos of the French Revolution. Madame deFarge's knitting needles still click in my imagination. With grave delight, she kept track of all the French aristocrats going to the guillotine. And the people in the real drama of the event had stories to tell themselves, making the history a collection of his stories and her stories. To this day, I am wary whenever my Hungarian mother-in-law gets her own needles out and commences with "I would like to say something about that, Craigie," as she begins another scarf to wrap around my neck.

The following year, Mr. Sullivan invited his senior class to read *Macbeth*. I read it quickly, wrote a pretty competent plot summary, handed it in and waited for my A. Instead, Mr. Sullivan invited me to read the play again. So I did. He asked me to write about it again. I did. He invited me to read the play again. The rest of the class was now reading *Romeo and Juliet*. At that point, I was reading *Macbeth* for the fourth time. I wrote another essay. I read the play again. I read the play eleven times before I realized that Frank expected a little more from me than a plot summary, no matter how comprehensive the summary became with each successive draft. Mumbling to myself, I read the play a twelfth time, noticing almost despite myself that there was a lot of blood in the play. Blood everywhere. Thus began my sense of language as a signifier, as meaning something more than just what it literally says. I read the play five more times, each time discovering new things: Macbeth has two personalities! Lady Macbeth is stronger than Macbeth, but weaker at the same time! Maybe Macbeth is just the best example of all the sick creeps lopping arms off in Scotland! Where is Fleance?!?

It was not what I read that mattered. Nor was it who I read that mattered. It certainly was not what Mr. Sullivan thought about what I read that mattered. The act of reading and then writing about what I read were the goals of Mr. Sullivan's unusual experiment. He forced me to discover my own voice in Shakespeare's world on my own. Coming from a rural high school in an economically depressed community, I arrived at college a literary beginner, my experiences with literature few but, thankfully, honest. I knew two things to be true about literature and they formed a simple conversation that to this day informs the way I think a curriculum and course should be developed for high school students: Literature is about life and also a celebration of language. This conversation did not change much despite college, graduate school, and my career as a teacher.

In college, I read every poem, play, story, and novel I could get my hands on. Along the way, I met every kind of teacher and student—stuffy, dramatic, political, intellectual—you can imagine. In graduate school, I read every book and essay about all those novels and plays I could understand. I studied all kinds of complex literary theories, all kinds of subtle ways to read books. And then as a teacher, I struggled with the many earnest arguments about political correctness: the calls from conservative thinkers for a traditional curriculum to save America's identity and the cries from new thinkers for a whole new curriculum to raise the oppressed. And despite all these persuasive people and ideas (or because I was just too dim to assimilate it all) I still thought of literature and composition in embarrassingly simple terms stemming from my time with Dale Nicholson who, when explaining his Swedish background, always began with the words "Fifty Svedes went into the weeds" and Frank Sullivan who said to me on more than one occasion, "You're so stupid you think a shoehorn is a musical instrument." For me, all good language tests the boundaries between realism and romanticism, between the objective world as we think we see it and the ideal world as we would like to see it.

So when confronted with the challenges of a diverse student body, a diverse faculty, and demands on the curriculum ranging from contemporary politics to grammar, I tried to recall who would be reading and writing in our department and why. I tried to recall my own days as a student, and I remembered that my journey, although inspired by teachers, was entirely my own.

There are basic rules about a curriculum in any high school discipline that every student and teacher should know.

- No curriculum in any discipline can cover every subject and represent every version of human experience.
- No single course should be judged by its content only. Nor should it be judged by its method only. A course and/or a specific literary work should be judged by a simple question: Does it provide an exciting opportunity to teach students how to read, write, and think?
- In any curriculum, ever-evolving balances are the order of the day, balances that constantly remind students and teachers that there are always other points of view defined by country, culture, religion, period, gender, genre, rhetorical style . . . ultimately by the next person to tell a story.
- Therefore, in an increasingly complex, rich world, a good curriculum imparts ways of discovering, assimilating, and using knowledge, instead of knowledge itself as something static and quantifiable.

Added to these basic rules are corollary rules about the works we include in a traditional curriculum.

- Understanding that the books we teach as teachers and read as students are important first as great literary efforts does justice to the classics of a Thomas Hardy and the new triumphs of a Leslie Marmon Silko.
- No work of literature should be treated solely as a political document or part of a political agenda. Politics are part of every culture's and community's creativity, but only part.

Winter in the Blood by Blackfoot Indian James Welch is not a diatribe. It is filled with Welch's tight-lipped brand of poetry. It tells the muted story of loss in the spirit of Hemingway's *In Our Time*. And while it certainly forces any sensitive reader to consider the plight of the American Indian, it does so in much the same way that Hemingway prompts us to consider the many ways someone can be a casualty of war, distant or immediate: by unfolding the drama of personal history and so making a world.

Ethnic-American and world literatures are not just "add-ons" in a curriculum. They contribute much to any curriculum interested in a literary-historical continuum in American and world letters. Consider, for instance, that many Hispanic, Asian-American, Native American, and African-American authors reintroduced faith and religion, magic and myth into American literature long after many Anglo writers gave up on these possibilities. Furthermore, ethnic American literatures in particular can be wonderful teaching texts for students interested in the art and craft of writing because the heroes of these stories are frequently desperate to find themselves in their native languages. In other words, the stories are about language and storytelling. And because they are so often preoccupied with either re-creating and affirming a cultural experience through story or finding a hero's place in an historical landscape, ethnic-American and world literatures are also rich with opportunities for experimental ways of teaching and learning, involving everything from writing about literature by telling your own story in poetry to teaching literature alongside history and biology teachers. And most important, these literatures ultimately serve to revitalize works teachers and students have read for years because their deepest meanings resonate with the universal music of all great literature, thus uniting voices, not separating them.

So if you are taking an English course in a boarding school and when looking at the faces in the room you see a measure of this global village, keep in mind that Cristina Garcia and Virginia Woolf might have something to say to one another and they both might have something to say to you. When I read Toni Morrison's *Sula* for the first time, I took a course with thirteen middle-aged black women who were studying to earn master's degrees while teaching in inner-city high schools. I was a very curious twenty-year-old fraternity president in my senior summer at Dartmouth College. The power with which Morrison spoke to each woman's experience of motherhood and sisterhood was stunning, especially when Morrison wrote of the violent ways we can love one another in hard times. I thought of what Sydney Carton was willing to do for love in a completely different world and time in the imagination of a completely different writer introduced to me in a rural classroom, and I realized that Toni Morrison could speak to me, too.

The word multicultural is all-inclusive. It means a poem from Brazil and a short story written by an Irish-Catholic Bostonian. It means William Faulkner and Toni Cade Bambara. It means Milan Kundera, Fumiko Enchi, and Eudora Welty. It means a little something by new writer Ethan Canin and a novel by Thomas Hardy. A multicultural course is one in which student and teacher hear a music they hadn't heard before even as they hear themselves in the new music. And excited by the sound, they hope to hear more. A multicultural curriculum is made up of such courses.

Craig Thorn is an instructor in English at Phillips Academy, where he has been a house counselor, adviser, administrator, and coach for twenty-one years. In addition to writing and editing books about education, he writes essays about literature and reviews of alternative rock music.

Focus

Bill Lowman
Idyllwild Arts Academy

As headmaster of a boarding school for young people who are talented in some aspect of the arts, I work with hundreds of young people who are impassioned learners. They are the next generation of artists who will speak for the finest in our culture through the media of dance, music, visual arts, writing, theater, and film. Parents who desire an excellent education for their children or see indications of interests/talent in the arts often ask many questions regarding the development of talent—when to suggest a certain musical instrument; when to start ballet training; when to start with reading; when to demand memorization; when to start throwing a baseball; when to start figure skating; when to begin chess lessons; how to know what level of pressure is healthy; how to know when to push and when not to; how early is too early; and on and on. On the other hand, I hear from many parents the view that specialization early in a child's life is too demanding. What they desire is that their children be well rounded and happy. How do you instill a love for learning in your child and yet not be an overbearing parent with an unhappy young person at home?

The answer, as you might expect, is a matter of balances. You must be realistic about the extraordinary impact you have as a parent. You are imprinting your most serious concerns and your deepest desires on your child's psyche from the moment of birth. Through a very interesting set of circumstances, I was honored to observe some of the preeminent brain mapping researchers from across the world at the Sante Fe Institute Consortium on "Increasing Human Potential." There, I saw concrete examples of what every mother knows and many doctors do not, that infants are lively learners from the moment of birth. From my work with Suzuki violin students and their parents, I had observed this to be true, but it was scientifically demonstrated that mere exposure to language alters the brain. Scientists estimate that a child's cognition changes more in the first five years of life than any other five-year period. They also confirmed that infants learn most effectively by imitating what others do. Even a newly born baby can imitate simple facial expressions and movements. Imitative learning seems to be wired into the human brain.

The Suzuki method of teaching instrumental music is called the mother-tongue approach and utilizes the listening and imitative skills of young children and the attachment of a child to the mother as teaching tools. It begins with the playing of easily recognizable music phrases on audiotapes. Many Suzuki parents play the tapes to the mother and child before the baby is born. Certainly they are played as soon as possible after birth. This remarkable method pioneered by a Japanese physician/violinist includes a great deal of listening, a lesson with a private instructor for mother and child, and daily practice under mother's supervision on the instrument. The learning that occurs can lead to an amazing capacity to perform and to memorize long musical phrases. It is no wonder that the method swept across America in the second half of the twentieth century. There are Suzuki programs in most of America's cities, teaching children how to memorize and how to learn—in some cases developing remarkable musicians.

The success of the Suzuki method and the scientific research at the Santa Fe Institute Consortium suggest that parents can nurture and develop specific talents from infancy. The little one already knows that you like football or baseball, listen to classical music, read aloud, and ponder meaning. In short, you have already helped to determine what educational path and what general interests your child will have! So, why wait? Behind every extraordinary young person is a parent who has either consciously or unconsciously pushed that young person to become a fine athlete, dancer, musician, or reader.

The second answer is to be realistic about your child's interests after he or she develops an individual life. Some children are very happy to continue with the interests of childhood and the positive aspects of parental involvement and family desires right through school, college, and on to a successful life. However, students can resist pressures to specialize early on. The pressures to succeed may be too much for young children and they may rebel against parents, and even turn away from genuine talents and interests they have. Similarly, however, students can and do branch out into areas that dismay those parents who are looking for a more generalized balance and a good future career. We often hear about students who suffer from too much pressure to succeed in one skill, but what about students who suffer from too much pressure to be "normal" or "well-balanced"?

Often, an inspiring teacher motivates a young student to try a specific field of study. Or a frustrated student finds an outlet in a new, potentially enriching experience outside or beyond the normal curriculum of a typical high school. What should parents do when a great biology teacher or a fabulous drama coach in the theater club has inspired their child? After parents who care, teachers are the next most important element in the development of extraordinary talents.

Stacie comes to mind as an example of a young woman who, like many young people who study the arts in the United States had taken all of the courses available at her school by the end of her sophomore year. She yearned to perform on stage and had already been the lead in most community and school productions. She found our school in her junior year and, after convincing her parents that she should leave the excellent school in her hometown, fell under the spell of the theater department chair, who had a strong influence on young actors and demanded complete obedience to her style and technique. Stacie attended our summer program and two years at the school, taking voice and diction, theater history, and several courses in acting as well as performing with the acting and technical company. She took every piece of advice the instructor had to offer, auditioned for every part, participated in every production, and offered her services for any other performance venues available. She continued the highest level of college preparatory academic study in addition to all her drama efforts. In spring semester of her senior year, she was rewarded for her academic excellence, her test scores, and her audition with acceptance at the Yale School of Drama. Stacie, in short, is a great example of how supportive parents, motivated mentors, and great passion all yielded a fulfilling result.

Yet, when it comes time for your child to break free of the all-pervasive influence of his parents and the dominant teacher, pay close attention to his communications with you. Scott came to the Idyllwild Arts Academy in his eighth-grade year as a young musician, to play the viola. He was referred to us from an inspirational teacher in his hometown area who wanted him to study at a boarding school with one of the best violists in the country. Scott was already a stereotypical musician, an excellent student at mathematics and languages who could easily transfer his symbolic understanding of musical notes and scores to other types of knowledge. Five years at a challenging school with a world-class youth orchestra and superior private instructors combined with Scott's talent and drive to take him to the top.

By the time he was a senior, Scott was recognized as one of the premier violists of his age in the world. He had won a major competition and was represented by professional management. However, his parents insisted that he stay in California and continue study with his teacher, a college professor who could stay with him at the next level. They wanted to make sure that he had a general education. As bright a student as he was talented, Scott had already (unbeknownst to us at school) hatched a very sophisticated plan to ensure that he would be able to enroll at the Curtis Institute of Music in Philadelphia, the most selective music conservatory in the country, and study with the violist in a famous string quartet. Scott basically sabotaged some of his courses and tests to ensure that he would not get into the kind of college his parents preferred. He accepted his full scholarship at Curtis. In keeping with Scott's independent personality, her transferred to The Juilliard School in New York City where he graduated and is now a successful performing musician as well as a college professor of music. While what Scott did was obviously inappropriate, his actions clearly reflected his overriding passion for his music. If his parents had recognized this passion, they may have been able to realize his dreams together. The irony is that Scott was generally brilliant. Failing chemistry and not completing the SATs in order to fulfill his real passion actually went against the very intellectual abilities his parents were anxious to exploit.

Actually, the more obvious forms of creative expression in the arts that might seem contrarian occur in more broadly creative arts like painting, filmmaking, and writing. While the musician, dancer, and actor seek perfection in every movement and phrase, the artist begins every day with a blank canvas on which he or she must create an entirely new thought or emotion for all to see. This is an attractive pursuit for a youngster who recently turned to the arts or who simply wants to blend popular culture with artistic expression. The young visual artist often has developed a "look" which includes a unique hair color and individualistic attire along with a sense of being an outcast. Such students are often lost in the normal school but can be amazing contributors to society and education with appropriate channeling of their visual skills and uniquely personal commentaries. We often call the performing musicians the re-creators and the others, creators. Each makes a different contribution to the world of the arts, but both are quite valuable. Parents need to pay attention to what brings their child to life, what seems to focus and energize them. The arts frequently speak powerfully to young people in search of a way to express themselves.

For parents inquiring about motivating older children, I recommend that you identify interests and respond to eagerness. An overly negative response to student interest will most often solidify that interest into full-blown love of the subject anyway. Why not keep an active, constructive role in your child's life by supporting what brings passion into their lives? Teenagers need something to care about. I cannot imagine a life without passion and dreams. I do not recommend a perfectly balanced life to any young person if it is solely the result of overbearing parents. At arts school we educate not only those who have been practicing the violin since age four, but those who are newly dedicated to sculpture, writing their first novel, or developing their own film script. The latter students often have chosen art school after much unhappiness in a "normal" school environment and significant disagreements with parents.

I often use a phrase from Goethe to describe life in a specialized school for the arts. In *Wilhelm Meisters Lehrjahre* he wrote, "One ought, every day at least, to hear a little song, read a good poem, see a fine picture, and, if it were possible, to speak a few reasonable words." Not a bad description for a twenty-four-hour-a-day, seven-day-a-week learning experience in arts academic and human development for passionate, dedicated youngsters.

William M. Lowman is the headmaster and founder of the Idyllwild Arts Academy. Prior to Idyllwild he founded the Nevada School of the Arts and worked for the University of Southern California School of Performing Arts. He received his bachelor of arts degree from the University of Redlands in history with related fields of music and civilization. He is past president of the International NETWORK of Performing and Visual Arts Schools, was a Klingenstein Visiting Fellow at Teachers College, Columbia University, and has been on the faculty of the Salzburg Seminar.

CONCLUSION: TWO LIFE EXPERIENCES IN BOARDING SCHOOL

Teaching at a Boarding School

Charlie Alexander
Groton Academy

It would seem that some of us who are fortunate enough to teach at boarding schools never have left school! Because my father was a schoolmaster, I grew up living in a dormitory at Belmont

Hill School until age six and at Middlesex School until I went off to college. While in college, I spent my summer months working at an outstanding small camp in Jaffrey, New Hampshire. In the fall of my senior year at Williams, I put together a résumé that forced me for the first time to put into writing what I thought were my goals and immediate plans. My list of possibilities in 1957 included officer candidate school, business school, and yes, teaching. As the fall progressed, I decided to interview for teaching jobs rather than pay yet another tuition bill for graduate school until I knew what I wanted to do with my life.

To my great delight, I was selected for a teaching fellowship at Phillips Academy, which provided a two-year experience involving one year at Andover and the following year at graduate school. I taught a Latin class under the guidance of a superb master teacher, Frank Benton; I did dormitory duty once a week with ninth-grade students; and I helped coach the varsity squash team and junior varsity baseball team. This combination of different contacts with students solidified my desire to teach. After a year at Harvard Graduate School of Education and then teaching at William Penn Charter School for another year, I received an offer to teach at Groton School. My wife and I leapt at the opportunity to be part of this fine small school.

One might ask, what makes this way of life so special? At a small school, my family has shared in the community life. I have been able to know students well as a teacher, coach, college adviser, academic dean, and adviser. I also served on the discipline committee with five students and two other faculty members. For many years, as a family we all went to plays, games, movies, and chapel together. Parents, alumni, and trustees have been regular guests in our home. My wife worked as an admissions officer for almost twenty years, coached JV girls' tennis, and now has sung in the school choir for twenty-five years. To this day we enjoy the friendship of many former students and their parents as we share common memories and experiences.

As I write these words in mid-August, I am excited at the thought of returning to school and sharing my life with students in the classroom, athletic field, and dormitory. Even after forty-four years in this life, I must acknowledge that I perhaps learn more from my students than they learn from me.

Charles Alexander has done virtually everything at Groton Academy. He is a living legend in New England boarding school education. He currently teaches in the classics department and serves as the dean of academic affairs.

Photographing Oneself

Nadia Sarkis '95
Phillips Academy

I have begun, in my last few weeks of high school, to take pictures. Looking past the standard smiling pose, I wander around campus and its surroundings like a visual predator. My choices for pictures are invariably eclectic in nature: a child leaning against a labyrinthine fort, a girl playing the cello, a door frame embroidered by cascading magnolias, a mannequin dressed as a bride in a rental shop. I strive to document my experiences through the countenance of others and the angles and contrasts of a school I have come to know quite well. In the pictures I craft in orange darkness, the latent quality of nostalgia emerges from the mysterious pools of darkroom chemicals. Harriet Doerr once beckoned her heroine to keep on striving until every view had a window to contain it. I find myself constantly drawing upon the richness of my surroundings (selfishly guzzling the sweetness) in order to see and be seen from many windows. While my time here shall soon end, I feel the need to compose a picture of myself at this school. Developing a frustrating thesis or talking with friends in a lazily verdant park, the fragments of experience fuse and crinkle, forming a spinal column from which I will continue to build an identity for myself. I wait for the day to capture this identity in a photograph.

My future looms ahead of me like a boundless path, and I squint before the overwhelming realization of my own possibility. My freedom inhabits a whimsical space, and I use various mediums as foils in order to develop a comprehension of this school. One of these foils is a campus magazine. The publication has accompanied me through the riddle of my education, allowing me to reflect, discuss, or just grumble about the tangle of school and life. The first article I wrote, in fact, was intended to be a character sketch on an Irish cousin of mine that I have never met. She is a Carmelite nun, known as a relation to me only through muted reference and oblique body language. I imagined how her life might be, shading in her childhood and weaving a creative fabrication about her work in Africa as a missionary. ("The wild grass swayed like a whip, but only had the sun to catch in its dry, green hands.") I suppose I adequately addressed the assignment, but the essay evolved into an exploration of my own time in Ireland as I tried to place myself within a strange context. My heritage roots itself in lonely moors and wily limericks, but also in butcher's smells and crosses' remembrance. I exploited the assignment, converted it into a reflecting pool, and then gazed at my reflection, hazy with confusion.

But then . . .

> In a lifting
> of wisps and scarves . . .
> with clandestine rose and violet, with opaline
> nuance of milkweed, a texture
> not to be spoken of above a whisper,
> began, all along the horizon, gradually to unseal
> like the lip of a cave
> or of a cavernous,
> single pearl-
> engendering seashell
> —Amy Clampitt

Unfortunately, I haven't developed with such gorgeous drama, but I did learn to take courage and heart in my passions. I no longer sequestered literature and art as lofty pastimes, but strove to make them components in my portrait. They served as windows and mirrors, and I took a long look. Writing about myself, I struggled to find the adjectives and adverbs to describe my aspect and action. I referred to the mirror's perception and the window's observation, and found snapshots, moments when pictures said more than words: lifting my head from Dante's circles of hell to find trees silhouetted by purple and orange (passionate clouds competing for my attention), getting up at five to watch the sun rise before my two friends posing as Greek goddesses, laughing through English class while learning grammar (quite a feat, let me tell you), lying on the floor and crooning along with Ella Fitzgerald on a night I should've done homework. Through me these images are threaded, and perhaps I can, as Doerr suggests, "weave chance and hope into a fabric that would clothe [me] as long as [I] live." Within the realm of this incredible possibility, my passions emerge. The skeleton of my identity assembles itself from these glimpses of self-acknowledgement.

This morning a few friends and I snapped pictures of each other for our college face books. Already we are asked to carve names and faces for ourselves in a new environment. My smile was glazed with uncertainty, and I felt uncomfortable under the len's objective eye. These last weeks of school shall be very well documented as memory has already begun to blot the days. We are reminiscent of moments before they pass, and scramble to preserve them into something tangible. Now I wish I had a picture from the beginning. Perhaps a picture of the night before my first day of school when I had a retainer lodged in my mouth and tried to respond to a question about my birthday (the retainer spit itself out, to my great dismay). I'd like to trace myself from those first images to the ones I posed for today. I'd like to see the evolution of a face on paper. The process of self-definition continues, however, and so I gratefully await the next photo opportunity.

Nadia Sarkis graduated from Andover with all sorts of writerly ambitions, some indulged, others yet to be satisfied. These days she's finishing up law school in Chicago. She has various schemes for her future. She just landed her job as a lawyer in Colorado. She wrote this piece in her senior spring at Andover. Some of her new poetry was recently published in the tenth anniversary edition of Andover's literary magazine, *The Courant*. At the time of this publication, she had just found a great job in Denver, Colorado.

CONCLUSION

You probably have noticed that the stereotype of the boarding school as an elite club for wealthy boys does not begin to describe the kinds of schools you have encountered here. Make no mistake; boarding school is not for everybody, but not because you have to be a brilliant scholar or all-star athlete in order to thrive at one. If you do not like the idea of living with lots of your peers on a campus or you really like the idea of putting distance between yourself and your school every day, then boarding at an independent school may not be for you. Boarding school is not just a group of impressive classrooms inside old buildings. Rather, boarding school is a living arrangement: a community with formal and informal rules. Furthermore, that community offers challenges (Can I write a four-page paper on *The Great Gatsby*? Is it possible to kayak through those rocks? Do I have any hope of learning how to play that sequence on the violin?) and opportunities (What am I doing on the side of this cliff? How can I possibly get along with a skinhead from Yonkers for a roommate? Do I really want to get to know Benedict Arnold this well just for a history research paper?) The way you answer these kinds of questions will determine what kind of boarding school experience you have. In short, you will get out of the boarding school community what you put into it.

There is one more very important quality of the boarding school community: friendship. On balance, friendships in boarding school are likely to be more rewarding and demanding than they are in public school. You share your second home in boarding school with roommates, dormmates, classmates, and schoolmates. You live with adults and frequently work with them side by side. What you learn about friendship by living in such a community cannot be quantified in a course of study guide or on a college board examination. We have devoted a lot of time in these pages to describing friendship in its many guises, but in the end you are still an interloper. Reading about the great experiences your peers have described, you probably have felt on more than one occasion, "I guess I had to be there." What is more, you have probably guessed that boarding school is not all about wonderful revelations and success stories. Well, both those reactions are understandable. If you choose to go to boarding school, you will have your own stories to tell, good and bad. Boarding school does not replace the trials and tribulations of middle school and high school with scrapbooks full of Kodak moments. Rather, it offers you the chance to experience those ups and downs in a supportive, focused environment from which you will emerge with a sense of accomplishment and a superior education inside and outside the classroom.

Because it offers the whole package, boarding school allows students to succeed in as many ways as there are ideas of success. If you can take responsibility for the things that make you passionate, then you and your school will find that unspoken contract that enables you to test your limits. It may be an extra hour on a tennis court, a fencing class, a teacher with whom you share a passion for African drumming. It may be gene splicing or makeup backstage for the production of Ibsen's *The Masterbuilder*. If you put your mind and heart into it, someone will be there to help you make it happen.

LIST OF CONTRIBUTING SCHOOLS

Andover (Phillips Academy) offers over 300 courses in all disciplines including a full arts program and eight languages. Located 25 miles north of Boston on a 500-acre campus, the school features a world famous museum of American art, dozens of athletic fields including a new hockey rink, a new science building, and a 120,000 volume library. The campus is fully wired so that the 1000+ students have immediate access to the Internet for course work and research. The school features an AP curriculum in all disciplines and the full range of extracurricular activities including a weekly newspaper, four other student publications, and a radio station.

> *www.andover.edu*
> Phone: 978-749-4000
> Address: 180 Main Street/Andover, MA 01810

The Andrews School serves a day and boarding population of girls in grades 6–12 from 8 states and 8 countries. Founded in 1910, we have served the mission of educating students to succeed as self-reliant women. Features nationally recognized equestrian program, and full academic curriculum. 6:1 student-teacher ratio. 360 acres, 30 minutes from Cleveland.

> *www.andrews-school.org*
> Phone: 440-942-3600   Fax: 440-753-4683
> Address: 38588 Mentor Avenue/Willoughby, OH 44094

Asheville School is a coeducational boarding/day school located in Asheville, North Carolina. Boarding 13–19. Traditional subjects, and art, music, drama. Independent project programs that have included horseback riding, SAT review, contemporary Russia. Mountaineering program features rock climbing, white-water kayaking, spelunking, and cross-country skiing in the Blue Ridge and Great Smoky mountains. Enrollment approximately 200 students.

www.ashevilleschool.org
Phone: 828-254-6354   Fax: 828-252-8666
Address: 360 Asheville School Rd/Asheville, NC 28806

Blair Academy in Blairstown, New Jersey, is a coeducational college preparatory school enrolling boarding and day students in grades 9–12 and a postgraduate year. Located near the Delaware Water Gap, Blair is less than 90 minutes from midtown Manhattan and is easily accessible via Interstate Route 80. Enrollment approximately 400+ students.

www.blair.edu
Phone: 908-362-2024   Fax: 908-362-7975
Address: PO Box 600/Blairstown, NJ 07825-0600

The Bolles School in Jacksonville, Florida, is a coeducational, college preparatory school enrolling over 1800 day students in early kindergarten through grade 12 and boarding students in grades 7 through postgraduate on four campuses. Bolles has one upper-school campus, (San Jose Campus), one middle-school campus, (Bartram Campus), and two lower-school campuses (Ponte Vedra Campus, and Whitehurst Campus). The Boarding Program enhances the Bolles experience by bringing students from over 25 different countries to Bolles. Bolles prepares students for the future by providing them with challenges that promote growth and development in academics, the arts, activities, and athletics. (from the website)

www.bolles.org
Phone: 904-733-9292
Address: 7400 San Jose Boulevard/Jacksonville, FL 32217

Brewster Academy is located on the shores of Lake Winnipesaukee in the resort community of Wolfeboro, New Hampshire, about 1½ hours from Boston. Brewster is widely recognized for its success in using advanced learning and information technologies to accelerate student growth in a vigorous college preparatory environment. Brewster provides its 360 students (grades 9–12 and postgraduate) with a personalized curriculum based on individual mastery and best-teaching practices in a sophisticated technology-rich learning environment. Eighty percent of our students are boarding students from 30 states and 18 different countries.

www.brewsteracademy.org
Phone: 603-569-7200   Fax: 603-569-7272
Address: 80 Academy Drive/Wolfeboro, NH 03894

Cate School is a coeducational, independent secondary (grades 9–12) boarding and day school located 12 miles south of Santa Barbara, California. Features a full academic program, including full complement of languages and language study abroad programs. Frequent excursions to places like Yosemite and Santa Cruz. The school enrolls 269 students.

www.cate.org
Phone: 805-684-4127   Fax: 805-684-8940
Address: PO Box 5005/Carpinteria, CA 93014

Chapel Hill-Chauncy Hall School is a college-preparatory day and boarding school that embraces differences in learning style and culture in a small, supportive community. We challenge young men and women to achieve their individual potential, experience academic success, and develop social and leadership skills. Grades 9–PG. Student-teacher ratio: 5 to 1. Enrollment is approximately 170 students.

www.chapelhill-chauncyhall.org
Phone: 781-894-2644   Fax: 781-894-8768
Address: 785 Beaver Street/Waltham, MA 02154

Cheshire Academy has been preparing students for college since 1794. Small classes and one-on-one instruction when appropriate. Comprehensive extracurricular program complements AP curriculum and independent study opportunities. Cheshire is near New Haven, Connecticut, between Danbury and Hartford off I-84. We have day students in all grades 6–PG and we board students in 9–PG.

www.cheshireacademy.org
Phone: 203-272-5396   Fax: 203-250-7209
Address: 10 Main Street/Cheshire, CT 06410

Choate-Rosemary Hall offers broad academic, athletic, and extracurricular opportunities on a 400-acre campus with state-of-the-art facilities. Enjoying a national and international reputation, the school boasts abroad programs in over half a dozen countries, a full AP curriculum, electives, and interdisciplinary courses. Enrollment is 800 plus students, grades 9–PG.

www.choate.edu
Phone: 203-697-2239
Address: 333 Christian Street/Wallingford, CT 06492

Colorado Rocky Mountain School is an independent boarding and day school that challenges students to excel in a college-preparatory academic curriculum balanced within a program of the arts, athletics, physical work, service to the community, and enriching wilderness experience. Approximately 175 students from 22 states and seven countries participate in small classes for grades 9–12. The school is located on a 365-acre working ranch near the town of Carbondale, 30 miles from Aspen.

www.crms.org
Phone: 970-963-2562   Fax: 970-963-9865
Address: 1493 Country Road/Carbondale, CO 81623

Concord Academy is a small, coed, college preparatory boarding and day school enrolling 340 students from the greater Boston area, the greater United States and around the world. Located near the center of historic Concord, the school provides a modern curriculum featuring electives and independent study in nearly all disciplines, and a visual arts program that includes ceramics, photography, film, filmmaking, textiles, and sculpture.

www.concordacademy.org
Phone: 978-402-2250
Address: 166 Main Street, Concord, MA 01742

Darlington School offers a coeducational, college preparatory education to boarders from ninth graders to postgraduates and to day students in prekindergarten through grade 12. Enrollment is approximately 900 students with 450 to 475 students at the Upper School. Located in Rome, Georgia, a community of about 84,000, Darlington sits at the center of a triangle formed by the cities of Atlanta, Chattanooga, and Birmingham. The school sits on 500 beautiful woodland acres. Darlington's distinctive buildings nestle around a spring-fed lake where, legend has it, the Spanish conquistador Hernando de Soto camped to trade with the Cherokee Indians.

www.darlingtonschool.org.
Phone: 1-800-368-4437
Address: 1014 Cave Spring Road/Rome, GA 30161

Deerfield Academy is in its third century of educating young people in preparation for college and beyond. Offering accelerated course tracks in all disciplines, Deerfield also offers several off-campus programs including SYA, the Mountain School, and the Maine Coast Seminar, the full range of interscholastic and intramural sports, and very active extracurricular activities. Enrollment is approximately 600 students, grades 9–PG, boarding and day. Campus is approximately 250 acres.

www.deerfield.edu
Phone: 413-774-1400   Fax: 413-772-1100
Address: Deerfield, MA 01342

Dublin School features small classes (8–10 students) with a core curriculum and AP curriculum for qualified students. Grades 9–PG. With an enrollment of approximately 100 students, Dublin offers students tutorials with a staff of trained professionals. Required athletic program. Outdoor excursions in the White Mountains.

www.dublinschool.org
Phone: 603-563-8584   Fax: 603-563-8671
Address: 18 Lehmann Way, Box 522/Dublin, NH 03444-0522

Exeter (Phillips Exeter Academy) offers a highly competitive academic curriculum, relying on the principle of the Harkness Table. Students and faculty collaborate in the educational endeavor around oval tables that promote student-initiated discussions. The rigorous academic program exposes students to seven disciplines, and provides students with the opportunity to mix breadth and depth in their studies. World-class facilities invite students to stretch themselves in a comprehensive sports and extracurricular program. Enrollment is approximately 1000 students;

13–15 students per classroom. Offers full-range independent study, off-campus study, AP curriculum.

www.exeter.edu
Phone: 603-772-4311   Fax: 603-777-4384
Address: 20 Main Street/Exeter, NH 03833-2460

Fay School educates students grades 1–9 in classes that average 11 students. Fay School enables children to become active participants in their education. Each student's specific needs and academic background are carefully considered when scheduling classes. A rotating schedule and more than 200 class offerings ensure maximum flexibility in designing study programs. Since 1866, Fay School has provided an outstanding education in a structured environment for students with diverse backgrounds and abilities. Today's 370 boys and girls represent many states and foreign countries. Fay accepts day students for grades 1–9, and boarding students for grades six through nine. (from the website)

www.fayschool.org
Phone: 508-485-0100   Fax: 508-485-5381
Address: 48 Main Street/Southborough, MA 01772

Fessenden School promotes a nurturing environment in a traditional atmosphere. The school represents a reliable and sturdy way to approach education. By traditional we mean enduring. Fessenden keeps and holds dear what has worked best over time; standards that are unapologetically high, social and academic structure and a regular routine, challenging sports, an appreciation of the arts, good adult role models, attention to manners, a sense of caring about the greater community, and a healthy respect for individual differences. These are as important today as they ever were. (from the website) All boys boarding (ages 10–15)/day school (5–15). Approximately 400 students. Grades K–9.

www.fessenden.org
Phone: 617-630-2300   Fax: 617-630-2303
Address: 250 Waltham Street/West Newton, MA 02465

Founded in 1763, **Governor Dummer Academy** is the oldest independent day and boarding school in the United States, educating young men and women, grades 9–12. We are located in Byfield, Massachussetts, 33 miles north of Boston and four miles from the Atlantic Ocean. In 2001–2002, our 372 students include 92 boarding girls, 133 boarding boys, 80 day girls, and 67 day boys, originating from 19 states as well as Australia, Canada, China, Czech Republic, Germany, Hong Kong, Indonesia, Korea, Iran, Japan, Thailand, and Taiwan. (from the website) The school boasts a new 50,000-volume library and a new state-of-the-art mathematics/science center.

www.gda.org
Phone: 978-465-1763   Fax: 978-463-9896
Address: One Elm Street/Byfield, MA 01922

Founded in 1884 by Rev. Endicott Peabody, **Groton School**'s original aims included the intellectual, moral, and physical development of its students in grades 7–12 toward preparation for both college and "the active work of life." Now a coeducational, primarily residential school of 165 girls and 186 boys in grades 8–12, we set for our students the highest standards of academic achievement, intellectual growth, ethical awareness and behavior, sportsmanship, athletic endeavor, and service to others. (from the website, words from outgoing head, William M. Polk) Grades 8–12. Founded: 1884. Setting: rural. Nearest major city is Boston. Students are housed in single-sex dormitories. 350-acre campus. 16 buildings on campus. Total enrollment: 354. Upper school average class size: 13. Upper school faculty-student ratio: 1:5.

www.groton.org
Phone: 978-448-7510   Fax: 978-448-9623
Address: Box 991 Farmers Row/Groton, MA 01450

The Hill School focuses on a traditional education, but places strong emphasis on individual growth in academic curriculum. Located in a rural setting in Pennsylvania. Recently coeduational ('98). Campus features new Academic Center, Student Center, and a 41,000-volume library. Enrollment 400+ students. Grades 8–PG, boarding and day.

www.thehill.org
Phone: 610-326-1000
Address: 717 East High Street/Pottstown, PA 19464

Holderness School offers a skills-based curriculum that emphasizes clear writing and thinking across disciplines. Full complement of academic offerings (AP) and sports. Boarding and day. 9–PG enrollment is 175 students, 30 states and international.

> *www.holderness.org*
> Phone: 603-536–1257   Fax: 603-536–1267
> Address: RR3 Box 18/Plymouth, NH 03264

Idyllwild Arts Academy is one of three independent, boarding high schools for arts in the United States. The school is located in the San Jacinto Mountains of southern California, approximately 100 miles east of Los Angeles. 265 students, grades 8–PG, 30 states and 20 countries enroll. They major in music, dance, theatre, visual arts, creative writing, moving pictures, or interdisciplinary arts. Auditions or portfolio presentations are required. The school's mission is to provide preprofessional training in the arts and a comprehensive college preparatory academic curriculum in an environment conducive to positive personal growth.

> *www.idyllwildarts.org*
> Phone: 909-659-2171, ext. 223
> Address: PO Box 38/Idyllwild, CA 92549

Founded in 1952 as an experiment in faculty-student governance and partnership, **Indian Springs School** still provides a model that says small is good, that the individual has worth, and that good citizenship is the prerequisite to good leadership. (from the website, Mel McKay, director) The school emphasizes collaborative learning and small class size. Much of the curriculum is student-centered. AP courses in core discipline. 350-acre campus. 250+ students. Intensive arts program. Near Birmingham, Alabama.

> *www.indiansprings.org*
> Phone: 205-988-3350   Fax: 205-988-3797
> Address: 190 Woodward Drive/Indian Springs, AL 35124

Lake Forest Academy's challenging curriculum prepares students for top colleges and universities. Located on a wooded 140-acre campus with lakes, Lake Forest focuses on education outside the classroom as well. Full interscholastic program; very broad extracurricular program. Student enrollment is approximately 300. Boarding/day, coeducational.

www.lfa.lfc.edu
Phone: 847-234-3210
Address: 1500 West Kennedy Road/Lake Forest, IL 60045

Loomise Chaffee School offer an elective program in all major disciplines, state-of-the-art art and athletic facilities, a 4:1 boarding student-to-faculty ratio, and extensive extracurricular opportunities. Enrollment is approximately 700, with a large day-student population and supportive parent group. From the website: "At Loomis Chaffee, we believe in a rich and varied curriculum, and you benefit from a dedicated faculty and superb facilities. Most of all, we believe in nurturing your intellectual and aesthetic growth."

www.loomis.org
Phone: 860-687-6400   Fax: 860-298-8756
Address: Windsor, CT 06095

From the website: "Founded in 1864, **Mid-Pacific Institute** is an independent, coeducational *college* preparatory school (bdg/day) for grades 6–12. Mid-Pacific is home to students from more than 17 countries around the world, and this internationalism promotes an understanding and respect for diversity that is essential in the global community of the 21st century. Mid-Pacific is recognized as an innovator in educational, technological, and artistic programs that develop lifelong learners and leaders." Last year, there were 1,083 pupils enrolled at Mid-Pacific Institute. They designated themselves in 111 different ethnic groups. Grades 6–12.

www.midpac.edu
Phone: 808-973-5004   Fax: 808-973-5099
Address: 2445 Kaala Street/Honolulu, HI 96822-2299

Milton Academy engages faculty and students in an intense and challenging preparation for college and for life, in an environment that stimulates and supports extraordinary intellectual and personal growth. In and out of class, faculty connect vitally with students—setting sights high, bringing opportunities to light, tackling big questions, affirming students' individuality, and building their confidence and skill. Not only do they succeed at the most competitive universities in the country, Milton graduates' awareness, creativity, and competence empower them to fully commit themselves to meaningful endeavors of all kinds, throughout the world. Enrollment is approximately 670 students, grades 9–12. Average class size: 14. Student/faculty ratio: 5 to 1.

> *www.milton.edu*
> Phone: 617-898-2227
> Address: 170 Centre Street/Milton, MA 02186

From the website: "A coeducational college preparatory school in western Massachusetts, **Northfield Mount Hermon** enrolls 900 boarders and 200 day students in grades 9–12 and postgraduate. With an innovative educational program, incredibly diverse and talented people, and world-class resources, the school enables students to learn better and grow more as people."

> *www.nmhschool.org*
> Phone: 413-498-3000
> Address: 206 Main Street/Northfield, MA 01360-1089

From the website: "**Oldfields School** is a small all-girls' college preparatory school serving 185 boarding and day students in grades 8–12. The diverse student population, which is 80% boarding, represents 26 states and 11 foreign countries. All students pursue a college preparatory course of study designed to challenge academic abilities and strengthen academic weaknesses. Within this framework, students are able to achieve their potential. The purpose of the Oldfields community is to provide an atmosphere in which students learn the value of self-discipline and self-respect. . . . Encouraging involvement and individual growth, Oldfields strives to help its students become confident, responsible, self-directed young women, well-equipped for their future." Enrollment is 185 students, 80% boarding. Located about 20 miles north of Baltimore.

> *www.oldfieldsschool.org*
> Phone: 410-472-4800   Fax: 410-472-3141
> Address: 1500 Glencoe Road/PO Box 697/Glencoe, MD 21152

The Peddie School is an independent college preparatory boarding school that as a community believes in the intellectual, social, and moral growth of each student. Our diverse faculty and students each strive for new levels of personal and educational achievement. Grades 8–PG. Enrollment is approximately 510 students, 60+% boarders. Located 8 miles from Princeton, 50 miles from Philadelphia and New York City. Average class size: 12 students. 6:1 student-faculty ratio. 42% on financial aid.

> *www.peddie.org*
> Phone: 609-490-7500   Fax: 609-490-0920
> Address: PO Box A/Hightstown, NJ 08520

Proctor Academy is a 4-year (9–12) coeducational boarding and day college-preparatory school with an enrollment of approximately 300 students. An extensive experiential learning curriculum complements the traditional core curriculum at Proctor. AP offerings in most disciplines. 2,300 acre campus. 4:1 student-teacher ratio. Emphasis on students' unique learning styles. 30 community service options. Enrollment is approximately 300 students.

> *www.proctornet.com*
> Phone: 603-735-6000
> Address: 204 Main Street/Andover, NH 03216

Putney School offers a progressive education that focuses on the learning process and experiential education. All students participate in an arts program and the work program. The school is nearly self-sustaining as part of the curriculum is farm work. The classes are small, and there are many opportunities for independent work. Enrollment is approximately 180 students. 5:1 student-faculty ratio.

> *www.putney.com*
> Phone: 802-387-6219   Fax: 802-387-5931
> Address: Elm Lea Farm/Putney, VT 05346-8675

St.Albans is a boys 9–12 college preparatory school located on a 60-acre part of the Washington Cathedral grounds. Offering special opportunities in music, the school also reflects its proximity to Washington, D.C., with a strong international student population. The school also boasts a rigorous athletic program for interested students. The school coordinates courses and social activities closely with its sister school, the National Cathedral School, also on the grounds. Episcopal teachings in the Christian faith.

http://staweb.sta.cathedral.org/
Phone: 202-537-6435
Address: Mount Saint Alban/Washington, DC 20016-5095

St. Andrews-Sewanee School is located on the Cumberland Plateau in the Smoky Mountains of Tennessee. In addition to the traditional liberal arts program, SAS offers outdoor and community programs, tuition-free courses at the University of the South, a year's study in the arts, and a year of religious study. Small, residential dorms; approximately 260 students; home of James Agee Library. Episcopal tradition.

www.sasweb.org
Phone: 931-598-5651
Address: 290 Quintard Road/St. Andrews, TN 37372

The only day school represented in the book, **St. John's School** is a K–12 school that offers a rigorous academic programs for students in the Houston area. With an enrollment of over 1200 students, the school offers a full complement of academic disciplines, sports, and arts. Graduating classes generally number 125–130. It is an interdenominational school. Encourages community involvement. Sophisticated website offers glimpses into actual courses. Honor code, our sense of family, and our traditions (even though we are only 56 years old) distinguish it from other local schools. (ages 5–18)

www.sjs.org
Phone: 713-850-0222   Fax: 713-622-2309
Address: St. John's School Admissions Office/2401 Claremont Lane/Houston, TX 77019

St. Mark's provides a college preparatory curriculum to 325 students on a 250-acre campus that features world-class facilities, including a recently built 500-seat performance hall. With an average class of 10 students and independent and advanced study opportunities in every discipline, the school offers academic challenges to motivated students. The school meets frequently for chapel and all-school meetings. A full complement of house counselors, advisers, student prefects and college counselors provide one-on-one support services for students. Grades: 9–12.

www.stmarksschool.org
Phone: 508-786-6000   Fax: 508-786-6120
Address: 25 Marlborough Road/Southborough, MA 01722

St. Stephen's Episcopal School offers a boarding education for grades 8–12, day for grades 6–12. A full college preparatory program, emphasizing English. AP courses in most disciplines. Overseas exchange program in several languages. 430-acre campus, single-sex dormitories. Fields all major sports. Private lessons available in many arts and a course in theology is required for graduation.

email address through peterson's guide to schools
Phone: 512-327-1213   Fax: 512-327-1311
Address: PO Box 1868/Austin, TX 78767

St. Timothy's School is an all-girl's school emphasizing personalized attention. With an enrollment under 100 students and a 4:1 ratio, the school seeks to educate the whole student. All girls play interscholastic sports in grades 9–11. In 12th grade, students are expected to play two interscholastic sports. Strong core curriculum with AP credit in most disciplines. Located in the Green Springs Valley (234 acres), the campus features a performing arts center, a gym, a 22,000 volume library, and indoor and outdoor riding rings.

www.sttimothyschool.com
Phone: 410-486-7400
Address: 8400 Greensprings Avenue/Stevenson, MD 21153

With over 100 courses in the curriculum, **Suffield Academy** offers a very competitive academic program for its 380 students in grades 9–12. Featuring a 350-acre campus in an old New England setting, the school has the full complement of facilities (athletic/residential/academic/and arts). The full curriculum includes the Leadership Program, which teaches students the skills necessary to lead their peers; the SOLO program is the outdoor component of the Leadership Program. The school takes advantage of its size by having frequent community gatherings in which faculty families participate.

www.suffieldacademy.org
Phone: 860-668-7315   Fax: 860-668-2966
Address: High Street/PO Box 999/Suffield, CT 06078

"Horace Taft chose [**Taft School**'s] school motto: *Non ut sibi ministretur sed ut ministret*—Not to be served but to serve. Today, Taft's 114 faculty members educate 570 boys and girls from 35 states and 25 countries. Our beautiful 220-acre campus features facilities that rival those of many small colleges, including a library with 56,000 volumes, a 45,000 square foot science and mathematics building, two theaters, two hockey rinks, and an 18-hole golf course." (from the website)

www.taftschool.org
Phone: 860-945-7777   Fax: 860-945-7808
Address: 110 Woodbury Road/Watertown, CT 06795-2100

"Founded in 1889, **The Thacher School** is a coeducational boarding high school located 85 miles north of Los Angeles, California. The School serves academically talented students who will benefit from a rigorous college preparatory experience. The faculty and students live and work closely together in a community in which cooperation, trust, honesty, and respect are the cornerstones of school life. Together, we commit to the belief that demands in the academic classroom, when combined with those of mountains and horses, of sports and the arts, produce independent minds, strong bodies, and powerful character. Academic excellence is the core of Thacher's program. The rigorous and traditional curriculum is comprised of 75 different courses including required courses, elective courses, honors-level classes, and 17 Advanced Placement courses. Classes are energized by scholarly and enthusiastic teachers and motivated students who respect each other's interests and talents. The average class size of 11 encourages lively intellectual exploration." (from the website) Weekly all-school meeting at which a different faculty member speaks. Well-established equestrian program.

www.thacher.org
Phone: 805-646-4377   Fax: 805-640-9490
Address: 5025 Thacher Road/Ojai, CA 93023

A very small, very competitive school, **Thomas Jefferson School** boast a median SAT verbal of 700 and math of 670, a long list of prestigious colleges to which students have matriculated, and an intimate residential program. Students live in cottage-style dormitories around campus. 75 students currently attend in grades 7–12. Average class size is 11 students. Novel approach to class time: short classes, long vacations, lots of freedom with study hours. Students and faculty frequently travel abroad together.

www.tjs.org
Phone: 314-843-4132   Fax: 314-843-3527
Address: 4100 South Lindbergh Blvd./Saint Louis, MO 63127

"Founded in 1870, the **Webb School** enjoys a long history as an independent, college-preparatory, coeducational boarding and day school. The 150-acre campus is located in a rural setting 50 miles southeast of Nashville. The school has 295 students in grades 6–12, with boarding students comprising a third of the population. At present, the school enrolls students from 16 states and 9 foreign countries." (from the website) Features a new 27,000 square foot athletic complex. Traditional boarding school curriculum, grades 6–12, 50 miles southeast of Nashville.

www.thewebbschool.com
Phone: 931-389-6049   Fax: 931-389-9473
Address: Sawney Webb Highway/Bell Buckle, TN 37020

Westtown School, located in Chester County, about 25 miles southwest of Philadelphia, was founded in 1799 by Philadelphia Quakers. It has always been a boarding school for girls and boys and with basic program for high-school-aged people. Now, about 25% of the students are Quaker and about the same for faculty and staff, it also has a lower and middle school as well as a child care and pre-school program. Total student population is about 700 with about 400 in the high school. There are about 295 boarders. Boarding can begin in 9th grade and is required of 11th and 12th graders.

www.westtown.edu
Phone: 610-399-0123   Fax: 610-399-3760
Address: Westtown Road/PO Box 1799/Westtown, PA 19395

Featuring a faculty fully engaged in all areas of student life, **Woodberry Forest** is an all boys 9–12 boarding/day college preparatory school located in central Virginia on a campus that features a 55,000 volume library and a golf course. The school offers a full AP curriculum, but also offers non-honors courses in all disciplines as well. An extensive athletic program (33 teams) provides opportunities for nearly every student to participate in an interscholastic sport, regardless of ability. Enrollment is approximately 370 students with about 70 full-time faculty, most of whom have graduate degrees. Located about 45 miles from Charlottesville.

www.woodberry.org
Phone: 540-672-6023   Fax: 540-672-0928
Address: Woodberry Forest, VA 22989

Wyoming Seminary is a coed boarding/day school (boarding: ages 14–19; day: ages 4–19 that offers a complete AP curriculum, summer programs in college placement, ESL, and sports camps. "The school's mission is to teach and prepare students for success in college and in life in a supportive environment shaped by the Judeo-Christian values of our Methodist heritage. A challenging curriculum; well developed music, art and athletic programs; highly skilled and experienced faculty; a diverse student body including members from more than 11 states and 25 countries; and well-equipped facilities all combine to provide our students with an outstanding educational experience." (from the website, statement from H. Jeremy Packard, head of school) Enrollment is approximately 780 students. Two campuses: upper school and lower school.

www.wyomingseminary.org
Phone: 570-270-2160 (upper school) 570-718-6610
Address: 201 North Sprague Avenue/Kingston, PA 18704-3593
    (upper school); 1560 Wyoming Avenue/Forty Fort, PA 18704-4298 (lower school)